I0042213

Lancaster County, Virginia

LAND RECORDS

1770–1782

Tawny

Waske

HERITAGE BOOKS
2018

HERITAGE BOOKS

AN IMPRINT OF HERITAGE BOOKS, INC.

Books, CDs, and more—Worldwide

For our listing of thousands of titles see our website
at
www.HeritageBooks.com

Published 2018 by
HERITAGE BOOKS, INC.
Publishing Division
5810 Ruatan Street
Berwyn Heights, Md. 20740

Copyright © 2009 Colonial Roots

All rights reserved. No part of this book may be reproduced or
transmitted in any form or by any means, electronic or mechanical,
including photocopying, recording or by any information storage
and retrieval system without written permission from the author,
except for the inclusion of brief quotations in a review.

International Standard Book Number
Paperbound: 978-16-8034-737-1

CONTENTS

iv

Introduction

In this volume the author has abstracted the essentials of the information contained in the deed books of the period 1770 to 1782.

The records for the most part pertain to land transactions, bills of sale (frequently slaves), bonds, reports on the value or loss of value of land relating to proposed roads and mills, and deeds of gifts. The polls listing the eligible voters in 1771 and 1774 are also contained here, giving us a virtual census of the freeholders.

Especially helpful to genealogists are the relationships revealed in these records. Often the names of wives, children and other relationships are shown.

The state of the records was given in a report on 7 Aug 1770 in which the subscribers by order of Lancaster court examined the clerks office & records ... and found no minutes of the orders of said court between Sept 1750 & Feb 1757. Nor Aug 1760 and Jun 1766. Nor any since Sep 1769. ...No orders of court recorded between Sep 1765 & Nov 1768 & many of the orders recorded between Nov 1768 & May 1770 are but in part. The Record Book containing orders of court from Oct 1743 to Feb 1752 is so much defaced since Aug 1745 that the said orders cannot be understood. No minutes ....found from Nov 1745 to Sep 1750. ....We do not find any appeals recorded since the year 1756 nor any Fee Book since Nov 1768 nor any executions at all recorded the bonds & other papers belonging to the office are so intermixed that it would take a long time to sort... - James Ball, George Heale, Richard Mitchell, & John Chinn.

These records are difficult to read. The author has made painstaking efforts to interpret the scribe's handwriting which sometimes proved impossible.

Other books of genealogical value pertaining to Lancaster County during the Colonial period:

Duvall, Lindsay O. *Lancaster County, Virginia, Court Orders and Deeds, 1656-1680. Virginia Colonial Abstracts, Series 2, Vol. 2.*

Lee, Ida J. *Abstracts of Lancaster County, Virginia, Wills. 1653-1800.*

Lee, Ida J. *Lancaster County, Virginia, Marriage Bonds 1652-1850.*

Lancaster County, Virginia, Will Book 28, Abstracts and Index of Wills Recorded 1796-1839.

Nottingham, Stratton. *The Marriage License bonds of Lancaster County, Virginia, From 1701 to 1848.*

Nottingham, Stratton, *Revolutionary Soldiers and Sailors from Lancaster County, Virginia: Muster Rolls and Pay Rolls of the Ninety-Second Regiment of Virginia Militia, Lancaster County, 1812.*

F. Edward Wright
Lewes, Delaware
2009

Glossary

Acre: A common measure of area, 43,560 square feet. There are 640 acres in a square mile.

Administration/administrator/administratrix: Administratrix is the feminine of administrator. When a person dies intestate (without a will), the estate is administered by an appointed administrator. An intestancy is often called an administration. The administrator usually is the person who sells the deceased's land.

Ad Quod Domnum: The name of a writ formerly issuing from the English chancery, commanding the sheriff to make inquiry "to what damage" a specific act, if don, will tend.

Agreement: Type of instrument (document) often related to land and recorded in deed books.

Appurtenance: An intangible right associated with land, such as an easement or right-of-way.

Assigns: Anyone to whom the grantee might assign the property in the future.

Bond: An agreement to pay a penalty if a certain obligation is not filled.

Certificate: Similar to a warrant.

Chain: The Gunter chain was used to measure distances by a surveyor in early America. It was made of one hundred straight pieces of metal (about seven inches long), connected by three small loops. The length between the center loops, a link, was 7.92 inches. The chain was sisty-six feet long. One hundred links equals four rods, each of which is sixteen and a half feet long.

Consideration: The amount of money or other item of value that's exchanged for land. Consideration includes love and affection.

Convey: To transfer title or ownership from one person to another.

Corner: The geographical anchor between two lines in a metes-and-bounds survey. Usually, but not always, this is the point at which there is a chsange of direction in lines. The corner may mention adjoining (abutting) landowners, whose property may run along one or both lines or may simply touch at this corner.

Dedimus: (potestatem) Latin for "we have the power" whereby commission is given to one or more private persons for the expedition of some act normally performed by a judge. It is granted most commonly upon the suggestion that a party, who is to do something before a judge or in a court, is too weak to travel.

Deed of Gift: A deed in which the monetary or practical consideration is less than the value of the land and in which "love and affection" may be mentioned.

Deed of Trust: A deed in which the grantee does not have full legal ownership. In some times and places, it was used instead of a mortgage.

Do.: The abbreviation for "ditto."

Dock the entail/intail: Land is entailed if someone wills it to the oldest son to the oldest son etc... To dock this means to break the link of descendancy.

Dower or **Dower of Rights:** The lifetime interest that the law allowed a widow to retain in the real property of her deceased husband in order to maintain herself and her children.

Dower Release: The specific statement, usually recorded directly following a deed, that the wife has been examined "privily" (alone, without the husband in the room) and has agreed to the sale of the land, including her dower rights.

Enfeoffed: To invest with a feudal estate or fee. Deed by which a person was given land in exchange for a pledge of service.

Entail: The restrictions placed on the transfer of real property.

Esquire: A term denoting social status.

Fee Simple: The type of title or ownership in which the owner can do whatever he wants with the land and can dispose of it in any way he likes.

Feoffment: The grant of an estate held in fee.

Gentleman: A member of the gentry, a descendant from an aristocratic family whose income came from the rental of his land. Later in the colonial period this address was used generally out of respect.

Halfpenny: British coin worth one half penny.

Head: The place at which a body of water originates.

Heir at Law: Oldest living son to whom the land descended if there were not a will.

Hereditaments: Property that can be inherited.

Hogsheads: A very large barrel used to transport tobacco or liquids. A tobacco hogshead measured 48 inches long and 30 inches in diameter. Fully packed with tobacco, it weighed about 1000 pounds.

Indenture: Originally, an instrument (document) that is written twice (or more) on the same sheet of paper, and then the copies were cut apart with a curvy or jagged line (to prevent forgery). This was used when both parties continued to have an interest in the terms of the agreement. Eventually, the term came to apply to the instrument, even if it wasn't done with two copies and a jagged cut.

Interlined: Written between the lines. The scribe might add at the bottom of a deed what was added to indicate that place where "^" appears and information added above the line was not a later addition by someone else.

Intestate, intestacy: A person who dies without a valid will.

Lease: The transfer of possession but not ownership. Any agreement that gives rise to a relationship of landlord and tenant.

Lease and Release: The type of transaction used, especially in areas under proprietorships, to transfer estate or possession. It involved two transactions, executed one day after the other, bbetween the same two parties, one of which is for a nominal sum, such as one dollar.

Line: The "sides" in a land description.

Link: 7.92 inches, 1/100 of a pole.

Livery and Seisin: See Seisin.

Meanders: The winding turns of a waterway. Used as a general term in land platting to describe a line that does not have both a distance and a direction. Down the meanders means with the direction of water flow; up the meanders means against the direction of water flow.

Messuage: A dwelling house. Sometimes indicates land with a dwelling house.

Metes-and-bounds: A description specifying the measures and boundaries of a parcel of land.

Moiety: One half of property or land.

Mortgage: When a person borrows money using land as a security.

Mouth: The place where a body of water empties into a body of water.

Moveables: All property not classed as heritable.

Pence: Plural of penny.

Penny: Equal to one hundredth of a pound.

Perch: 16.5 feet. Equivalent to a pole or rod.

Plantation: Property with land under cultivation or growing crops. It carries no connotation of size, wealth, or slaves. It didn't even have to have a house on it.

Plat: The drawing and accompanying text, usually prepared by a surveyor, showing the boundaries of a piece of property, commonly showing lines with direction and distance, corners with geographical features and adjoining property owners.

Pole: 16.5 feet. Equivalent to a perch or rod.

Pound: A basic unit of money in Great Britain equal to 100 pence.

Power of Attorney: The instrument (document) giving a person the right to act for another person, usually to transact specific business.

Quitrent: A fixed annual payment or rent, somewhat like a tax, that the landholder paid to the government or proprietor.

Relict: A widow or widower; the surviving spouse.

Remainder: the part of the estate that is left after a prior interest ends.

Rod: 16.5 feet. Equivelant to a perch or pole.

Seisin, seizin: A common-law term meaning possession or tenure of property. The transfer of tenure was called livery of seizin (delivery) and was done literally and physically, when the holder of the tenure stood on the land in the presence of neighbors and give the new holder a piece of dirt and a twig. "delivery of Turf & Twigg"

Shilling: English coinage valued at 1/20th of a pound or twenty shillings in one pound.

Tenement: A dwelling house; also used to refer to real property irrespective of the presence of a house.

Testable, test: Capable of making or witnessing a will.

Turf and Twig: See Seisin.

Vizt: a contraction of videlicet, to wit; meaning that is to say.

30 May 1770. Valuation of work done. We have valued the work done by the carpenters of Thomas Pinckard Gebt, vizt. A shop and covering the dwelling house where Humphrey Simons kuved with nails at six pounds, fifteen shillings, and seven pence. Recorded 19 Jul 1770. [Wit:] William Lawson, Jonathan Wilder, Nathaniel Wilder. Recording of above Valuation by Test Thomas B. Griffin Cl. Cur [Page 1]

16 Aug 1770. Bill of Sale. Burges Smith.... of Lancaster County. In consideration of the sum of one hundred pounds ....paid in hand by William Sydnor of the same county. Receipt ....acknowledge ...and do aquit and discharge the said William Sydnor, his heirs, executors, and administrators. ....Heirs, executors, and administrators of Burges Smith grant, bargain and sell unto William Sydnor, his heirs, executors and administrators the following Negroes to wit: Winney and Betty and their future increase .....assigns forever to his and their only proper use and behoof and to no other use, intent or purpose whatsoever. The said Burgess Smith ..for myself, my heirs, executors, and administrators covenant, promise and grant to with the said William Sydnor at all times, forever, hereafter, to warrant and defend the said Negro slaves and their future increase.....and assign forever against the lawfull claim of all and every person or persons whatsoever. [Wit:] Oswald Newby, Eliza Mactier. Recorded by Test Thomas B. Griffin, Cl Cur. [Page 1]

16 Aug 1770. Bill of Sale. John Heath of the county of Northumberland in the colony of Virginia Merchant am held and stand firmly bound to Bridgar Haynie of the county of Lancester....just sum of one thousand pounds. The condition of above Bridgar Haynie hath for the valuable consideration of ninety-eight pounds purchased of the above bounder John Heath three negroes. A negro woman named Miram, a negro girl named Sarah, and a negro boy named Abel. Now...Bridgar Haynie, his heirs, executors, and administrators, or assigns, shall at all times forever hereafter enjoy a peaceful and quiet possession of the said Miram, Sarah, and Abel and all (their) future increase. (This will) sufficiently warrant from the claim and demand of the said John Heath, his or any other person whatsoever, then the above obligation to be void and of no effect...[Wit] Robert Hening, James Tapscot, and Holland Haynie. 16 Aug 1770 Recorded Test Thomas B Griffin Cl Cur. [Page 2]

9 Dec 1769. Deed. ...Between William Blackerby of the county of Northumberland of the one part & Johnson Riveer of the county of Lancaster of the other part. ...Johnson Riveer who married the daughter of the said William Blackerby. ...William Blackerby doth ....absolutely give, grant, convey, & confirm unto the said Johnson Riveer ....forever all that tract piece or parcel of land...lying in the said county of Lancaster which descended unto him by the death of his father, James Blackerby, bounded on the lands of Capt Merryman

Payne, Robert Jones, and the main branch of Morattico Swamp containing by estimation twenty-five (25) acres...with all [that is included on the land] [Wit:] Thomas Williams, John Riveer, & Thomas Bell. Recorded 16 Aug 1770 by Test Thomas B. Griffin Cl Cur. [Page 2, 2a & 3].

7 Aug 1770. Record. We the subscribers by order of Lancaster court examined the clerks office & records ... do not find any minutes of the orders of said court between Sept 1750 & Feb 1757. Nor Aug 1760 and Jun 1766. Nor any since Sep 1769. ...No orders of court recorded between Sep 1765 & Nov 1768 & many of the orders recorded between Nov 1768 & May 1770 are but in part. The Record Book containing orders of court from Oct 1743 to Feb 1752 is so much defaced since Aug 1745 that the said orders cannot be understood. No minutes ....found from Nov 1745 to Sep 1750. ....We do not find any appeals recorded since the year 1756 nor any Fee Book since Nov 1768 nor any executions at all recorded the bonds & other papers belonging to the office are so intermixed that it would take a long time to sort....[Wit:] James Ball, George Heale, Richard Mitchell, & John Chinn. Recorded 16 Aug 1770 by Test Thomas B. Griffin Cl Cur. [Page 3 & 3a]

17 Aug 1770. Record. ..Court of Lancaster. Whereas Thomas Lawson hath a suit depending against me [John Fleet], in your said court of scandal. .....I declare I never knew any scandalous action of him either by word or deed. If I said any such thing, I confess I was wrong, therefore with his consent will pay all costs concerning said suit and have it dismissed. Recorded 17 Aug 1770 by Test Thomas B. Griffin Cl Cur. [Page 3a]

30 Jul 1770. Bill of Sale. ....Burgess Ball of Lancaster County for & in consideration of the sum of one hundred & eighty pounds....paid by James Ball of the said county. The receipt I do acknowledge & every part thereof do forever acquit & discharge the said James Ball, his heirs, executors, & administrators granted, bargained & sold.....forever the following slaves to wit, Scipio, Moses, Daniel, Spencer, Alice and her child Molly, Will, Nan, Harry, & Sue...slaves now in the possession of said James Ball, as tenant by the courtesy of England at whose death the same would descend to me. ...[Afore mentioned slaves] & their future increase unto the said James Ball, his heirs, executors, administrators & assigns forever to his & their only proper use & behoof ....signed, sealed & delivered in the presence of Mungo Harvey, James Selden, William Heale. Recorded 20 Sep 1770 by Test Thomas B. Griffin, Cl Cur. [Pages 3a & 4]

21 Apr 1770. Deed of Mortgage. Indenture made.....tenth year of the reign of His Majesty King George the Third, between Burges Smith of the county Lancaster...and James Ball of the same county ...for the sum of one hundred

and fifty pounds...[for sale of] granted slaves and their future increase, Milly, Molly, Sisly, Spencer, Sam, John, & Peter ...unto said James Ball, his heirs, executors, administrators, & assigns...provided nevertheless, that whereas, there is sui[?] now depending in the general court of the colony of Virginia brought by Mr. Rodham Kenner against the said Burges Smith for all the lands in Lancaster which descended to him on the death of his mother, Frances, and which the said Burges Smith has sold & conveyed unto the said James Ball part of the said lands as mentioned and contained in an Indenture of Bargain & Sale made between the said Burges Smith and Alice, his wife, of one part and the said James Ball, of the other bearing even date ... and hath received of the said James Ball, ...the sum of one hundred and fifty pounds...covenanted & agreed between the said parties that in case the said Kenner shall be finally cast in the said suit both in Virginia and Great Britain & the said Burges Smith, his heirs & assigns thereby .... Shall and may be lawful for the said Burges Smith, his heirs, executors, administrators, & assigns to repossess the said hereby slaves and their future increase and enjoy the same as if the indenture had never been made. [Wit:] George Heale, James Ewell, Burges Ball, Peter Conway. Recorded 20 Sep 1770 by Test Thomas B. Griffin, Cl Cur. [Pages 4, 4a & 5]

20 Sep 1770. Deed of Bargain and Sale. ...Tenth year of the reign of King George the Third between James Ball of the county of Lancaster, gentlemen of one part & John Schon of the same county, planter, of the other part. Witness that the said James Ball & in consideration of the sum of twenty pounds, current money, to him in hand paid by the said John Schon at or before the sealing & delivery of these....[for] all that tract or parcel of land which the said James Ball purchased from Mr. Burges Ball in the said County of Lancaster and is bordered .....?..at the head of the creek called Fishing Creek on which Norris's Mill stands & wining thence N48 & W72 Pole to a stump near the marsh in Kirks Line then S66 & W36 ½ pole to a hickory then S10 & W68 pole along a line of the said John Schon to the dividing line between this land & the land formerly purchased by said James Ball, then along said line to creek, then up the said creek the several meanders to the beginning, containing fifty-three (53) acres .... [Wit:] William Yerby, Matt Myars, Abraham White. Recorded 20 Sep 1770 by Test Thomas B. Griffin, Cl Cur. [Pages 5, 5a, & 6]

20 Sep 1770. Deed of Bargain and Sale. Between Merryman Payne of the county of Lancaster and Bushrod Riveer of the same county. For the sum of thirty pounds, ... all that tract or parcel of land in the county of Lancaster, being part of a tract of land owned by Merryman Payne, commonly called his Forrest Plantation bounded, beginning in the road near Mrs. Payne's, at a stake & running southwesterly to a stake in the middle of Coach Road to a marked white oak at a corner near Peter Riveer's then N76 E81 ¼ to a corner near Agnes Robertson's containing 75 acres, 1 rood & twenty-five pole. [Wit:] John

Taylor, Edward Carter, Peter Riveer. Recorded by Test Thomas B. Griffin, Cl Cur. [Pages 6, 6a, & 7]

18 Oct 1770. Deed. Benjamin Cundiff & Saryanne, his wife of Christ Church Parish, in the county of Lancaster & John Wormeley of the said Parish in the same county, Lancaster... one hundred and seventy-five pounds....[for] two hundred acres of land beginning at a corner White Oak standing a little below Colln Selden's Mills, then running southeast one hundred and thirteen poles along a line of marked trees dividing this land from Edwin Conway's to a stake in the said line. Then south forty-nine degrees, west two hundred fifty-seven poles to another stake, then northwest to the mouth of a small branch at the marsh. Then along the marsh & creek (at the head of Corotoman River to the place it begun. [Wit:] James Gordon, James Tapscot, George Gordon. Recorded 18 Oct 1770 by Test Thomas B. Griffin, Cl Cur [Pages 7, 7a, 8, & 8a]

19 Apr 1770. Report & Settlement. Johnson Riveer, guardian of George Nichols, with that part of the Orphan's Estate in the hands of James Robinson, ...subscribers met & found in the hand of said Robinson sixteen pounds, five shillings, which sum he refused to pay said Riveer ...given 19 Sep 1770. [Wit:] John Chinn & Joseph Norris. Recorded 20 Sep 1770 by Test Thomas B. Griffin, Cl Cur. [Page 8a]

17 Apr 1769. Commission and Certificate. Lancaster, George the Third by grace of God, Great Britain, France, & Ireland....to John Fleet & Richard Edwards, whereas, Henry Hinton, by his certain Indenture of Bargain & Sale...hath sold & conveyed unto William Steptoe of Lancaster County...the estate of ten acres of land ...in the Parish of Christ Church in the county of Lancaster, where Ann Hinton, wife of Henry, cannot conveniently travel to said county court to make acknowledgement & acquittal of rights...[court was allowing a person to personally go to her and get her acknowledgement & acquittal of the said land]. [Wit:] Thomas B. Griffin 21 Sep 1770. 12 Oct 1770. Ann Hinton, privately and apart from her husband, gave acknowledgement and relinquished said land. [Wit:] John Fleet and Richard Edwards. Recorded 18 Oct 1770 by Test Thomas B. Griffin. [Page 8a & 9]

3 May 1770. Bill of Sale. John Heath of Northumberland County... for the consideration of a large sum of money due Mr.'s Clay and Midgley for goods in trade account also a sum due himself agree to ship one hundred threads hheads[hogsheads] tobacco on ships Bettsey and Henry by 20th July. John Heath also, makeover, bargain, & sell to Captain Henry Parry, their attorney, thirty negroes as security for what may be due them. [Names of the thirty negroes are as follows:] Daniel, Daniel, Daniel, George, James, Tom, James Crab, Harry, Dennis, Robin, Tom again Fellows, Stepney, Simon, London, Kendall, Cate,

Winney, Famey, Bett, Martha, Ellich, Milley, Lilah, Bett (a woman), Hagar, Jane, Milley (a girl), Rose, Jude. [Wit: Benjamin George] Test Thomas Pollard. Recorded 19 Oct 1770 by Test Thomas B. Griffin, Cl Cur. [Page 9 & 9a]

15 Nov 1770. Bond. Richard Edwards and Thomas Pinckard are bound...in the sum of one thousand pounds ....whereas Richard Edwards is constituted & appointed Sherif of county of Lancaster...by commission from the honourable William Nelson, President of this colony. [Wit: Thomas B. Griffin and Thomas Pinckard. Recorded 15 Nov 1770 by Test Thomas B. Griffin, Cl Cur. [Page 9a]

15 Nov 1770. Bond. Richard Edwards and Thomas Pinckard... sum of five hundred pounds to be paid... The above obligation is such whereas above bound Richard Edwards is Sherif of Lancaster county by commission from the honourable William Nelson, President of this colony, shall collect all ..fines...due His Majesty in the said county and will pay the same to the officers of His Majesty revenue on or before the second Tuesday in June annually and shall be truly and faithfully execute the said office of Sheriff. Signed Richard Edwards and Thomas Pinckard. [Wit:] Thomas B. Griffin. Recorded 15 Nov 1770 by Test Thomas B. Griffin, Cl Cur. [Page 9a & 10]

18 Dec 1770. Deed. Between Jesse Chilton and his wife Ann, of Lancaster County one part and William Chilton of same county of the other part. ...sum of four hundred pounds current money of Virginia, ...for a tract of land equaling about four hundred acres which descended to Robert Newsum from his father, Robert Newsum who dying without male heir descended in copartnership to his two daughters, Anne & Jemima who is now intermarried with Edward Blakemore....and the sd Anne to the above named Jesse Chilton which sd /half part is now intended to be sold containing two hundred acres divided from the other half bounded on one side by the Rappahannook and by the lands of the said Blakemore and George Chitwood. Jesse Chilton and his wife Ann, within eight months of date hereof [will produce] the Levery and Seisen endorsed by witnesses. [Wit:] Dale Carter. Recorded 20 Dec 1770 by Test Thomas B. Griffin, Cl Cur. [Page 10, 10a, & 11]

3 May 1770. Bill of Sale. Samuel Rollings of Parish of North Farnham in the county of Richmond, Taylor, in consideration of bond to Nicholas Flood of the said county bearing the date 9 Oct 1765, for twenty pounds conditioned for payment of ten pounds also for bond ... to Merryman Bryant of the said county, 30 Jan 1768 for ten pounds-for payment of five pounds and security for payment of said sums in two bonds ...do deliver one nine cart and one pair of new cart wheels, yoke ring, & staple belonging to same value-one pound. Two draught

oxen, one red and one brown about six years old-five pounds, nine head of sheep value – forty shillings, sixteen head of hogs value-forty shillings, three feather beds, rugs, blankets, sheets, bolster, and beadstead value-ten pounds, three iron pots, five pewter dishes, one dozen pewter plates value-thirty shillings, all chests, casks, table, chairs, now being & remaining in my dwelling in said county-goods & chattel to be used by Nicholas Flood unless redeemed by me by the payment of thirty pounds. ...Samuel Rollings ...delivery of two draught oxen and cart wheels, yoke, and part of the above bargained promises. [Wit:] John Randall. Recorded 20 Dec 1770 by Test Thomas B. Griffin, Cl Cur. [Page 11 & 11a]

17 Jan 1771. Bill of Sale, Livery with Seisen. Between Samuell Brumley and Elisabeth, his wife of Lancaster county and William Brumley of said county in consideration of seventy pounds current Virginia money .....for tract or parcel of land whereon the said William Brumley now lives. [This land] in said county containing fifty-nine acres and a half, binding on the lands of Col. James Ball, Capt. Henry Tapscot, and Mrs. Ellison Oliver. ... Memorandum on day of sale all promises....to named William Brumley by within named Samuell Brumley by delivery of the handle of door of the mansion house, in presence of Jas Newby, William Brent, and John Newby. Recorded 17 Jan 1771 by Test Thomas B. Griffin, Cl Cur. [Pages 12 & 12a]

17 Jan 1771. Bond. Samuell Brumley of Lancaster county, am held and stands bound unto William Brumley of said county, sum of one hundred and forty pounds, current money of Virginia. [Wit:] Jas. Newby, William Brent, and John Newby. Recorded 17 Jan 1771 by Test Thomas B. Griffin, Cl Cur. [Page 12a & 13]

13 Dec 1770. Bill of Sale. John Wormsley of Lancaster County and Parish of Christ Church, have bargained, sold, and delivered unto Bailie George and John Hill of said county and parish, two negro girls, Winney and Lett for consideration of one hundred pounds Virginia currency. [Wit:] Thos Brent and James Tapscott. Recorded 7 Jan 1771 by Test Thomas B. Griffin, Cl Cur. [Page 13]

21 Jun 1770. Deed of Mortgage. Between Thomas Pollard of Parish of Christ Church and county of Lancaster and Thomas Newton and son, merchants of the Burough of Norfolk. ...for sum of three hundred and seventeen pounds, eleven shillings, and ten pence paid by said Thomas Newton and son....[for] tract of land which said Thomas Pollard purchased of John Steptoe on which Thomas Pollard now lives. ...containing one hundred forty acres bounded on the land of the late James Gordon, by the land of Henry Tapscot, and the glebe of the aforesaid parish. ....[Thomas Pollard will pay Thomas Newton and son] three

hundred seventeen pounds, eleven shillings, and ten pence ...with interest as aforesaid at the day and time before mentioned for payment thereof according to the true intent and meaning of these presents five pr centum pr annum on the tenth day of December... [Wit:] Test Henry Tapscot, Bailie George, and David Boyd. Recorded 20 Dec 1770, further proved & recorded 17 Jan 1771 by Test Thomas B. Griffin, Cl Cur. [Pages 13a & 14]

18 Oct 1770. Notice. Subscribers met and land of a road for the complainant William /Schofield. Beginning at the Westside of said Schofield Plantation, running over his line on John Yerby's land ten foot, to a bottom above his son, William Shofield's Schofield house, ...crossing the line on his own line and to a bottom above his son, Thomas Shofield, as the path now runs, then up said path to main road. 14 Jan 1771- Wit: James Kirk & John Morridoth. Recorded 17 Jan 1771 by Test Thomas B. Griffin, Cl Cur. [Pages 14 & 14a]

9 Feb 1771. Bill of Sale. William Hinton of Christ Parish and county of Lancaster in consideration of the sum of two hundred sixty pounds...paid by Messrs Gilmour, Rowand, and Barrett....[for] one schooner rigged vessel the Elizabeth Burthen forty-eight tons, eighteen months old, built in Gloucester County...said William Hinton do oblige myself, my heirs, etc to warrant & defend property of said schooner to said Gilmour, Rowand, and Barrett under the penalty of five hundred pounds money aforesaid. [Wit:] John Doak, Bailie George, Hancock Eustace, Jno Clayton. Recorded 21 Feb 1771 by Test Thomas B. Griffin, Cl Cur. [Page 14a]

23 Aug 1770. Deed of Mortgage. Between Burges Smith of Lancaster county and Burges Ball of same county Gent. In consideration of the sum of one hundred sixty pounds, eleven shillings, and three pence...paid by Burges Ball [for] the following slaves – Long Tom, Short Tom, Margery and her youngest child Little Kate, Ben and Solomon. Burges Ball entered himself security for the said Burges Smith bond bearing date 16 Aug 1771 for one hundred pounds, eleven shillings, and three pence with interest from said date payable to John Belfield and Richard Mitchell guardians of Milly and Nancy Tarpley orphans of Majr Travers Tarpley. .... Burges Ball is security, ...the aforesaid granted slaves and their future increase ....[shall be returned] to Burges Smith as if Indenture had never been made. [Wit:] Jas Ball, Tesse Ball, and Peter Conway. Recorded 21 Feb 1771 by Test Thomas B. Griffin, Cl Cur. [Pages 14a & 15]

21 Feb 1771. Record. Between Edwin Conway, Harry Carter, and William Sanders have visited the road thru John Carter's land, ... and agree that it may be altered in the manner said John Carter proposes... without inconvenience or detriment to those who live adjacent to that road or to the publick. Recorded 21 Feb 1771 by Test Thomas B. Griffin, Cl Cur. [Page 15a]

17 Jan 1771. Report. Summons of the sheriff of Lancaster Court...subscribers met, were duly sworn, and in company of surveyor viewed and valued an acre of land belonging to Charles Lee (which was petitioned for by Rawleigh Shearman to be the value of twelve shillings. We have valued the marsh belonging to Charles Lee, between the said Lee and William Hathaway and think damage to said marsh will sustain in consequence of a mill being built agreeable to above order, to be the value of ten shillings...likewise have considered the inconveniences atend the sloping of the landings above said acre of land of Charles Lee's not to be worth anything in consideration of a mill. Witnessed on 15 Feb 1771 by Thomas Brent, Roger Kelly, Mosses Davis, Anthony Garton, Benjamin Kelly, William Martin, Nicholas Currell, William Yerby, Thomas Hunton, Maurice Brent, John Yerby, and Harry Currell. Recorded 21 Feb 1771 by Test Thomas B. Griffin, Cl Cur. [Page 15a]

20 Mar 1771. Deed with Livery and Seisen. Between William Chilton of Christ Church Parish in Lancaster County and Jesse Chilton of same parish and county. William Chilton in consideration of four hundred pounds ...[from] Jesse Chilton... [for] two hundred acres of land lying in said parish and county, bounded by the lands of Edward Blakemore and George Chitwood and is one moiety or half part of a tract of land containing about the quantity of four hundred acres which descended to Ann Chilton, wife of said Jesse Chilton, the present purchaser and her sister Jemima Blakemore, wife of aforesaid Edward Blakemore as a binder from their father Robert Nesum estate... deced [Wit:] Gavin Lawry, Edward Blakemore, and Dale Carter. Recorded 21 Mar 1771 by Test Thomas B. Griffin, Cl Cur. [Pages 15a, 16 & 16a]

10 Dec 1770. Deed with Livery and Seisen. Between John Eustace and Alice Corbin his wife of Northumberland county of one part and John Meredeth of Lancaster county of the other part. Said John Euslace and Alice Corbin in consideration of the sum of two hundred and nineteen pounds, thirteen shillings, and nine pence paid by the said John Meredeth ....to a certain tract of land ...being in the Parish of Christ Church and county of Lancaster containing one hundred seventy-five and three quarters acres, lately purchased by the said John Eustace of Col. Charles Carter of county of King George and known by the name of Poplar Neck beginning (by a survey and plot by Griffin Garland 17 Mar 1769) opposite to Dymers Gate thence to a stump by the creek side near the warehouse, thence cross the mouth of a cove and up the meanders of the Mill Creek to a line dividing this land from the said Dymers a little below the main road from thence S1d 30m E181 pole to the angle of four trees and from thence to the place of the beginning. [Wit:] Thos Rowand, George Norris, Thos Rob, Jno Nichols. Recorded 21 Mar 1771 by Test Thomas B. Griffin, Cl Cur. [Pages 16a & 17]

25 Feb 1771. Deed with Livery with Seisen. Between George Garland of the county of Richmond of one part and Edmond Wilcox gent of the county of Amherst on the other part. In consideration of the sum of forty pounds... paid by the said Edmond Wilcox ... (for) a negro wench named Chloe...and her future increase... [Wit:] Caty Tarpley, John Mackay, & Burges Smith. Recorded 17 Mar 1771 by Test Thomas B. Griffin, Cl Cur [Page 17 & 17a]

21 Mar 1771. Deed with Livery with Seisen. Between Richard Mitchell and Ann his wife of county of Lancaster of one part and John Chinn of same county of the other part. In consideration of the sum of sixty pounds... paid by the said John Chinn... being one moiety of a grist mill lately erected on Momtico Run by James Ball and Joseph Chinn gent and one acre of land on each side the said Run thereunto adjoining with their and every of their appurtenances, the acre of land on the north side of said Run bounded according to an Indenture of Feoffment granted by Richard Nash and Hannah his wife to the said Joseph Chinn and James Ball and the other acre bounded by the lines run by a jury and the county surveyor pursuant to an order of Lancaster court with all... right title interest claim and demand whatsoever of the said Richard Mitchell and Ann his wife in and to the said grist mill and land and promises to have and to hold said moiety of said grist mill land and promises with all and singular their appurtenances unto said John Chinn... [Wit:] Jas Ball, Thads McCarty, John Pullen, and James Warrick. Recorded 21 Mar 1771 by Test Thomas B. Griffin, Cl Cur [Pages 17a & 18]

5 Mar 1771. Deed with Receipt. Between George Hoate of the county of Lancaster gent and Sarah his wife of the one part and Mungo Harvey of the same county of the other part. In consideration of the sum of five hundred and seventy pounds by the said Mungo Harvey... for two tracts or parcels of land scituate in the said county of Lancaster, to wit, all that tract or parcel of land whereon the [blank] George Hoate now dwelleth on the west side of the westward branch of Corotoman River and by him purchased of Joseph Whorten, John Davis, William Glascock gent and Easther his wife, and William Mountague gent containing by estimation two hundred acres... and all that tract of land purchased by said George Hoate at two different times of James Webb containing by estimation eighty four acres... and are bounded according to the several Deeds of Conveyance made unto the said George Hoate by the aforesaid persons... Mungo Harvey ...shall or may from the said first day of December rest quietly and peaceably have, hold, possess... the two said hereby granted parcels of land and promises with all rights... thereunto belonging clear and free ... from all form or grants, dowers, or other incumbrances whatsoever except the Quitrents thereafter becoming & us to the Chief Lord of the Fee... [Wit:] Jas Ball, James Webb, John Dye, Jesse Ball, & John Chinn. Received day of Indenture of within named Mungo Harvey the sum of five hundred pounds... in

full consideration for the within named two parcels of land & premises. [Wit:] Jas Ball, James Webb, John Dye, Jesse Ball, & John Chinn. Recorded 21 Mar 1771 by Test Thomas B. Griffin, Cl Cur [Pages 18, 18a, & 19]

5 Mar 1771. Report. James Ball, John Chinn and Jesse Ball gent whereas George Hoate gent and Sarah his wife by their certain Indenture of Bargain and Sale bearing date 5 Mar 1771 have sold and conveyed unto Mungo Harvey merchant two tracts of land containing two hundred eighty four acres with the appurtenances lying and being in Church Christ Parish in said county of Lancaster and whereas Sarah Hoate the wife of said George Hoate cannot conveniently travel to our county court of Lancaster to make acknowledgement and relinquishment of her right in said land. Therefore, we do give unto you, or any two of you, full power to receive acknowledgement and relinquishment which the said Sarah Hoate shall be willing to make before you of her right in the land aforesaid... Wit: Thomas B. Griffin, Clerk of our said court at the courthouse aforesaid 7 Mar 1771. [Pages 19 & 19a]

15 Mar 1771. Commission and Certificate. We the subscribers having... examined the within named Sarah Hoate privately and apart from her husband the within named George Hoate gent, do hereby certify the said Sarah Hoate doth freely and voluntarily without persuasions or threats of her said husband acknowledge her right of dower to the two tracts of land mentioned in a Deed of Conveyance from the said George Hoate and his wife Sarah unto Mungo Harvey Merchant...sealed.. 15 Mar 1771. {Wit:] Jas Ball, John Chinn, & Jesse Ball. Recorded 21 Mar 1771 by Test Thomas B. Griffin, Cl Cur [Page 19a]

18 Apr 1771. Report. In obedience to an order of court directed to us to view a road between Mr. George Carter and Mr. William Chilton we have found no inconveniency but rather a dryer road. [Wit:] Richard Stephens and John Biscoe. Recorded 18 Apr 1771 by Test Thomas B. Griffin, Cl Cur [Page 19a]

21 Feb 1771. Deed with Receipt. Between Jesse Robinson of county of Lancaster planter and Joanna his wife of the one part and Oswald Newby of the same county planter of the other part. ...In consideration of the sum of eleven pounds five shillings ... by Oswald Newby ... all that piece or parcel of land situate in said county of Lancaster and is bounded as followeth, beginning at a stone on the west side of the main road that leads by Doctr Robertsons to Machans Bridge being a corner between said Jesse Robinson and Robert M Tire and running thence S78 W39 ½ pole to a red oak near the swamp, a corner between the said Robinson, Newby, Neasom, and Chattin thence N24 W11 ½ P up the swamp to a black oak in the line between the said Robinson and Chattin thence N9 E8 P to a chestnut on the east of the said road and corner between the said Jesse Robinson and Doctr Robertson and Chattin, thence along the said road

to the beginning corner thence containing twelve and a half acres... [Wit:] Jas Ball, Jesse Ball, Bridgar Haynie. Court held 21 Feb 1771, Deed with Receipt thereon indorsed from Jesse Robinson and Joanna his wife to Oswald Newby was acknowledged in court... ordered to lye for his wife's acknowledgement till next court. Recorded 18 Apr 1771 by Test Thomas B. Griffin, Cl Cur [Pages 19a, 20 & 20a]

20 Mar 1771. Deed with Livery with Seisen. Between John Eustace gent and Alice Corbin his wife of Northumberland county of the one part and Elmour Dogget of the county of Lancaster of the other part. In consideration of the sum of one hundred twenty pounds... paid by the said Elmour Dogget ... [for] tract or parcel of land situated and lying and being in the Parish of Christ Church and county of Lancaster containing and survey made by Griffin Garland, one hundred and fifty eight acres of land lately purchased by the said John Eustace of Col Charles Carter of the county of King George and known by the name of Brick House Tract. Beginning by a survey and plot by Griffin Garland dated 17 Mar 1769 at the line between John Yerby's line bought of the said Eustace at the main road and thence west to the corner of the said Yerbys near to a Branch and thence down the Branch being the line between Eustace and Haynes to Haynes corner and thence S E to the crossing of the Mill Run and thence up the main road to the beginning... [Wit:] Thomas Rowand, Thomas Rob, & John Merrideth. Recorded 18 Apr 1771 by Test Thomas B Griffin, Cl Cur. [Pages 20a & 21]

8 Mar 1771. Deed with Livery with Seisen. Between John Eustace and Alice Corbin his wife of Northumberland County of the one part and Richard Hutchings of the county of Lancaster of the other part. ...In consideration of the sum of two hundred pounds... paid by the said Richard Hutchings ... [for] tract or parcel of land situate and lying being in the county of Lancaster and the Parish of Christ Church containing two hundred seventy three and three quarters acres of land lately purchased of Col Charles Carter of King George county and known by the name of the Brick House tract beginning by a survey and plot made by Griffin Garland dated 14 Mar 1769. Beginning at a large black gum near the road that leads from the Grant Mill to the Rappahannock then W to a long bottom thence to the main branch thence S S E down the meanders to the main road, thence N up the said road to the beginning, then begin at a locust tree near Mr. Pinckards corner Hicory thence down the Fleet Bay Road to George Flowers line thence N to the creek, thence up the creek to the head and thence W to said hicory.... Recorded 18 Apr 1771 by Test Thomas B. Griffin, Cl Cur [Pages 21 & 21a]

6 Mar 1771. Deed with Memorandum with Livery with Seisen... Between John Cundiff of Lancaster county and Wiccomica Parish, of the one part, and John

Heath of the said Parish and county of Northumberland of the other part... In consideration of the sum of seventy five pounds... [for] two tracts or parcels of land containing by estimation one hundred and sixty two acres... one of which said tracts, was purchased of Charles Marsh by the said Cundiff and the other of William Galloway by the said Cundiff, both said tracts are situate and lying in the Parish of Wiccomica and county of Lancaster bounded as by deeds from Marsh and Galloway to the said Cundiff... that Anne Cundiff, wife of said John Cundiff, shall relinquish her Right of Dower of in and of said two tracts of land within six months after the date hereof, in due form of law... [Wit:] William Brown, Thomas Heath, & Joanne Everitt. Memorandum before acknowledged in court, that William Galloway is to have his life [?]/ in one hundred acres which he has possession of, and Judith his wife her Right of Dowery in the same tract. Test William Downing. [Wit:] John Heath & John Cundiff. 6 Mar 1771 Livery and Seisen of within two mentioned tracts of land was made and given by said John Cundiff to said John Heath... in presence of William Brown, Thomas Heath, Joanna Everitt, and Ezekiel Lunceford. Recorded 18 Apr 1771 by Test Thomas B. Griffin, Cl Cur. [Pages 21a, 22, & 22a]

12 Apr 1771. Report. We subscribers having (by virtue of said county court) viewed the cannon of the old fort at Queens Town, are of the opinion that the five we saw (the others being under water) are fit for the service they were at first intended... James Ball & Ja Ewell. Recorded 18 Apr 1771 by Test Thomas B. Griffin, Cl Cur. [Page 22a]

21 Feb 1771. Allotment of Dower. We the subscribers thereby required have laid off and allotted to Sarah Maughan, her dower in the land of Henry Davis, decd. Beginning at a marked tree near the head of a round cove and running along the line of the said land by marked trees to a corner apple tree, thence by another line of marked trees to a long cove. Containing by estimation a third part of the said tract. We also possess her with the kitchen, the room at the end of the dwelling house, and the hen house with a third of the Tobacco House, a third of the Corn House, and two apple trees next the house. Given under our hands this 28 Feb 1771 by Ja Ewell, Jas Newby, & John Taylor. Recorded 18 Apr 1771 by Test Thomas B. Griffin, Cl Cur. [Page 22a]

18 Apr 1771. Report. We the subscribers have met and possessed Jesse George with one third part of John Simmons estate, decd, witnessed 9 May 1771 by John Fleet, Raw Shearman, & Thos Carter. Recorded 16 May 1771 by Test Thomas B. Griffin, Cl Cur. [Page 23]

21 Mar 1771. Report. James Kirk, Benjamin George, and John Nichols have met and divided the estate of William Waugh, decd, and possessed Bartley James with his wifes part thereof as followeth, vuzt, To movables Edney

Tapscot keeps £10.8.4 ¾ . To cash in Charles Hammonds hand 30 with lawfull interest. 16 Apr 1771 by James Kirk, Berry George, & John Nichols. Recorded 16 May 1771 by Test Thomas B. Griffin, Cl Cur. [Page 23]

18 Apr 1771. Report. Pursuant to an order of said county court, ... subscribers having met and viewed the road that Capt Payne petitioned for, and the new road Mr. Mercer has proposed to be made, are of opinion that the new road that Mercer wants to make for the said Payne will be prejudicial to the said Payne and Mercer both, and that the old road with some mending, or a small turn around a vally will be the best of the two, to either person that has been proposed... report made 15 May 1771 by Wm Armes, Richd Overstreet, Jno Biscoe. Recorded 16 May 1771 by Test Thomas B. Griffin, Cl Cur. [Page 23]

May 1771. Deed with Livery of Seisen. Between John Lock and Frances his wife of Wiccomica Parish in the county of Lancaster of the one part and Meredith Mahanes of the same parish and county of the other part... in consideration of the sum of seventy five pounds...[for] sixty eight acres and a half of land situate lying and being in the parish of Wiccomica in the county of Lancaster and bounded as followeth vizt. Binding on the land of Mr Thomas Edwards and on the land of Mr Robert Pinckard and on the land of Mr Benjamin George and the land of Mr William Pasquet containing sixty eight acres and a half... [Wit:] George Edwards, Daniel Kent, & James Lock. Recorded 16 May 1771 by Test Thomas B. Griffin, Cl Cur. [Pages 23, 23a, & 24]

16 May 1771. Deed with Livery of Seisen. Between Richard Hutchings of county of Lancaster and Joanna his wife of one part and William Dogget Junr of the same county on the other part... in consideration of the sum of fifty pounds... paid by the said William Dogget Junr... [for] the quantity of forty five acres of land situate in the county of Lancaster and parish of Christ Church... which falls to the said Joanna wife of said Richard Hutchings one of the parties to these presents in copartnership with the rest of her sisters, children of Ann Dogget, decd, the widow of Benjamin Dogget, decd, the said forty five acres of land be the same more or less (yet undivided)...Richard Hutchings and his wife Joanna are now lawfully instituted to an absolute right in the above forty five acres... will in a legall manner acknowledge these presents before the court of said county of Lancaster within eight months from the date hereof that the same may be recorded. [Wit:] Test John Mason & Margret Dogget. Recorded 16 May 1771 by Test Thomas B. Griffin, Cl Cur. [Pages 24 & 24a]

16 May 1771. Acknowledgement. I, the above named John Heath, do hereby acknowledge the consideration for the above conveyance to be one hundred pounds sterling, due to the above named Henry Parry, and also nine hundred seventy three pounds, twelve shillings, and two three farthings sterling due to the

above said Richard Clay and Thomas Midgley Morebanks of Liverpool, except the article of charge in their account for loss of cottons from Kendall £3 g.10, and also the article in said acct for goods shipt by the Molly marked RYC £25.8.1 which two articles are to be referred to persons in Liverpool mutually chosen by the said parties. Test Jas Ball. Recorded 16 May 1771 by Test Thomas B. Griffin, Cl Cur. [Page 24a]

18 Apr 1771. Report. In obedience to an order of the county court of Lancaster, ...We the subscribers hath this day met and settled the estate of John Angell, decd and find a balance of two shillings and eight pence due George Edwards as [?] intermarried with Mary Angell, widow of the deceased John Angell and one third part of a negro fellow named James valued at sixty pounds current money of Virginia ...[Wit:] Anthony McQukas [?], James Kirk, and Edwin Conway. Recorded 16 May 1771 by Test Thomas B. Griffin, Cl Cur. [Page 25]

17 May 1771. Report. ...We the subscribers have viewed the outlet at Sarah Mahons and William Davis's proved it upon the line to the satisfaction of them both... [Wit:] Jesse Ball & Burges Smith. Recorded 17 May 1771 by Test Thomas B. Griffin, Cl Cur. [Page 25]

19 Nov 1770. Bill of Sale. George Tillery of Richmond county for and in consideration of Thomas Glascock having become my security to the executors of the estate of William Oliver, decd in a certain sum of money amounting to forty nine pounds which said sum was put in suit and there is now an execution against the body of him, the said Thomas and myself, the said George... pays and deliver unto said Thomas Glascock his heirs & assigns one Negro woman named Cate, two boys named Joe and Abel, and one negroe girl named Hannah... I, the said, George Tillery, my executors, ...or any of us do and shall well and truly pay or cause to be paid the whole or any balance that may be due at the time of such payment on the said execution for forty nine pounds principal with all interest arisen and to and with all other charges whatsoever, on the first day of December next the date hereof for redemption of said conveyed negroes that this Bill of Sale to be void or else to remain in full force. [Wit:] Wm Stonum and Rawh Downman. Recorded 20 June 1771 by Test Thomas B. Griffin, Cl Cur. [Pages 25 & 25a]

20 Jun 1771. Deed of Gift with Livery of Seisen. Between Thomas Percifull of Wiccomico Parish and county of Lancaster, of the one part, and Elijah Percifull of St Stephens Parish and county of Northumberland of the other part... the said Thomas Percifull as well for and in consideration of five shillings to him in hand paid by the said Elijah Percifull at and before the sealing and delivery of these said presents, as for and in consideration of the natural love and affection which he hath and beareth unto his son Elijah Percifull, hath given... all that tract or

parcel of land situate lying and being in the parish of Wiccomico and county of Lancaster containing one hundred acres ... and bounded as followeth. Beginning at a corner tree of Col James Balls land thence running to a corner tree of Thomas Brent thence to a corner tree between Brent, Carter, & Percifull thence down the branch to James Wallaces line in the great swamp and from thence to the beginning tree... [Wit:] William Brown, Edwin Kent, & Thos Brent, Senr. Be it remembered the day and year first within written, Livery and Seisen of the within mentioned tract or parcel of land, with all and every of the appurtenances was made, given and done by within mentioned Thomas Percifull unto the within mentioned Elijah Percifull by the delivery of Turf and Twig upon the promises in name of the whole. [Wit] Thos Brent, Senr, Edwin Kent, & Thos Brent, Junr. Recorded 20 Jun 1771 by Thomas B. Griffin, Cl Cur. [Pages 25a & 26]

20 Feb 1771. Bill of Sale. ...Nicholas Currell of the county of Lancaster and parish of Christ Church, have bargained, sold and delivered unto John Roberts of the same county and parish, one negroe girl named Anne for the consideration of forty five pounds...[Wit:] Bailie George & Samuel Hinton, Junr. Recorded 21 Jun 1771 by Test Thomas B. Griffin, Cl Cur. [Page 26 & 26a]

20 Jun 1771. Deed of Gift. ...Merryman Payne Senr of the county of Lancaster... for and in consideration of the natural love and affection which I bear for my son John Payne of the aforesaid county for divers good causes and valuable considerations... for and in consideration of the sum of five shillings current money doth hereby give... unto the said John Payne after the death of me and my wife, Catharine Payne the one half of my land or plantation being the part whereon I now live... [Wit:] George Wale, Elias Edmonds, Richd Stephens, Jesse Chilton, & James Newby. Recorded 20 Jun 1771 by Test Thomas B. Griffin, Cl Cur. [Pages 26a & 27]

13 Jun 1771. Deed with Receipt. ...between James Robinson and Agnes Robinson Junr of county of Lancaster of the one part, and Andrew Robertson, of the same county of the other part. Witnesseth that the said James Robinson and Agnes Robinson for and in the consideration of the sum of fifty four pounds current to them paid at or before the sealing and delivery of these presents, the receipt... have given... the said Andrew Robertson... all that tract or parcel of land situate in the said county of Lancaster whereon Agnes Robinson the elder, now dwelleth, being a parcel of land devised by Giles Robinson unto his wife the said Agnes Robinson the elder during her life and at her decease to his two sons Jesse and Giles equally, and the said Jesse sold & conveyed his part thereof unto the said James Robinson & said Giles devised his part thereof unto said Agnes Robinson Junr, & is bound as followeth. Beginning on the main road at a corner that divides the same from the land of said Andrew Robertson (formerly

Randolph Miller's) and running thence along their line S85 E64 pole to another corner of said land, thence S10 W to a swamp or branch that divides this land from the land of said Andrew Robertson, thence down the said swamp or branch, to the line of the said Andrew Robertson (formerly Joseph Heale's) thence along the said line N11 ¼ W127 P to the aforesaid road, thence down the said to the beginning, containing by estimation one hundred and eight acres... [Wit:] Johnson Riveer, Robert Belvard, & Jesse Robinson. Received the day of the date of the within indenture... of Andrew Robertson the sum of fifty four pounds... in full consideration for the within mentioned parcel of land & premises. [Wit:] Johnson Riveer, Robert Belvard, & Jesse Robinson. Recorded 18 Jul 1771 by Test Thomas B. Griffin, Cl Cur. [Pages 27a & 28]

18 Jul 1771. Deed of Bargain and Sale. ...between George Phillips of the parish of Wiccomico and county Northumberland of the one part, and John Yerby of the parish of North Farnham and county of Richmond and George Yerby of the parish of North Farnham and count of Richmond of the other part... in the consideration of the sum of two hundred pounds... paid by the said John Yerby and George Yerby... [for] tract or parcel of land whereon the said George Phillips now lives situate lying and being in the parish of Wiccomico and county of Northumberland containing by estimation two hundred and forty acres... assigns forever to... the said John Yerby and George Yerby... nevertheless, and upon condition that whereas one Thomas Taff hath brought and commenced an action in Richmond county court against the aforesaid John Yerby and George Yerby for the recovery of certain lands and tenements late the property of John Woodbridge Gent. deceased, and now in the possession of the aforesaid John Yerby and George Yerby... on the [blank] day of January in the year of our Lord one thousand seven hundred and seventy became bound as security for the aforesaid George Phillips in a bond to one Traverse Downman, Late of the parish of Wiccomico and county of Northumberland for the payment of two hundred sixty five pounds ... Now if at and upon the end and trial of the aforesaid action of the said Thomas Taff... shall be cast in his said action or suit and the right of inheritance and fee of the said lands late the property of the aforesaid John Woodbridge deceased, shall be determined by the judgement of the aforesaid county court of Richmond to be lawfully vested in the aforesaid John Yerby and George Yerby that then and from thenceforth this present indenture and everything therein contained shall cease determine and be utterly void herein anything before contained to the contrary notwithstanding, and the said George Phillips doth by these presents for himself, his heirs and assigns covenant and grant to and with the said John Yerby and George Yerby their and every of their heirs... that if the said Thomas Taff shall prevail in his action or suit now commenced and prosecuted in Richmond county... for recovery of said lands and tenements... by his said action and suit and upon the trial and determination thereof then he the said George Phillips his heirs and assigns shall

and will... truly pay... unto the aforesaid John Yerby and George Yerby the just and full sum of two hundred pounds... with interest to be computed on sixty seven pounds ten shillings thereof from the first day April last past before the date of this present indenture till April in the year of our Lord one thousand seven hundred seventy two, and afterwards on the whole sum of two hundred pounds without any deduction or abatement for taxes... and also the said George Phillips doth by these presents covenant and grant to the aforesaid John and George Yerby that in case the aforesaid Thomas Taff shall be cast in his said action... then the said George Phillips his heirs or assigns shall and will well and truly pay... the aforesaid John Yerby and George Yerby lawful interest on the aforesaid two hundred pounds to be computed as last aforesaid, and also the said George Phillips doth for himself, his heirs and assigns by these presents covenant and grant to and with the aforesaid John Yerby and George Yerby... shall and may from time to time and at all times after default shall be made in performance of the previous conditions or covenants herein before contained... and is hereby... agreed upon by and between all the said parties... it is so declared that the said George Phillips... shall and may until default shall be made in performance of any or all of the previous conditions or covenants aforesaid... have... the aforesaid tract or parcel of land... Lastly it is agreed by and between all the said parties to these presents that upon the said George Phillips executing a mortgage or other sufficient security of any other part of his estate for the purposes herein before mentioned to the aforesaid John Yerby and George Yerby... which shall be adjudged by the said John Yerby and George Yerby... of equal value to the estate hereby bargained and sold that then this present indenture shall cease and be void... [Wit:] William Brown, George Norris, & John Carter. Recorded 18 July 1771 by Test Thomas B. Griffin, Cl Cur. [Pages 28, 28a, 29, 29a & 30]

24 Jun 1771. Deed of Bargain and Sale. ...Between John Heath of the parish of Wiccomico and county of Northumberland in the colony of Virginia merchant of the one part and Richard Clay and Thomas Midgley of the Borough of Liverpool in Great Britain merchants and partners of the other part... For and in consideration of the sum of nine hundred and twenty three pounds, twelve shillings and two pence, three farthings lawful money of Great Britain, to him [John Heath]... paid by the said Richard Clay and Thomas Midgley at or before the ensealing and delivery of these presents... [for] a tract or parcel of land... whatson the said John Heath now dwelleth situate lying and being in the parish of Wiccomico and county of Northumberland aforesaid containing by estimation one hundred acres and which was purchased by the said John Heath of George Oldham and Winifred his wife as by deed bearing date [blank] day of [blank] ...1750 of record in the county court of Northumberland relation being thereto... all that mortgage and tract of land... situate lying and being in the parish of Wiccomico and county of Northumberland aforesaid and containing... one

hundred acres and adjoining and contiguous to the said first mentioned tract of land and which was purchased by the said John Heath of and from William Garlington Junior and Elizabeth his wife by deed bearing date [blank] of record in the county court of Northumberland...situate lying and being in said parish of Wiccomico county of Northumberland aforesaid containing... one hundred acres and adjoining and contiguous to the aforesaid tract of land on which the said John Heath now liveth and dwelleth and was purchased by the said John Heath of and from William Heath as by deed bearing date [blank] of record in the aforesaid county court of Northumberland relation being thereto had may more fully and at large appear and all that Water Grist Mill with the appurtenances and one acre of land to the said Water Grist Mill appropriated which said acre of land was purchased by the said John Heath of Isaac Gaskins and together with the said Mill is situate lying and being in the said parish of Wiccomico and county of Northumberland and all that messuage and tract of land with the appurtenances situate lying and being in the said parish of Wiccomico and county of Northumberland aforesaid containing by estimation one hundred acres and which was purchased by the said John Heath of and from Joseph Kent at two different purchases by deeds bearing the date [both blank]... and tract of land situate lying and being in the said parish of Wiccomico and county of Northumberland containing by estimation two hundred and eighty acres and which was purchased by the said John Heath of and from Traverse Downman by deed [blank]... of record in the county court of Northumberland aforesaid... tract of land with appurtenances situate lying and being in the aforesaid parish of Wiccomico and county of Lancaster containing by estimation two hundred and forty five acres and which was purchased by the said John Heath of and from Edwin Conway Genl by deed... [blank] of record in the county court of Lancaster... and tract of land situate lying and being in said parish of Wiccomico and county of Lancaster aforesaid containing by estimation one hundred and sixty acres and which was purchased by the said John Heath of and from John Cundiff by deed... [blank]... on record in said county of Lancaster... and tract of land situate lying and being in the parish of Northfarnham and county of Richmond containing by estimation one hundred and forty three acres which was purchased by the said John Heath of and from the aforesaid Traverse Downman by deed... [blank]... of record in county court of Richmond... and also the following slaves by the following names and distinctions Vizt. Hursts Daniel, Richmond Daniel, Mahanes's Daniel, Dennis Torn, and Robin sons of Cate, Copedge's Tom, Peter, George, Stephney, Harry, James Crab, James called Thomas's James, Moll and Dennis her son, Affa and her three children Milley, Tom, and Scipio, Martha, Dinah, Bett a woman, Old Nan, Cate, Judy and Rose, daughters of Cate, Old Winny, Esther and her son Edmond, Lilah and her four children Fame, Lisman, Moses, and Mark, Hagar and Jane, a woman daughter to Hagar, and George son of Hagar, Tabb and her four children in North Carolina whose names are unknown except Manuel, Young Nan and her seven children vizt. Milley, London, Kendall, Isaac, Traverse, Sarah and Phillis, Simon and Allick, sons of Affa, and Stephen a mulatto boy, and the present and future increase of the aforesaid female slaves...[all land and slaves] unto the said Richard Clay and Thomas Midgley...assigns in manner following that is to say that he the said John Heath is now the true and lawfull owner of said messuages lands water grist mill tenements, hereditaments premises... the said John Heath... shall well and truly pay or cause to be paid unto the said Richard Clay and Thomas Midgley... the full sum of nine hundred seventy three pounds twelve shillings and two pence three farthings... upon the first day of May next... with interest on the same from the first day of May until said sum... shall be fully paid and satisfied. [Wit:] David Blackwell, David Boyd, & Margaret Boyd. Recorded 17 Jul 1771 by Test Thomas B. Griffin, Cl Cur. [Pages 30, 30a, 31, 31a, & 32]

24 Jun 1771. Bond. John Heath of parish of Wiccomico and county of Northumberland am held and firmly bound to Richard Clay and Thomas Midgley of the Borough of Liverpool in Great Britain merchants and partners in nineteen hundred and forty seven pounds four shillings and five pence and one half penny lawfull money of Great Britain to be paid to said Richard Clay and Thomas Midgley... if the above John Heath... shall well and truly pay the said Richard Clay and Thomas Midgley... nine hundred and seventy three pounds twelve shillings and two pence three farthings... on or before the first day of May [1772]... then this obligation to be void or else to remain in full force and virtue. [Wit:] David Blackwell, David Boyd, and Margaret Boyd. Recorded 17 Jul 1771 by Test Thomas B. Griffin, Cl Cur. [Page 32 & 32a]

18 Jul 1771. Deed with Receipt. Between Mungo Harvey Mercht. of the county of Lancaster of the one part and Samuel Angell Wheelwright of the same county of the other part... for and in consideration of sum of sixty pounds... tract of land situated in the said county of Lancaster purchased by the said Mungo Harvey of John Davis who purchased the same of one John Wilkins bounded by the lands of Giles Robinson, Aaron Robinson, Thomas Chinn, and the main branch of Mrs. Margaret Balls Mill pond containing one hundred and sixteen acres... to have and to hold... to the said Samuel Angell... the first day of January next... Recorded 18 Jul 1771 by Test Thomas B. Griffin, Cl Cur. [Side note:] Delivered original to Jas Angell one of the heirs of Sam Angell herein mentioned 22 May 1872. [Pages 32a, 33 & 33a]

23 Sep 1771. Receipt. ...Between Richard Chichester of the county of Fauquier Gent of the one part and James Ewell of the county of Lancaster Gent of the other. Whereas the said Richard Chichester did on the first day of October [1765] for and in consideration of the sum of one thousand and eighty five pounds... at publick auction, sell unto the said James Ewell two certain tracts or

parcels of land lying in the county of Lancaster aforesaid containing the one devised unto the said Chichester by his father Richard Chichester Esqr Decd who purchased the same of Robert Carter Esqr and others executors in trust of the last will and testament of Andrew Jackson decd by deeds of lease and release bearing date twenty ninth and thirtieth days of April [1719] four hundred acres... the other purchased by said Richard Chichester of Capt William Payne by indenture bearing date eighteenth day of June [1764] containing one hundred acres be it more or less in the whole five hundred acres... recorded in the county court of Lancaster... said Richard Chichester did engage by bond to warrant and defend said land... and first day of December [1766] execute a deed for said land. Witnesseth that for the more effectual securing and suremaking of said lands... said James Ewell his heirs and assigns the said Richard Chichester for and in consideration of the sum of one shilling sterling to him in hand paid by said James Ewell and also in consideration of the said sum of one thousand and eighty five pounds and also in consideration of his said bond, the said Richard Chichester hath given... unto said James Ewell... tracts or parcels of land... [Wit:] Rawh Downman, James Selden, John Selden & James Ball. Recorded 17 October 1771 by Test Thomas B. Griffin, Cl Cur. [Pages 33a & 34]

18 Jul 1771. Report. ... value the damage as followeth, the land of John Boyd we valued to five shillings and six pence and the land of Bartholomew Dameron we valued to five shillings giving under our hands and seal, this twenty second day of July 1771. [Wit:] Oswald Newby, Johnson Riveer, William Dunaway, John Davis, George Norris, Spencer George, James Norris, John Bean, Richd Goodridge, Jesse Robinson, James Hill, & Jonathan Bullen. Recorded 16 Aug 1771 by Test Thomas B. Griffin, Cl Cur. [Page 34a]

24 Aug 1771. Deed of Bargain and Sale... between Richard Edwards of the county of Lancaster, Gent and Anne his wife of the one part and Thomas Rouand of Northumberland county of the other part... the said Richard Edwards and Anne his wife in consideration of the sum of four hundred pounds... all that tract of parcel of land whereon the said Richard Edwards now dwelleth and which was devised unto him by his father Thos Edwards Gent deced situate lying and being in Flash Bay Nash in the said county of Lancaster, and is bounded as followeth. Beginning at a marked pine tree (said to be the beginning corner) upon Hathaways Creek, and running thence down the meanders of the said creek to the mouth of Swans Bay, thence along and up the meanders of the said bay to a point that makes the Fleets Bay, thence down the Fleets Bay to the great bay of Chesapeak, thence up the said bay to a point that makes the mouth of Indian Creek, thence up the meanders of said creek to a marked corner pine between this land and the land of Capt Hugh Brent, thence south 37 W to the beginning containing... two hundred acres... [Wit] J. Eustace, Robert Gilmour,

Hugh Brent, Saml S. McCroskey, & James Armstrong. Recorded 19 Sep 1771 [by] Fost [?] .

Richard Mitchell, Hugh Brent, and Thomas Lawson, Gent Whereas Richard Edwards Gent and Ann his wife by their certain Indenture of Bargain and Sale bearing date the twenty fourth of August last past, have sold and conveyed unto Thomas Rouand... whereas Ann Edwards the wife of the said Richard Edwards cannot conveniently travel to our county court of Lancaster to make acknowledgment and relinquishment of her right in the said land. Therefore we give unto you or any two or more of you, full power to receive the said acknowledgment and relinquishment ... sending then there the annexed indenture and this writ. Witness Thomas B Griffin clerk of our said court at the courthouse aforesaid the twenty first day of October [1771]. By virtue of the within commission to us directed, we the subscribers did personally go to the said Ann Edwards and did examine her as to the indenture hereunto annexed, separately and apart from her husband the within named Richard Edwards, whose answer was that she freely and willingly execute the indenture hereunto annexed without any persuasions or threats by her said husband and she is willing that the same be recorded among the records of Lancaster County court given under our hands and seals this 17th Dec 1771. [Wit:] Rich Mitchell, Hugh Brent, & Thomas Lawson. Recorded 19 Dec 1771 by Test Thomas B Griffin, Cl Cur. [Pages 34a, 35, 35a, & 36]

3 June 1771. Articles of Agreement... between William Armes of the county of Lancaster of the one part and Hugh Walker of the county of Middlesex of the other part... said William Armes for and in consideration of the sum of five pounds... paid by the said Hugh Walker... a certain parcel or point of land situate lying in the said county of Lancaster. Beginning at the mouth of a small creek known by the name of Arm's Creek and so along the river side up to a cove of said creek where is and stands several stakes formerly a water fence and two acres of high land part of his the said Arms's Tract to be laid off just as said William Arms and Hugh Walker can agree... whereof the parties to these presents have interchangeably set their hands and affix their seal [Wit:] William Mountague, James Mountague, and Southy Darby... 21 Nov 1771, This writing from William Armes to Hugh Walker was proved... by the oath of Southy Darby and ordered to lye for further proof. Test Thomas B Griffin, CSC. Recorded 19 Dec 1771. This writing from William Armes to Hugh Walker was fully proved in court by the oaths of William Mountague and James Mountague Gent and they further proved the said Armes was quite sober and in his proper senses... by Test Thomas B Griffin, CSC. [Page 36]

21 Nov 1771. Deed of Bargain and Sale with Receipt...between Johnson Riveer of the county of Lancaster and Alice his wife of one part and Thomas Ball of the same county Planter of the other part... the said Johnson Riveer and Alice his

wife for and in consideration of the sum of twenty five pounds... tract or parcel
of land situate in the said county of Lancaster which formerly belonged to
Merryman Payne and William Blackerley and by them sold and conveyed... to
said Johnson Riveer and is bounded on the lands of Robert Jones beginning at a
red oak on the west side of the Coach Road and runs along Robert Jones's line,
to the main branch and then up the branch to the Coach Road and thence down
the road to the beginning containing fifty five acres... [Wit:] James Kirk Junr &
Edwin Lunceford. Recorded 21 Nov 1771 by Test Thomas B Griffin, CSC.
[Pages 36, 36a, & 37]

14 Jan 1772. Agreement...in the suit in ejectment depending in the said county
court between Burges Ball Plaintiff and James Ewell Defendant it is agreed
between the said parties that the bounds between the two plantations devised by
Richard Chichester Esqr , that is, the plantation called Newsoms unto his son
John under whom the said Burges Ball claims in right of Mary his wife and the
plantation called Fairweathers unto the son Richard under whom the said James
Ewell claims be settled and forever hereafter established as followeth.
Beginning at the mouth Fairweathers Creek, thence up the middle branch thereof
which runs by the said Ewell's peach orchard to a cove issuing up the east side
thereof, thence up the said cove to a holly tree at the head thereof, thence N 70 E
to a red oak close on the west side of the main road and at the corner of the said
Burges Ball's fence, thence the same course continued to Sharps line and that
the said suit be discontinued and each party to pay their own costs in this suit
expended. Nevertheless, that this agreement shall not bar the said James Ewell
of his remedy against the said Richard Chichester the son or his heirs in case he
or they shall hereafter inherit the said plantation called Newsoms... [Wit:] Test
Jas Ball, Lettice Ball, & Ann Ball. Recorded 16 Jan 1772 by Test Thomas B
Griffin, Cl Cur. [Page 37]

31 Dec 1770. Letter of Attorney. Know all men by these presents that I
Christopher Hare of Taunton in the county of Somerset... nephew and devises
named in the last Will and Testament of Jeremiah Greenham late of Richmond
county Rappahanock River Virginia Planter deceased ... authorized and
appointed...James Ball of Lancaster county Rappahanock River Virginia
aforesaid Esq my true and lawfull attorney and hereby give to him full power
and authority in my name and hand and for my use to enter into and upon all
those three plantations situate lying and being in Richmond county Rappahanock
River aforesaid containing in the whole about three hundred ten acres of tobacco
land together with all the houses thereon erected late the lands of the said
Jeremiah Greenham deceased and situate lying and adjoining to the lands late of
John Woodbridge Gent decd and to ask sue demand for recover and receive all
and every sum and sums of money... due or belong to me from any person or
persons in Virginia aforesaid and on non payment and non delivery thereof for

me and in my name to use and take all proper methods according to the laws and customs of Virginia aforesaid for obtaining and recovery of the same and on payment or delivery thereof to my said attorney to release and discharge the person and persons so paying and delivering the same... hereby further authorize and impower my said attorney to sell and dispose of the said plantations and all the houses and stock thereon to any person or persons as he shall think fit for the greatest price that can or may be gotten... [Wit:] Rr Hoare, Notary Publick, at Taunton aforesaid & Rr Hoare Junr Borough and town of Taunton in the county of Somerset. These are to certify all whom it may concern that Roger Hoare the younger, of Taunton in the county of Somerset, Gent hath this day made oath before me one of his Majestys Justices of the peace in and for the said borough and town that he did see the within named Christopher Hare sign seal and deliver the within written letter of attorney and the names Rr Hoare and R Hoare Junr the witnesses attesting the same are the proper hands writing... [Wit:] Thos Hancock, Mayor. Recorded 16 Jan 1772 by Test Thomas B. Griffin, Cl Cur. [Pages 37, 37a, & 38]

15 Jan 1772. Deed of Feoffment with Receipt of Livery with Seisin. ...between John Wormsley and Ann his wife of the parish of Christ Church and county of Lancaster of the one part and Robert Hening Junr of the same parish and county of the aforesaid of the other part... the said John Wormsly and Ann his wife for and in the consideration of the sum of one hundred and eighty pounds...paid by the said Robert Hening at and before the sealing and delivery of these presents... all that tract or parcel of land situate lying and being in the parish and county aforesaid whereon Apphia Boatman now lives containing by estimation two hundred acres... vizt the bounding line begins at a corner white oak standing a little below Capt James Selden's Mill from thence it runs south east one hundred and thirteen poles along a line of marked trees dividing this land from the lands of Peter Conway to a stake in the said line thence south forty nine degrees west two hundred and fifty seven poles to another stake, thence north west to the mouth of a small branch at the marsh thence along the said marsh and creek at the head of the Corotoman River to the place where it first begun... [Wit:] Robert Gilmour, James Gordon, Bridgar Haynie & William Brown. Recorded 16 Jan 1772 by Test Thomas B. Griffin, Cl Cur. ***Side note – The original delivered to Lewis Hening the son and heir at law of Robert Hening July 20th, 1792 by Test James Gordon, CLC.*** [Pages 38, 38a, & 39]

21 Dec 1771. Deed of Feoffment with Livery of Seisen and Receipt... between Doctor Joseph McAdam Gent and Sarah Ann his wife of the parish of St Stephen and county of Northumberland of the one part and William Brown of the parish of Christ Church and county of Lancaster of the other part... said Joseph McAdam and Sarah Ann his wife for and in the consideration of the sum of five hundred and twenty pounds... paid by the said William Brown... [for]

tract or parcel of land situate lying and being in the parish of Wiccomoco and county of Lancaster which the aforesaid Joseph McAdam purchased of Edward Sanders (being part of a larger tract formerly belonging to Edward Sanders father of the aforesaid Edward Sanders and by the said Edward Sanders the father made over by Deed of Gift to Edward Sanders the son as by said deed of gift... bearing date on or about the fifth day of March 1742/3 and a Deed of Bargain and Sale from the aforesaid Edward Sanders the son to the aforesaid Joseph McAdam bearing date [unknown] 1764 both properly proved and recorded among the records of Lancaster court...) containing by estimation one hundred and ninety acres... [Wit:] Harry Carter, Thomas Ellet, Edwin Conway, Charles Lock, & Samuel Brooks... Recorded 16 Jan 1772 by Test Thomas B. Griffin, Cl Cur. [Pages 39, 39a, 40, & 40a]

21 Nov 1771. Indenture of Mortgage... between John Heath of the parish of Wiccomoco and county of Northumberland in the colony of Virginia merchant of the one part and Nicholas Flood of the parish of Northfarnham and the county of Richmond of the other part. Whereas the above mentioned John Heath did on the seventeenth day of September... 1770 execute an indenture or Deed of Mortgage to Nicholas Flood of fifty two Negro slaves and eight messuages and tracts of land for the security of the payment of eight hundred and sixty pounds... which the said John Heath was indebted to said Nicholas Flood which said Indenture or Deed of Mortgage was proved and recorded in the general court on the twenty second day of April 1771. Recourse being thereto had many more fully and at large appear and whereas the above named Nicholas Flood... hath advanced and lent to the said John Heath at sundry different times several sums of money the balance of which after the deduction of the store account of the said John Heath amounts to five hundred and seventeen pounds twelve shillings and seven pence for the security of the payment of which... effectually to secure the payment of the said sum of two hundred and seventeen pounds twelve shillings and seven pence and also for the more effectuate security of the payment of the further sum of four hundred pounds... now advanced and lent to the said John Heath by the said Nicholas Flood for which the said John Heath hath made and executed a bond of equal date with these presents wherein the said John Heath stands bound to the said Nicholas Flood in the sum of eight hundred pounds... the said bond and condition recourse being thereto had may morefully and at large appear. Now this indenture witnesseth that the said John Heath as well for and in consideration of the first mentioned sum of two hundred seventeen pounds twelve shillings and seven pence entered on the back of the above mentioned indenture or Deed of Mortgage as for and in consideration of the said bond and conditions amounting in the whole sum of six hundred and seventeen pounds twelve shillings and seven pence... for the better security of the said Nicholas Flood... in the payment of the said sum [above mentioned] and also in consideration of the further sum of ten shillings to him the said John

Heath by the said Nicholas Flood at or before the ensealing and delivery of these presents... [for] tract of land with the appurtenances whereon the said John Heath now dwelleth situate lying and being in the parish of Wiccomico and county of Northumberland aforesaid containing by estimation one hundred acres and which was purchased by the said John Heath of George Oldham and Winnefred his wife as by deed bearing date [blank] 175? Of record in county court of Northumberland... and also all... tract of land with appurtenances situate lying and being in the said parish of Wiccomico county of Northumberland aforesaid containing by estimation one hundred acres and adjoining and contiguous to the said first mentioned tract of land and which was purchased by the said John Heath of and from William Garlington Junr and Elizabeth his wife by deed bearing date... [blank] of record in the county court of Northumberland and... tract of land with the appurtenances situate lying and being in the said parish of Wiccomico and county of Northumberland aforesaid containing by estimation one hundred and forty acres and adjoining and contiguous to the aforesaid tract of land on which the said John Heath now dwelleth... which was purchased by the said John Heath of and from William Kent[?] as by deed bearing date ...[blank] of record in the said county court of Northumberland... and all that Water Grist Mill with appurtenances and one acre of land to the said Water Grist Mill appropriated which said acre of land was purchased by the said John Heath of Isaac Gaskins and together with the said mill, is situate lying and being in the said parish of Wiccomico and county of Northumberland aforesaid... and tract of land with the appurtenances situate lying and being in the parish of Wiccomico and county of Northumberland aforesaid, containing by estimation one hundred acres and which was purchased by said John Heath of and from Joseph Kent at two different purchases by deed bearing date... [blank]...of record in the general court... and tract of land with the appurtenances situate lying and being in said parish of Wiccomico and county of Northumberland containing by estimation two hundred and eighty acres, and which was purchased by said John Heath of and from Traverse Downman and George Conway by deed bearing date...[blank] of record in the county court of Northumberland... and tract of land with the appurtenances situate lying and being in the said parish of Wiccomico and county of Lancaster containing by estimation two hundred and forty five acres and which was purchased by the said John Heath of and from Edwin Conway Gent by deed bearing date... [blank] of record in the county court of Lancaster... and tract of land with the appurtenances situate lying and being in the said parish of Wiccomico and county of Lancaster aforesaid containing by estimation one hundred and sixty acres and which was purchased by the said John Heath of and from John Cundiff by deed bearing date... [blank] of record in the in the said county court of Lancaster... and tract of land with the appurtenances situate lying and being parish of Northfarnham and county of Richmond containing by estimation one hundred and forty three acres, and which was purchased by said

John Heath of and from the aforesaid Traverse Downman by deed bearing date... [blank] of record in the county court of Richmond... and tract of land with all its appurtenances situate lying and being in the parish of [blank] and county of Hallifax (formerly Edgcomb County) in the province of North Carolina containing by estimation six hundred and fifty acres which was purchased by the said John Heath of and from Samuel Huckaby and David Fluker by deed bearing date... [blank] of record in county court of Hallifax... and also the following negroe slaves, by the following names and distinctions, Vizt. Daniel, Richmond Daniel, Mahanes Daniel, and Dennis Tom, and Robin, the sons of Kate, Cappedges Tom, Peter, George, Stepheny, Harry, James Crab, James called Thomases James, Moll and Dennis her son, Affa and her three children, Vizt Milley, Tom, and Cipio, Martha, Dinah, Beth, a woman Old Nan, Kates Judy and Rose, daughters of Kate, Old Winny, Easter and her son Edmund, Lydia and her four children, Vizt Fame Elias, Mosses and Mark, Hagar, and her daughter Jane, and her son George, Tab and her four children, Vizt Elismond, Emanuel, [blank], in North Carolina Young Nan and her seven children, Vizt Milley, London, Kendall, Isaac, Traverse, Sarah and Phillis, Simon and Elloch, sons of Affa, and Stephen a mulatto boy, Isaac, Will, Little Jude and her daughter Massey, Winny, Minah, and Jos a shoemaker, and present and future issues and increase of aforesaid female slaves, together with all the rights members and appurtenances of the aforesaid... land... together with the present and future increase of the said sixty negroe slaves and also one Tea Sloop Burthen about thirty tons called the Judith with one six[?] hogshead flatt[?] both almost new with all their tackle, furniture, and apparel, compleat and the Regester of the said sloop, which said vessels are now in the Bay of Chesapeak commanded by John Waddey, also fifty head of Neat cattle full grown and twenty head of young Neat cattle, also forty head of sheep, two grey horses, two bay horses, two black horses, and a bay mare and a bay filly, also twelve feather beds with twelve pair blankets, twelve pair sheets and one quilt or counterpain or other covering to each bed, and six sets of curtains, belongings to the same beds and also one Eight Day Moon Clock quite new, also three hundred and fifty barrels of Indian corn, and also all the tobacco made at the different plantations of the said John Heaths above mentioned supposed to be about twenty thousand weight, but which is not yet inspected. Together with all the future increase of the said cattle, sheep, and mares... unto the said Nicholas Flood... and the said John Heath will not send the said sloop Judith on a voiage to sea without the consent of the said Nicholas Flood... therefore according to the true intent and meaning of these presents with interest on the same from the sale of these presents, untill the said sum of six hundred and seventeen pounds twelve shillings and seven pence shall be fully paid and satisfied. [Wit:] David Blackwell, David Boyd, Jane Swan, & Mills Ball. Received of the within named Nicholas Flood the day of the sale of the within written Indenture the sum of six hundred and seventeen pounds twelve shillings and seven pence...being the consideration money within mentioned. I say received by me...John Heath Witness David Boyd & Jane Swan. Recorded 19 Mar 1772 by Test Thomas B. Griffin, Cl Cur. [Pages 40a, 41, 41a, 42, 42a, & 43]

22 Apr 1771. Memorandum in the nature of a Mortgage. Whereas the within named Nicholas Flood hath advanced and lent unto the within named John Heath several sums of money at different times since the seventeenth day of September 1770 at which time the said John Heath executed the within indenture or Deed of Mortgage Vizt. The said Nicholas Flood did on the 20th day of September in the said year 1770 advance and lend unto the said John Heath twenty three pounds eight shillings and ten pence and the said John Heath did on the second day of June last past assume to pay a bond of Thomas Waddey's for twenty pounds nine shillings and nine pence to the said Nicholas Flood, also on the second day of June last past advance and lend unto said John Heath the further sum of twelve pounds seven shillings and six pence and the said Nicholas Flood did also on the fifth day of June last past advance and lend unto the said John Heath the further sum of one hundred and fifty nine pounds sixteen shillings and nine pence. And the said Nicholas Flood did also advance and lend unto the said John Heath on the third day of July last past the further sum of one hundred and four pounds twelve shillings and eight pence amounting in the whole to the sum of three hundred and twenty pounds fifteen shillings and six pence out of which is to be deducted the store account of the said John Heath with the said Nicholas Flood, from the fifth day of June in this present year till the twentieth of November amounting to one hundred and three pounds two shillings and eleven pence so that the ballance of two hundred and seventeen pounds twelve shillings and seven pence remains due to Nicholas Flood. And whereas the said John Heath did at the different times of the said Nicholas Flood advancing and lending unto him the said differnt sums of money, engage and oblige himself to make sufficient security to the said Nicholas Flood for the same on the within mortgaged estate of lands and slaves. Now these presents witness that for and in consideration of the said sum of two hundred and seventeen pounds twelve shillings and seven pence... to the said John Heath in hand will and truly be paid by the said Nicholas Flood at or before the ensealing and delivery of these presents... and every part and parcel of the said lands and every of them with their and every of their appurtenances and all the said negroe slaves and all their future issus and increase shall from the twentieth day of September in the year 1770, and from the first second and fifth day of June and from the third day of July all in this present year 1771, as are above mentioned and from henceforth stand and remain and be charged and chargeable with and be a security to the said Nicholas Flood... for the payment of the said further sum of two hundred and seventeen pounds twelve shillings and seven pence...with lawfull interest for the same of the first day of January now next without any deduction or abatement whatsoever out of the same... [Wit:] Jane Swan, Mills

Ball, David Boyd, & David Blackwell. Recorded 19 Mar 1772 by Test Thomas B. Griffin, Cl Cur. [Pages 43 & 43a]

14 Mar 1772. Letter of Attorney. Know all men by these presents that I Thomas Young of Craven County in the province of South Carolina. Eldest son and heir at law of Robert Young who was the second son and devisee of Thomas Young decd late of the county of Lancaster in the colony of Virginia, do hereby nominate constitute and appoint William Sydnor and Jesse Ball of the said county of Lancaster Gent my true and lawfull attorneys, for me and in my name to dock the intail of a certain parcel of land and water grist mill, on or near the head of Morattico Creek containing by estimation fifty acres... which was devised unto the said Robert by his father the aforesaid Thomas Young decd, and to sell and execute deeds for conveying a fee simple estate in the parcel of land and mill with their appurtenances to such person or persons... my said attorneys... shall think proper... [Wit:] Jas Ball, Thads McCarty, Robert Chinn, & Jas Newby. Recorded 19 Mar 1772 by Test Thomas B. Griffin, Cl Cur. [Page 44]

15 Feb 1772. Deed of Bargain and Sale. Between James Ball of the county of Lancaster of one part and John Norris of the same county of the other part... James Ball for and in consideration of the sum of eleven pounds five shillings... [paid by] John Norris...[for] in said county of Lancaster, being part of a tract of parcel of land lately purchased by the said James Ball of Charles Carter Esq and is bounded as followeth, begining at a markd Mulberry tree in the line between the said Ball and Norris, and running thence Northerly to a marked small Dogwood between two marked Sassafras trees near the head of a small branch thence down the eastern side of the said branch by a line of a markd tree to Stoneham's line, thence Easterly along the line between the said Stoneham and Ball to the corner stake between the said Stoneham, Ball and Norris. Thence S42 West to the beginning containing by estimation fifteen acres... [Wit:] Jesse Ball, Jean Ker & Judith Ball... Recorded 19 Mar 1772 by Test Thomas B. Griffin, Cl Cur. [Pages 44 & 44a]

25 Sep 1771. Deed of Gift. ...Richard Boatman of the county of Lunenburg, in the colony of Virginia, sent greeting... for and in consideration of the natural love and affection which I have and bear unto Nancy Palmer my sister as also the sum of five shillings in hand paid the receipt whereof I do hereby acknowledge have given and granted... unto the said Nancy Palmer one negroe woman named Kate and one negroe girl named Kate and her increase also one negroe boy named Tom... [Wit:] George Chilton and Dale Carter... Recorded 16 Apr 1772 by Test Thomas B. Griffin, Cl Cur. [Pages 44a & 45]

25 Sep 1771. Deed of Gift. ... Richard Boatman of the county of Lunenburg... for and in consideration of the natural love and affection which I have and bear unto my mother Apphia Boatman, as also the sum of five shillings... [and] one negroe boy named Harry... [Wit:] George Chilton and Dale Carter. Recorded 16 Apr 1772 by Test Thomas B. Griffin, Cl Cur. [Page 45]

16 Apr 1772. Between William Steptoe of the parish of Christ Church and county of Lancaster of the one part, and Robert Gilmour of the parish of Wiccomicco and county of Northumberland of the other part... William Stepcoe for and in the consideration of the sum of five pounds seven shillings and six pence... paid by the said Robert Gilmour... [for] two acres and a half of land... thereof situate lying and being in the parish of Christ Church and county of Lancaster near the crossroads at Stepcoe's. Ordinary and bounded as followeth begining at a large persimon tree standing on the road side from thence runing S 84 W to a stake twenty poles, thence N 6 W twenty poles to another stake thence N 84 E to a scrubby oak by the roadside twenty poles and from thence along the road side to where it began... Recorded 16 Apr 1772 by Test Thomas B. Griffin, Cl Cur [Pages 45a & 46]

28 Xber 1769. Bond. Know all men by these presents that we John Eustace and Alice Corbin Eustace of the county of Northumberland are held and firmly bound unto Enoch George of the County of Lancaster in the just sum of thousand pounds current money to be paid unto the said Enoch George... The conditions of this obligation is such that whereas Enoch George of the aforesaid county of Lancaster hath this day of the aforementioned John Eustace bought one negroe woman named Winney... [Wit:] James Armstrong and Fortunatus Sydnor... Recorded 16 Apr 1772 by Test Thomas B. Griffin, Cl Cur. [Pages46 & 46a]

Apr 1772. Deed. Between John Eustace and Alice Corbin his wife of Northumberland county of the one part and John Yerby of Lancaster county of the other part... John Eustace and Alice Corbin his wife for and in the consideration of the sum of one hundred pounds...paid by the said John Yerby... [for] tract or parcel of land situate lying and being in the parish of Christ Church in the county of Lancaster being tract or parcel of land which the said John Eustace lately of the gentlemen trustees of Col. Charles Carter known by the name of the Brick House Tract. Beginning at a stake in the main county road where it crosses a branch called Dicks Branch, thence down the road to a sychamore tree planted, thence north seventy degrees west one hundred and seventy poles to a parsimon in a bottom at the head of a branch, thence north twenty five degrees east to Dicks Branch aforesaid which line divides this land from the lands the said Yerby purchased of the said trustees, thence down the said Dicks Branch the several meanders thereof to the begining containing by estimation one hundred and fifty five acres... [Wit:] James Armstrong and Edward Smith... Recorded 16 Apr 1772 by Test Thomas B. Griffin, Cl Cur. [Pages 46a & 47]

20 Apr 1772. Receipt. Received of Col. Burges Smith fourteen pounds two shillings and one penny half penny cash for the Quit.. of one thousand and twenty six acres of land due for the years 1761, 62, 63, 64, 65, 66, 67, 68, 69, 70, & 71. [Wit:] Test Wm Sydnor. By James Newby-collector. Recorded 21 May 1772 by Test Thomas B. Griffin, Cl Cur. [Page 47]

14 Feb 1772. Deed of Bargain and Sale. ...Between Jonathan Pullen of the county of Lancaster Planter and Betty anne his wife of the one part and Joseph Chinn Gent of the same county of the other part... the said Jonathan Pullen and Bettyanne his wife for and in the consideration of the sum of one hundred pounds... paid by the said Joseph Chinn... [for] tract or parcel of land situate in the said county Lancaster whereon the said Jonathan Pullen now dwelleth. Bounded as followeth, begining at a stake, corner between said Pullen and Chinn and runing along their line S by W 96 poles, thence W by N 186 p to the land of Thomas Stott thence N by E 96 p down a branch to a corner stake in said branch near the mouth thereof thence to the begining containing by estimation one hundred acres... which said parcel of land was sold and conveyed by Andrew Jackson unto Mary relict of Henry Pullen decd... by Indenture bearing date twelfth day of October 1698, and by Bryan Pullen heir at law of the said Henry devised unto Mary his wife in Fee and by her devised unto her son the said Jonathan Pullen... [Wit:] Thomas Dunaway, James Warrick, & James Bush. Recorded 16 Apr 1772 by Test Thomas B. Griffin, Cl Cur. [Pages 47, 47a & 48]

16 Nov 1771. Deed of Bargain and Sale. Between William Sanders of the parish of Wiccomico and county of Lancaster of the one part and Mary Sanders of the aforesaid parish and county of the other part... William Sanders for and in consideration of the sum of fifty pounds... paid by the said Mary Sanders... [for] eleven head of cattle, one cart and wheels, one roan mare about 10 years old, and a colt of the said mare eight months old, one grey horse – three years old, six ews and two weathers, one dozen pewter plates, three pewter dishes, two pewter basons, two iron pots, one cast bed and furniture of him the said William Sanders, all bargained promises are now in the possession of the said William Sanders. To have and to hold the said cattle along with all the other goods and chattels above by these presents bargained and sold unto the said Mary Sanders... as her own... provided always and upon condition that if the said William Sanders... do and shall well and truly pay or cause to be paid unto the said Mary Sanders... the just and full sum of fifty pounds... at any day and time within the space and term of five years next ensuing after the date hereof... and lastly it is agreed between the said parties that he the said William Sanders...

shall or may lawfully have... use occupy possess and enjoy all and singular aforesaid goods and promises till breach or nonperformance of the condition or proviso aforesaid shall be made he or they not abusing or misusing the same without the Let Trouble hindrance or denial of the said Mary Sanders... and also it is agreed by and between the said parties to these presents that upon the said William Sanders executing another mortgage of any other part of his estate that shall by the said Mary Sanders... be adjudged equal in value to the goods and premises herein and hereby mortgaged to her... [Wit:] Craven Everit, Henry Lowry, and Chloe Sulavan. Recorded 18 Jun 1772 by Test Thomas B. Griffin, Cl Cur. [Pages 48 & 48a]

18 Jun 1772. Deed of Bargain and Sale. ...Between Henry Tapscott of the county of Lancaster merchant and Mary his wife of the one part, and Bailie George of the same county planter of the other part... Henry Tapscott and Mary his wife, for and in consideration of the sum of two hundred pounds... paid at or before the sealing and delivery of these presents, the receipt whereof the said Henry Tapscott doth hereby acknowledge and of every part doth acquit and discharge the said Bailie George... [for payment] tract or parcel of land situate in the said county of Lancaster, which formerly belong to Richard Chichester Esq and by him given to Priscilla Palmer by indenture bearing date 12 Mar 1710 and on the death of said Priscilla, the same discarded unto her son and heir at law John Reeves who sold and conveyed the same by indenture bearing date 3 Sep 1756, unto the said Henry Tapscott and is bounded on the lands of James Gordon, Thomas Pollard, and on Carters Creek containing by estimation one hundred acres... [Wit:] Bridgar Haynie, Nicho George, & Robt Hening. Received the day of the sale of the within indenture of the within Bailie George the sum of two hundred pounds... in full consideration for the within mentioned granted parcel of land and premises. [Wit:] Bridgar Haynie, Nicho George, & Robt Hening. Recorded 18 Jun 1772 by Test Thomas B. Griffin, Cl Cur. [Pages 48a, 49, & 49a]

18 Jun 1772. Bill of Sale. ...I, Edwin Conway of Lancaster County in Virginia for the consideration of thirty two pounds... to him in hand paid, the receipt whereof ... Edwin Conway... sell and confirm unto Thomas B Griffin one mulatto boy slave called Arthur, alias, Arthur Currie... [Wit:] Thomas Shearman. Recorded 18 Jun 1772 by Test Thomas B. Griffin, Cl Cur. [Page 49a]

26 Dec 1771. Agreement. ...Between John Wormsley and Ann his wife of the parish of Christ Church and county of Lancaster of the one part, and Robert Hening Junr of the aforesaid parish and county of the other part as followeth. First the said John Wormsley and Ann his wife for and in consideration of the sum of one hundred and eighty pounds... to be paid as is herein after mentioned

and agree with the said Robert Hening that the said John Wormsley and Ann his wife shall and will at the proper costs and charges in the law of the said Robert Hening within six months after the date hereof by such conveyances ways and means in the law as the said Robert Hening or his council learned in the law shall reasonably advise devise and require, well and sufficiently grant convey and assure to the said Robert Hening his heirs and assigns or to whom he or they shall appoint and to such used as he or they shall direct all that tract or parcel of land situate lying and being in the parish of Christ Church and county of Lancaster containing by estimation two hundred acres be the same more or less whereon Effie Boatman now lives which said tract of land the said John Wormsley purchased of Benjamin Cundiff... the said Robert Hening shall and will immediately upon the said conveyance or conveyances... cause to be paid to the said John Wormsley and Ann his wife... the sum of one hundred and eighty pounds as and for the... said tract of land and promises above mentioned in manner following, to wit, the sum of fifty pounds immediately upon the aforesaid conveyance being executed and fifty pounds more in April 1772 and forty pounds more in October 1772 and the remaining forty pounds... on the first day of April 1773 and further it is agreed by and between the parties to those presents that the said Robert Hening... shall and may on or before the first day of January next ensuing after the date hereof enter into and upon one half of the aforesaid tract of land and premises with the appurtenances and from thence take and receive the rents profits and issues thereof to his and their own proper use and uses into the other half of aforesaid tract of land and premises above mentioned which is now possessed and enjoyed by the aforesaid Effie Boatman. Immediately upon the death of the said Effie Boatman and afterwards take and receive the rents... forever... it is covenanted and agreed upon by and between the parties to these presents that the said John Wormsley shall have good right full power and lawfull authority for and during the term of his natural life to cut mow and carry away... all the marsh or marshes belonging to the aforesaid tract of land as much hay straw or other grass as the said John Wormsley shall want for... the use of his own horses and cattle... the said John Wormsley and Ann his wife and the said Robert Hening do bind themselves... in the penal sum of one thousand pounds... firmly by these presents... [Wit:] William Brown, Nicholas George, and Janeta Brown. 19 Jun 1772 oath of William Brown given, 16 Jul 1772 oath of Nicholas George and recorded by Test Thomas B. Griffin, Cl Cur. [Pages 49a, 50, 50a]

10 Jun 1772.   Bill of Sale. I, Merryman Payne of the county of Lancaster for a valuable consideration to me in hand paid, have this day bargained sold and delivered and by these presents do bargain sell and deliver unto Merryman Payne Junr a young negro wench named Pleasant and her future increase... [Wit:] Jno Briscoe & Richd Overstreet. 16 Jul 1772 recorded by Test Thomas B. Griffin, Cl Cur. [Page 50a]

1772. Deed of Bargain and Sale. ...Between William Steptoe of county of Lancaster of the one part and Thomas Pollard of the same county of the other part... William Steptoe for and in the consideration of the sum of twenty one shillings [from Thomas Pollard for]... one small piece parcel or tract of land situate in the said county of Lancaster bounded as followeth. Beginning at the sign post and bounded by the road to a chestnut, from thence to a stake and then crossing the road to a peach tree and then to the aforesaid post containing two acres... [Wit:] Lawson Hathaway, James Pollard, & John Campbell. 18 Jun 1772 received of within named Thomas Pollard the sum of twenty one shillings... [and] memorandum peaceable possession Seisen of the land and premises in the within deed was given and delivered unto the within named Thomas Pollard by the within named William Steptoe... [Wit:] Lawson Hathaway, James Pollard, & John Campbell. 18 Jun 1772 recorded by Test Thomas B. Griffin, Cl Cur. [Pages 51 & 51a]

16 Jul 1772. Deed. ...Between William Schofield of the parish of Christ Church and county of Lancaster of the one part and William Schofield Junr of the said parish and county son of the aforesaid William Schofield of the other part... the said William Schofield the father as well for and in consideration of the natural love which he hath and beareth unto his said son... hath given... all that tract or parcel of land situate lying and being in the parish of Christ Church and county of Lancaster containing by estimation ninety six acres whereon the said William Schofield the father now lives... which... the said William Schofield the father lately purchased of Ebbin Porter... Nevertheless, and it is the true intention and meaning hereof that the said William Scholfield the father, ... to himself full power and lawfull authority to have hold use occupy possess and enjoy all and singular the aforesaid tract or parcel of land with the appurtenances and to take and receive to his own proper use and behoof the rents issues and profits thereof for and during the full time and term of his the said William Schofield the father's natural life... [Wit:] Thomas James, Geo Wale, & William Wale. 16 Jul 1772 recorded by Test Thomas B. Griffin, Cl Cur. [Pages 51a & 52]

8 Feb 1772. Deed. Between Sarah Wale widow and relict of George Wale decd of the parish of Christ Church and county of Lancaster of the one part and William Wale son of the aforesaid Sarah Wale and George Wale decd of the same county and parish aforesaid of the other part... the aforesaid George Wale decd did in and by his Last Will and Testament bearing date 23 Mar 1767, among other things give and devise as follows, "Item it is my will and desire that my loving wife Sarah Wale may live and enjoy herself with every part and parcel of my estate of what nature or kind soever during her natural life or widowhood" and also "Item I give my son William Wale all my land in Nantepoison to him and the male heirs of his body lawfully begotten." Now the said Sarah Wale in and for the consideration of the natural love and affection

which she hath and beareth unto her son the said William Wale and also for divers other good causes and considerations her thereunto moving she... hath granted... unto the said William Wale... all the estate... [Wit:] George Horton Junr, Joanne Wale, Thomas Lawson, Thomas Rowand. 16 Jul 1772 oaths from Thomas Lawson Gent and Thomas Rowand and 20 Aug 1772 acknowledged by Sarah Wale and recorded by Test Thomas B. Griffin, Cl Cur. [Pages 52a & 53]

4 Jan 1772. Deed. Know men by all these presents, I, Merryman Payne of the county of Lancaster for and in consideration of the love good will and affection which I have and do bear towards my loving son Nicholas Payne of the said county have given and granted... unto the said Nicholas Payne a negroe wench named Moll and her son Abraham with her future increase. [Wit:] Stockley Towles & John Chowning. Recorded 20 Aug 1772 by Test Thomas B. Griffin, Cl Cur. [Page 53]

19 Aug 1772. Deed of Bargain and Sale. ...Between George Goodridge of the county of Lancaster of the one part and John Goodridge of the same county of the other part... the said George Goodridge for and in consideration of one negro wench named Cate, one Do Nell, and one bay horse to him in hand paid by the said John Goodridge at or before the sealing and delivery of these presencs the receipt whereof he doth hereby acknowledge and of every part doth hereby forever hereby acquit and discharge the said John Goodridge... hath granted bargained and sold... by George Goodridge... unto John Goodridge... all that parcel of land in the said county of Lancaster bounded as followeth. Begining in a swamp at a corner white oak of Mr. George Heale's from thence a strate course along a line of marked trees to a corner red oak between the said Heale and Mr. Richard Ball, thence a strate course to a corner maple of the said Ball's standing in the swamp thence up the said swamp joining the land of Richard Cundiff to a branch that divides this land from the land of John Goodridge thence up the said branch to the head from thence to the head of another branch thence down the said branch and swamp to where it first began one hundred and fifty acres... [Wit:] Thos Gaskins, Jesse Ball, and Richard Hull. Recorded 20 Aug 1772 by Test Thomas B. Griffin, Cl Cur. [Pages 53, 53a, & 54]

19 Aug 1772. Bond. Know men by all these presents that I, George Goodridge of the county of Lancaster am held and stand bound unto John Goodridge of the same county in the sum of one hundred eighty and four pounds current money which payment well and truly to be made unto the said John Goodridge. The condition of the above obligation is such that if the above bounden George Goodridge... shall and will at all times hereafter well and truly perform fulfill and keep all and singular the articles clauses covenants and agreements mentioned and contained in a certain Indenture of Bargain and Sale made between the said George Goodridge of the one part and the said John Goodridge

of the other part... [Wit:] Patrick Connolly and Thomas Brent. Recorded 20 Aug 1772 by Test Thomas B. Griffin, Cl Cur. [Page 54]

26 Dec 1771. Writing. Whereas there was an agreement between the late Mr. William Hathaway decd that James Currell father of Isaac Currell did in the lifetime of the said Hathaway promise and agree, and doth at this time promise and agree that if the above named Isaac Currell should intermarry with Dolly Hathaway that the said James Currell do agree and freely give all his estate both real and personal after his decease and Sarah Currell his present wife... [Wit:] Henry Lawson, Thomas Lawson, and John Hathaway. Recorded 20 Aug 1772 by Test Thomas B. Griffin, Cl Cur. [Page 54a]

15 Sep 1772. Deed of Gift with the Livery of Seisen. ...Between Elizabeth Davenport of the county of Richmond widow of the one part and Rawleigh Davenport son of the said Elizabeth of the other part... the said Elizabeth Davenport for and in consideration of the natural love and affection that she hath for her said son and for divers other good causes her thereunto moving, hath given granted... unto said Rawleigh Davenport all that tract or parcel of land situate in the county of Lancaster whereon the said Rawleigh Davenport now dwelleth, bounded on the north side of the main road that leads from Capn Jesse Ball's Mill to Mrs. Margaret Ball's Mill and on the lands of Mr. George Heale containing by estimation one hundred acres be it more or less which descended unto the said Elizabeth on the death of her uncle John Heale... thereunto belonging or in any wise appertaining unto the said Rawleigh Davenport to and for the use and benefit of the said Elizabeth Davenport during her natural life and at her decease to and for the use and benefit of him the said Rawleigh Davenport... [Wit:] Oswald Newby, Thomas Flint, and William Mitchell. Memorandum- Quiet and peaceable possession and Livery of Seisen of the within mentioned granted parcel of land was had and given by the within named Elizabeth Davenport unto the within named Rawleigh Davenport by the delivery of the handle of the door of the chief mansion thereon... [Wit:] Oswald Newby, Thomas Flint, and William Mitchell. Recorded 17 Sep 1772 by Test Thomas B. Griffin, Clt. [Pages 54a & 55]

17 Sep 1772. Deed with Receipt. ...Between Merryman Payne of the county of Lancaster Gent, of the one part, and Peter Riveer of the same county of the other part... the said Merryman Payne for and in consideration of the sum of eight pounds... paid by the said Peter Riveer [for]... all that tract piece or parcel of land situate in the said county of Lancaster, being part of a tract of land formerly belonging to the said Merryman Payne commonly called his Forrest Plantation, and is bounded as followeth, begining at a stake in a small branch and runing thence by a line of marked trees N 84 degrees E to a marked red oak on the side of the Coach Road thence northwardly up the said road 32 ½ pole, thence S 76

½ W or such a course as will strike the back line 7 ½ pole from the begining stake, thence S 1 degree W to the said stake containing twenty one acres... [Wit:] Henry Tapscott and Johnson Riveer. Received the day of the date of the within Indenture of the within named Peter Riveer the sum of eight pounds... [Wit:] Henry Tapscott and Johnson Riveer. Recorded 17 Sep 1772 by Test Thomas Ber-d Griffin, C Curt. [Pages 55, 55a, & 56]

17 Sep 1772. Deed with Receipt. ...Between Merryman Payne of the county of Lancaster Gent of the one part and Robert Jones of the same county of the other part... the said Merryman Payne for and in consideration of the sum of eight pounds... paid by the said Robert Jones... [for]... all that piece parcel or tract of land situate in the said county of Lancaster binding on a parcel of land formerly purchased by the said Robert Jones of the said Merryman Payne, on the west side of the Coach Road, on the land lately purchased by Peter Riveer of the said Merryman Payne, and on the land lately on now belonging to Charles Carter Esqr, called Pea Vine Neck, containing twenty one acres... [Wit:] Henry Tapscott and Johnson Riveer. Received the day of the date of the within Indenture of the within named Robert Jones the sum of eight pounds... [Wit:] Henry Tapscott and Johnson Riveer. Recorded 17 Sep 1772 by Test Thomas B. Griffin, Cl Cur. [Pages 56 & 56a]

24 Apr 1772. Deed with the Livery of Seisen and Receipt. ...Between Mungo Harvey and Priscilla his wife of the county of Lancaster of the one part and Jonathan Pullen of the same county of the other part... the said Mungo Harvey and Priscilla his wife for and in consideration of the sum of two hundred and seventy pounds... paid by the said Jonathan Pullen... [for] all that tract or parcel of land situate lying and being in the aforesaid county of Lancaster which the said Mungo Harvey purchased of William Thatcher and bounded on the lands of William Dogget James Hill, Robert Nicken, Judith Fendla, and Charles Carter Esqr containing by estimation one hundred and thirty acres... to the said land belonging or in any wise appertaining, with all right, title, interest, claim or demand of them the said Mungo Harvey and Priscilla his wife in and to the same (saving to the said Mungo Harvey the use of that part thereof which Leanna Purcel the mother of the above mentioned William Thatcher now holds as her Dower during her natural life, in lieu of her dower) in consideration of which dower the said Mungo Harvey and Priscilla his wife... doth oblige themselves to let the said Jonathan Pullen... have the use of the same quantity of land for and during the life of the said Leanna Purcel out of a piece or parcel of land which the said Mungo Harvey purchased of James Hill and in such part thereof will be most convenient to the said Jonathan Pullen... (which said land now adjoins above mentioned land)... the said Mungo Harvey and Priscilla his wife... doth further agree to and with the said Jonathan Pullen... that they will when thereunto required by the said Jonathan Pullen... within eight months from the

date hereof acknowledge these presents in due form of law in the county court of Lancaster the said Mungo Harvey and Priscilla his wife doth oblige themselves when thereunto required by the said Jonathan Pullen... to make and do execute... in writing... an absolute Fee Simple... [Wit:] Joseph Rosson, John Overstreet, John Dunaway, & Andrew Robertson. Memorandum that on the day of the within date quiet and peaceable possession was made and given for the within mentioned land and promises by the within named Mungo Harvey and Priscilla his wife by the delivery of the handle of the door of the chief mansion house on the said land to the within named Jonathan Pullen [Wit:] Joseph Rosson, John Overstreet, & John Dunaway.

Received on the day of the within named date of the within named Jonathan Pullen the sum of two hundred seventy pounds... in full consideration for the within mentioned granted parcel of land and premises. [Wit:] Joseph Rosson, John Overstreet, & John Dunaway.   Recorded 20 Aug 1772 by Test Thomas B. Griffin, Cl Cur. [Pages 57, 57a, & 58]

4 Sep 1772. Commission of Certificate. To Richard Mitchell, John Chinn, Jesse Ball, James Selden and John Taylor Gent. Whereas Mungo Harvey and Priscilla his wife by their certain Indenture of Bargain and Sale bearing date 24th day of April 1772, have sold and conveyed unto Jonathan Pullen one tract of land containing one hundred and thirty acres more or less with the appurtenances lying and being in the said county of Lancaster and whereas Priscilla Harvey wife of Mungo Harvey cannot conveniently to our county court of Lancaster to make acknowledgement and relinquishment of her right in the said land. Therefore we do give unto you, or any two or more of you full power to receive the acknowledgement and relinquishment which the said Priscilla Harvey shall be willing to make before you of her right in the land aforesaid contained in the aforesaid Indenture... we therefore command you, that you personally go to the said Priscilla Harvey and receive her acknowledgement and relinquishment of the same and examine her privily and apart from the said Mungo Harvey her husband, whether she does the same freely and voluntarily without his persuasion or threats, and whether she be willing that the same should be recorded in our said county court of Lancaster and when you have received her acknowledgement and relinquishment and examined her as aforesaid that you distinctly and openly certify us thereof in our said county court under your hands and seals sending then there the annexed Indenture and this writ witness Thomas B Griffin clerk of our said court, at the courthouse aforesaid the twenty fourth day of July in the twelfth year of our reign. We the subscribers, having by virtue of the within commission examined the within named Priscilla Harvey privately and apart from the within named Mungo Harvey her husband and do hereby certify that she doth freely and voluntarily without the threat and persuasions of her husband acknowledge her right to the parcel of land and appurtenances contained in the deed within mentioned which is hereto annexed, and that she is

38

willing the said deed may be recorded in the county court of Lancaster. Given under our hands and seals this fourth day of September 1772... [Wit:] Jesse Ball and John Taylor. Recorded 17 Sep 1772 by Test Thomas B Griffin, Cl Cur [Page 58]

A poll taken for Richard Mitchell Novr 25th, 1771. Column 1: James Ball, James Selden, John Chinn, George Heale, James Newby, Joseph McAdam, Henry Tapscott, Edwin Conway, Burges Ball, John Heath, Benjamin Kelly, William Mason, Thomas Heydon, Edney Tapscott, William King, Charles Hammonds, John Heydon, John Bailey, Richard Ball, Jacob Currell, James Kirk, William Yerby, John Yerby, William Dogget Junr, William Mott, Paul Sullivant, James Hill, William Chilton Junr, John Nichols, Harry Carter, George Edwards, Charles Lee, James Kirk Junr, Enoch George, Richard Lock, Bushrod Riveer, William Griggs, Thomas Pinckard, John Connolly, Samuel Angell, Oswald Newby.
Column 2: David Currie, John Leland, Andrew Robertson, William Hubbard, James Gordon, Hugh Brent, Thomas Rob, William Sanders, Burges Smith, Moses George, Thomas Brent, John Eustace, James Currell, Bailie George, James Brent, John Biscoe, Augustin Rice, Joshua Hubbard, Richard Mitchell, James Waddell, John Norris, John Clutton, Benjamin George, James Pinckard, Spencer George, John Mason, Moses Davis, George Connolly, Dale Carter, Moses Chilton, George Webb, William Pasquet, John Bean, Jesse Robinson, Fortunatus Sydnor, Edwin Fielding, John James, Henry Carter, George Stonham, John Sexon.
Column 3: George Chitwood, James Norris, Anthony Sydnor, Martin George, Samuel Yopp, John Fleet, William Chowning, Roger Kelly, John Riveer, Gavin Lawry, Robert Chinn, William Steptoe, Samuel Brumley, Anthony Garton, Nicholas Brent, William Galloway, Thomas Lawson, Harry Currell, Henry Lawson, Harry Currell, Henry Lawson, William Martin, Benjamin Garton, Henry Mayes, John Yerby, Thomas Carter Junr, Lazarus George, Thomas Pitman, Richard Cundiff Junr, John Yerby, John Goodrich, John Pope, John Davis, George Bean, John Taylor, James Simmons, William Mitchell, George Carter, George Brent, Thomas Hammonds, George Davis, Thaddeus McCarty.
Column 4: Isaac James, James Fendla, Richard Hutchings, Maurice Brent, John Carter, Peter Riveer, Elias Edmonds, William Dunaway, Thomas Dunaway, Richard Stott, John Die, Jesse Robinson, Thomas Garner, Thomas Flint, Edward Carter, Thomas Pollard, Thomas Edwards, Elmore Dogget, William Davis, William Bean, William Riveer, Richard Stephens, Thomas Stott, Rawh Davenport, Henry Towles, Richard Hinton, Bartley James, Edward Blakemore, John Chowning, John Rogers, William Brumley, John Cundiff, William Stott, John Longwith, Joseph Norris, Thomas Everitt, James Wallice, Johnson Riveer, James Tapscott, Richard Edwards. **Thomas McCarty – 161.

Lancaster, to wit, Richard Edwards Esqr, Sheriff of this county, this day made oath before me that the writing herein contains a true copy of the poll taken for Richard Mitchell the 25th November 1771. [Wit:] Thos Pinckard, December 9, 1771. [Pages 58a & 59]

A poll taken for Charles Carter November 25, 1771.

Column 1: James Ball, James Selden, John Chinn, George Heale, James Newby, Joseph McAdam, Henry Tapscott, Edwin Conway, Burges Ball, John Heath, Benjamin Kelly, William Mason, Thomas Heydon, Edney Tapscott, William King, Charles Hammonds, John Heydon, John Bailey, Jacob Currell, James Kirk, William Yerby, John Yerby, William Dogget Junr, William Mott, Paul Sullivant, James Hill, William Chilton Junr, John Nichols, Harry Carter, George Edwards, Richard Hinton, Bartley James, Edward Blakemore, William Brumley.

Column 2: Charles Lee, James Kirk Junr, Enoch George, Richard Lock, Bushrod Riveer, William Griggs, Thomas Pinckard, Revd David Currie, Revd John Leland, Andrew Robertson, William Hubbard, James Gordon, Hugh Brent, Thomas Rob, William Sanders, Burges Smith, Moses George, Thomas Brent, John Eustace, James Currell, Bailie George, James Brent, John Biscoe, Joshua Hubbard, Richd Mitchell Junr, Revd James Waddell, John Norris Senr, John Clutton, Benjamin George, James Pinckard, William Stott, John Longwith, James Norris, Thomas Everitt.

Column 3: Spencer George, John Mason, Moses Davis, George Connolly, Dale Carter, John Bean, Fortunatus Sydnor, Edwin Fielding, John James, Henry Carter, George Chitwood, Joseph Norris, Anthony Sydnor, Martin George, Samuel Yopp, John Fleet, William Chowning, Roger Kelly, John Riveer, Gavin Lawry, Robert Chinn, William Steptoe, Samuel Brumley, Anthony Garton, Nicholas Brent, William Galloway, Thomas Lawson, Harry Currell, Henry Lawson, William Martin, John Connolly, Oswald Newby, George Stonham, John Sexon.

Column 4: Benjamin Garton, Henry Mayse, John Yerby, Thomas Carter, Lazarus George, John Yerby, John Pope, John Davis, John Taylor, James Simmons, William Mitchell, George Carter, William Schofield, George Brent, Thomas Hammonds, Isaac James, James Fendla, Richard Hutchings, Thomas Schofield, Maurice Brent, John Carter, William Edwards, Peter Riveer, Elias Edmonds, Edward Carter, Thomas Pollard, Elmore Dogget, James Pinckard, Richard Stephens, Thomas B. Griffin, Thaddeus McCarty, Richard Edwards, James Tapscott.   Bridgar Haynie – 135.

Lancaster, to wit, Richard Edwards Esqr Sheriff of this county, this day made oath before me that the writing herein contains a true copy of the poll taken for Charles Carter, November 25, 1771. [Wit:] Thos Pinckard, December 9, 1771. [Pages 59 & 59a]

A poll taken for Richard Ball November 25, 1771.
Column 1: Augustin Rice, Moses Chilton, George Webb, William Pasquet,
Jesse Robinson, Thomas Pitman, Richard Cundiff Junr, John Goodrich.
Column 2: George Bean, William Schofield, Thomas Schofield, William
Edwards, William Dunaway, Thomas Dunaway, Richard Stott, John Die.
Column 3: Jesse Robinson, Thomas Garner, Thomas Flint, Thomas Edwards,
William Davis, James Pinckard, William Bean, William Riveer.
Column 4: Rawh Davenport, John Chowning, John Cundiff, James Wallice,
Johnson Riveer, Samuel Angel, George Davis.   James Tapscott – 31.
Lancaster to wit Richard Edwards Esqr Sheriff of Lancaster, this day made oath
before me that the writing herein contained is a true copy of the poll taken for
Richard Ball November 25, 1771. [Wit:] Thos Pinckard December 9, 1771.
[Page 59a]

17 Nov 1772. Deed of Livery with Seisen and Receipt. ...Between Thomas
Stott and Betty his wife, of the county of Lancaster and the parish of Christ
Church of the one part and Richard Mitchell of the county and parish aforesaid
of the other part... the said Thomas Stott and Betty his wife for and in
consideration of the sum of forty pounds... paid by the said Richard Mitchell...
for divers other good causes and considerations the said Thomas Stott and Betty
his wife thereunto... moving have... sold... unto the said Richard Mitchell... one
certain piece parcel or tract of land situate, lying and being in the county of
Lancaster and the parish of Christ Church containing by estimation forty acres...
and bounded as followeth vizl begining at a stone standing in a line which
divides the aforesaid Mitchell's land from the land which the aforesaid Thomas
Stott formerly sold to John Carpenter decd thence nearly a west course to a
forked walnut tree standing at the head of a gulley near the said Thomas Stott's
spring, thence down the gulley and spring branch to Morattico Creek, thence up
the several courses of the said creek untill it intercepts the aforesaid Mitchells
line, thence up the said line to the first mentioned begining... the said Thomas
Stott and Betty his wife will within eight months from the date hereof in due
form of Law acknowledge these presents in Lancaster County court... [Wit:]
John Tapscott, Samuel Dunaway, Sarah Stonum, & Grace Stonum.
Memorandum that on the day of the within date quiet and peaceable possession
was made and given by the within named Thomas Stott and Betty his wife to the
within named Richard Mitchell by the delivery of Turf and Twig on the within
land in presence of John Tapscott, Samuel Dunaway, Sarah Stonum, & Grace
Stonum.   Received on the day of the within date the sum of forty pounds being
the consideration to be paid for the within mentioned land and premises. [Wit:]
John Tapscott, Samuel Dunaway, Sarah Stonum, & Grace Stonum.   Recorded 19
Nov 1772 by Test Thomas B. Griffin, Cl Cur. [Pages 59a, 60, & 60a]

19 Nov 1772. Bond. Know all men by these presents that we John Chinn, George Heale, and Richard Mitchell are held and firmly bound unto our Sovereign Lord King George the Third in the sum of five hundred pounds to be paid to our said Lord the King his heirs and successors. To which payment well and truly be made we bind ourselves... jointly and severally firmly by these presents sealed with our seals... The condition of the above obligation is such that whereas the above bound John Chinn is constituted and appointed Sheriff of the county of Lancaster during pleasure by commission from his Excellency the Governor of this colony under the seal of the said colony dated the 29th day of October last if Therefore the said John Chinn shall well and truly collect all Quitrents, Fines, Forfeitures, and amerciments accruing or becoming due to his Majesty in the said county and shall duly account for and pay the same to the officers of his Majesty's revenue for the time being, on or before the second Tuesday in June annually and shall in all other things truly and faithfully execute the said office of Sheriff during his continuance therein. Then the above obligation to be void, otherwise to remain in full force and virtue. Signed sealed and delivered in the presence of the court by John Chinn, Geo Heale, & Richd Mitchell. Recorded 19 Nov 1772 by Test Thomas B. Griffin. [Page 61]

19 Nov 1772. Bond. Know all men by these presents. That we John Chinn, George Heale, and Richard Mitchell are held and firmly bound unto our Sovereign Lord King George the Third in the sum of one thousand pounds, to be paid to our said Lord the King his heirs and successors. To which payment well and truly to be made, we bind ourselves... jointly and severally firmly by these presents sealed with our seals... The condition of the above obligation is such that whereas the above bound John Chinn is constituted and appointed sheriff of the county of Lancaster during pleasure by commission from his Excellency the Governor of this colony, under the seal of said colony dated the 29th day of October last. If therefore the said John Chinn shall well and truly collect and receive all officers fees and dues put into his hands to collect and duly account for and pay the same to the officers to whom such fees are due respectively at such times as are prescribed and limited by Law, and shall well and truly execute, and due return make, of all Processes and Precepts to him directed and pay and satisfy all sums of money and tobacco by him received by virtue of any such processes to the person or persons to whom the same shall be due his or their Exors... , and in all other things shall truly and faithfully execute and perform the said office of Sheriff during the time of his continuance therein. Then the above obligation to be void otherwise to remain in full force and virtue. Signed sealed and delivered in presence of the Court by John Chinn, Geo Heale, & Richd Mitchell. Recorded 19 Nov 1772 by Test Thomas B. Griffin, Cl Cur. [Pages 61 & 61a]

20 Nov 1772. Bond. Know all men by these presents. That we Edwin Fielding and William Norris of the county of Fauquier and Joseph Norris and Richard Mitchell of the county of Lancaster are held and firmly bound unto William Nutt administrator of William Dymer Gent late of the county of Lancaster decd in the full and just sum of two thousand pounds current money of Virginia. To which payment well and truly to be made to the said William Nutt, we bind ourselves and each of us... jointly and severally firmly by these presents... The condition of the above obligation is that whereas Capn William Dymer of the county of Lancaster departed this life without Will and the above named William Nutt qualified himself as administrator of the Estate of the said William Dymer and whereas the said Estate is to be equally divided between the said William Nutt and the above bound Edwin Fielding, and as the said Fielding is desirous of having his part of the said decd Estate delivered to him. Now if the above bound Edwin Fielding, William Norris, Joseph Norris, and Richard Mitchell... shall forever save and keep harmless the aforesaid William Nutt... and truly pay or cause to be paid unto the said William Nutt... one half of all legal debts and charges which the said William Nutt may be put to as administrator aforesaid, which shall be demanded of the said William Nutt... on account of the Estate of the said William Dymer and shall truly and faithfully pay or cause to be paid unto any person or persons and half of any claim or claims which they by Law may have a right to demand of the said William Nutt... as administrator aforesaid. Then this obligation to be void otherways to remain in force. [Wit:] Test Thomas B. Griffin. Signed by Edwin Fielding, Wm Norris, Joseph Norris, & Richd Mitchell. Recorded 20 Nov 1772 by Test Thomas B. Griffin, Cl Cur. [Pages 61a & 62]

17 Dec 1772. Deed with Receipt. ...Between Fortunatus Sydnor of the county of Northumberland and Elizabeth his wife of the one part and William Chowning of the county of Lancaster of the other part. Whereas Elias Edmonds Sharp late of the said county of Lancaster deceased was in his lifetime seis'd in Fee of two parcels or tracts of land situate on Corotoman River in the said county of Lancaster, one of the said tracts containing by a late survey two hundred and sixty five acres, the other tract containing two hundred and three acres by the said survey and died so seis'd without issue and intastate upon whose death the said two parcels of land descended unto his four sisters, the aforesaid Elizabeth, Thomazine, Sarah and Anne in equal portions... the said Fortunatus Sydnor and Elizabeth his wife for and in consideration of the sum of one hundred and seventy pounds ten shillings... [paid by William Chowning]...the said Fortunatus Sydnor and Elizabeth his wife... do fully and absolutely... sell... unto the said William Chowning... one full fourth part of the aforesaid tracts of land containing one hundred and seventeen acres... the said William Chowning... shall and may at all times forever hereafter quietly and peaceably have... and enjoy the said granted parcel of land and premises with its

appurtenances and every part thereof clear and free, and clearly and freely discharged of and from all former grants mortgages dowers title of dowers or other incumbrances whatsoever, (except the dower thereof of a Sarah Bond widow of Thomas Sharp the father of the aforesaid Elias Edmonds Sharp during her natural life only, and also except the Quitrents hereafter becoming due for the same to the Chief Lord of the Fee) and that they the said Fortunatus Sydnor and Elizabeth his wife... shall and will at all times warrant and defend the same against the lawfull claim lett, hindrances... grant and to and with the said William Chowning that they, the said Fortunatus Sydnor and Elizabeth his wife, at the time of sealing and delivery of these presents have in right of the said Elizabeth an absolute and indefeasible estate in Fee Simple in the said hereby granted parcel of land and premises...the aforesaid one hundred and seventeen acres unto the said William Chowning... at the proper costs and charges in the Law of them...[Wit:] Rich'd Mitchell, Spencer George, & Robert Hening... Received the same day of the date of the within Indenture of the within named William Chowning the sum of one hundred and seventy pounds ten shillings in full consideration for the within mentioned granted parcel of land. [Same witnesses as above]. Recorded 17 Dec 1772 by Test Thomas B. Griffin, Cl Cur. [Pages 62, 62a, & 63]

8 Jan 1773. Deed of Lease. ...Between Edwin Fielding of the parish of Leeds, and the county of Farquier of the one part and William Nutt of the parish of Wiccomico and county of Northumberland of the other part... Edwin Fielding for and in consideration of the sum of five shillings... paid by the said William Nutt at and before the ensealing and delivery of these presents... [for] one undivided moiety of all these two tracts of land and two plantations of which William Dymer late of the parish of Christ Church and county of Lancaster Gentleman deceased... one of which said tracts of land being the dwelling plantation of the said William Dymer at the time of his death with the appurtenances containing by estimation five hundred acres... situate lying and being in the parish of Christ Church and the county of Lancaster... to have and to hold the said undivided moiety of all the aforesaid Messuages, Lands... and every part and parcel thereof... unto the said William Nutt... from the first day of January this instant for and during and unto the full end and term of one whole year from thence next ensuing and fully to be compleat and ended. Yielding and paying therefore at the expiration of the said year one ear of Indian corn if the same shall be lawfully demanded. To the intent that by virtue of these presents and of the statute for the transfer in the actual possession... the said William Nutt may be enabled to accept and take a Grant and Release of the Reversion and Inheritance thereof to him... [Wit:] David Boyd, Thomas Norris, & Thos Shearman. Recorded 21 Jan 1773 by Test Thomas B. Griffin, Cl Cur. [Pages 63 & 63a]

9 Jan 1773. Deed of Release. ...Between Edwin Fielding of the parish of Leeds and the county of Farquier of the one part and William Nutt of the parish of Wiccomico and the county of Northumberland of the other part... Edwin Fielding for and in the consideration of the sum of three hundred and fifty pounds and ten shillings... paid by the said William Nutt at or before the ensealing and delivery hereof the receipt... (in his actual possession now being by virtue of a bargain and sale to him thereof made for one whole year by Indenture bearing date the day next before the day of the date of these presents and by force of the statute for transferring uses into possession)... one undivided moiety of all these two messuages two tracts of land and two plantations of which William Dymer late of the parish of Christ Church and county of Lancaster Gentleman deceased died siezed one of which said two tracts of land being the dwelling plantation of the said William Dymer at the time of his death with the appurtenances containing by estimation five hundred acres... lying and being in the parish of Christ Church and county of Lancaster aforesaid... [Wit:] David Boyd, Thomas Norris, & Thos Shearman. Received the day of the date of the within Indenture of the within named William Nutt the sum of three hundred and fifty pounds ten shillings... [Wit:] David Boyd & Thos Shearman. Recorded 21 Jan 1773 by Test Thomas B. Griffin, Cl Cur. [Pages 63a, 64, 64a, & 65]

21 Jan 1773. Bond. Know all men by these presents that I, Edwin Fielding of the parish of Leeds and the county of Farquier am held and firmly bound unto William Nutt of the parish of Wiccomico and the county of Northumberland in the full and just sum of seven hundred and one pounds... to be paid to the said William Nutt... The conditions of this obligation is such that if the above bound Edwin Fielding... in certain Indentures Bipartite bearing even date with these presents and the above written obligation made or mentioned to be made between the said Edwin Fielding of the one part and the above named William Nutt of the other part according to the true intent and meaning of the said Indentures. Then the above obligation to be void otherwise to remain in full force power and virtue. [Wit:] David Boyd & Thos Shearman. Recorded 21 Jan 1773 by Thomas B. Griffin, Cl Cur. [Pages 65 & 65a]

21 Dec 1772. Lease. ...Between John Turbeville of the parish of Cople and the county of Westmoreland Gentleman and Martha his wife of the one part and John Hunton of the parish of Wiccomico and the county of Northumberland Joiner of the other part... John Turbeville and Martha his wife for and in consideration of the sum of five shillings... paid by the said John Hunton... [for] all that Messuage or Tenement and tract of land commonly called and known by the name of Turbevilles Quater also all those islands commonly called and known by Musqueto or Broken Islands containing by estimation four hundred and ninety acres more or less situate lying and being in the parish of Christ Church and county of Lancaster and bounded as followeth to wit. Begining at a

corner white oak standing near Musqueto Creek side a corner to the said tract of land and the land now belonging to Richard Hinton formerly Samuel Hinton deceased, from thence along a line of marked trees which divides the land of the said Hinton farm from this across the neck to a marked Hiccory standing near Fleet's Bay Creek side from thence up and along the said Fleets Bay Creek side to a marked Pine a corner to the said tract of land and the land of Thomas Hunton, from thence along a line of marked trees dividing the said tract of land from the land of the said Thomas Hunton across the neck to a line tree of Thomas Lawsons land, from thence along a line of marked trees which divides this land from the land of said Thomas Lawson still across the neck to a marked pine tree standing near Musqueto Creek side from thence across Musqueto Creek to Musqueto Point, from thence across the said point to Rappahannock River from thence down Rappahannock River side to the begining oak including all the aforesaid lands and also the creek called Musqueto Creek and also all that Messuages or Tenement and tract of land commonly called and known by the name of Black Sows Neck situate lying and being in the neck called Nanty Poison Neck in the parish of Christ Church and county of Lancaster aforesaid containing by estimation fifteen acres more or less and bounded by a line of the land of Roger Kelly formerly that of Hugh Kelly... unto the said John Hunton... from the first day of this instant December for and during and unto the full end and term of one whole year from thence next ensuing and to be fully compleat and ended. Yielding and paying therefore at the expiration of the said year one Pepper Corn if the same shall be lawfully demanded... [Wit:] George Hunt, John Pope Junr, Fortunatus Stonum, & John Schon. Recorded 21 Jan 1773 by Test Thomas B. Griffin, Cl Cur. [Pages 65a, 66, & 66a]

22 Dec 1772. Deed of Release. ...Between John Turbeville of the parish of Cople and the county of Westmoreland Gentleman and Martha his wife of the one part and John Hunton of the parish of Wiccomico and the county of Northumberland of the other part... John Turbeville and Martha his wife for and in consideration of two hundred and ninety acres of land lying adjoining in the counties of Northumberland and Richmond being the tract of land the said John Hunton now liveth conveyed in fee simple by the said John Hunton to the said John Turbeville by deed bearing even date with these presents and also for and in consideration of the sum of one hundred and fifty pounds five shillings... paid by the said John Hunton at or before the ensealing and delivery of these presents... (in his actual possession now being by virtue of a bargain and sale to him thereof made for one whole year by Indenture bearing date the day next before the day of the date of these presents and by force of the statute for transferring uses into possession)... forever all that Messuage or Tenement and tract of land commonly called or known by the name of Turbevilles Quater also all those islands commonly called or known by the name of Musqueto or Broken Islands containing by estimation four hundred and ninety acres more or less being

situate lying and being in the parish of Christ Church and county of Lancaster and bounded as followeth to wit begining at a corner white oak standing near Musqueto Creek side a corner to the said tract of land and the land now belonging to Richard Hinton formerly Samuel Hinton deceased, from thence along a line of marked trees which divides the land of the said Hinton from this across the neck to a marked Hiccory standing near Fleets Bay Creek side, from thence upon and along the said Fleets Bay Creek side to a marked pine a corner to the said tract of land and the land of Thomas Hunton, from thence along a line of marked trees dividing the said tract of land from the land of the said Thomas Hunton across the neck to a line tree of Thomas Lawsons land, from thence along a line of marked trees which divides this land from the said Thomas Lawson, still across the neck to a marked pine tree standing near Musqueto Creek side, from thence across Musqueto Creek to Musqueto Point, from thence across the said point to the Rappahannock River, from thence down the Rappahannock River side to the begining oak including all the aforesaid lands and also the creek called Musqueto Creek and also all that Messuage or Testament and tract of land commonly called or known by the name of Black Sows Neck situate lying and being in the neck called Nanty Poison Neck in the parish of Christ Church and county of Lancaster aforesaid containing by estimation fifteen acres more or less and bounded by a line of the land of Roger Kelly formerly that of Hugh Kelly with the rights... [Wit:] George Hunt, John Pope Junr, Fortunatus Stonum, & John Schon. Received the day of the date of the within written Indenture of the within named John Hunton the sum of one hundred fifty two pounds five shillings...[same witnesses]. Also I [Jno Turberville] hereby acknowledge to have received of the within named John Hunton a Deed of Conveyance in Fee Simple duely executed by the said John Hunton and Frances his wife for the two hundred and ninety acres of land within mentioned bearing even date with the within mentioned Indenture being the other and remaining part of the consideration within mentioned. [Same witnesses as above]. Recorded 21 Jan 1773 by Test Thomas B. Griffin, Cl Cur. [Pages 66a, 67, 67a, & 68]

24 Dec 1772. Commission and Certificate. George the Third... to Richard Lee Esqr, John Augustine Washington, Thomas Chilton, George Turberville, Joseph Lane and Joseph Pierce Gentl, Whereas John Turberville Gentl and Martha his wife by their certain Indentures of Lease and Release bearing date the 21st and 22nd daies of December instant have sold and conveyed unto John Hunton one tract of land containing five hundred and five acres more or less lying and being in Lancaster County and whereas the said Martha Turberville the wife of the said John Turberville cannot conveniently travel to our County Court of Lancaster to make acknowledgement and Relinquishment of her right in the said land. Therefore we give unto you or any two of you full power to receive the acknowledgement and Relinquishment which the said Martha Turberville shall

be willing to make before you of her right in the land aforesaid contained in the aforesaid Indentures which is hereunto annexed. And we therefore command you that you personally go to the said Martha Turberville and receive her acknowledgement and Relinquishment of the same and examine her privily and apart from the said John Turberville her husband...Witness Thomas B. Griffin Clerk of our said Court at the courthouse aforesaid the twenty fourth day of December... By virtue of a commission to us directed from the court of Lancaster County, bearing date the twenty fourth of December 1772 and hereunto annexed. We did personally go to Martha Turberville wife of John Turberville Gentleman, and did examine her separate and apart from her said husband touching her Relinquishment of her Right of Dower of in and to the lands and tenements, and Islands conveyed in the Deeds hereunto annexed; and she declared that she did the same freely and voluntarily without the persuasion or threats of her said husband, and that she is willing that the said Deeds of Lease and Release shall be recorded in the county of Lancaster. Given and certified under our hands and seals this twenty fourth day of December 1772. [Wit:] John Augn Washington and Jos Lane. Recorded 21 Jan 1773 by Test Thomas B. Griffin, Cl Cur. [Pages 68a & 69]

22 Dec 1772. Bond. Know all men by these presents that I John Turberville of the parish of Cople and county of Westmoreland am held and firmly bound unto John Hunton of the parish of Wiccomico and county of Northumberland in the sum of two thousand pounds... to be paid to the said John Hunton... The condition of this obligation is such that if the above boundon John Turberville... shall in all things well and truly observe... all and singular the covenants... which on the part and behalf of the said John Turberville... ought to be observed... in certain Indentures Bipartite bearing even date with the above written obligation made or mentioned to be made between the said John Turberville and Martha his wife of the first part and the above named John Hunton of the second part according to the true purport intent and meaning of the said Indentures. Then the above obligations to be void otherwise to remain in full force power and virtue. [Wit:] George Hunt, John Pope Junr, & Fortunatus Stonum. Recorded 21 Jan 1773 by Test Thomas B. Griffin, Cl Cur. [Page 69]

25 Nov 1772. Deed of Mortgage. ...Between William Steptoe of the parish of Christ Church and county of Lancaster of the one part and John Maxwell of the county of Northumberland and William Brown of Lancaster county of the other part... the said William Steptoe in and for the consideration of the sum of sixty eight pounds fifteen shillings and eight pence... paid by the said John Maxwell and William Brown... [for] all that Messuage Tenement Plantation tract or parcel of land situate lying and being in the parish of Christ Church and county of Lancaster wherein and whereon the said William Steptoe now liveth and dwelleth... provided always and it is agreed by and between the parties to these

presents that if the said William Steptoe... shall well and truly pay or cause to be paid unto the said John Maxwell and William Brown... the just and full sum of sixty eight pounds fifteen shillings and eight pence in and upon the first day of May next ensuing the date hereof, with lawfull interest from the date hereof and without any deduction taxes... or other impositions whatsoever either ordinary or extraordinary, that then and from thenceforth these presents and everything contained therein shall cease determine and be void... and the said William Steptoe... doth covenant... to and with the said John Maxwell and William Brown... parcel of land and premises above mentioned... and further that the said William Steptoe... shall and will well and truly pay or cause to be paid unto the said John Maxwell and William Brown... all and every lawfull and reasonable charge and expense whatsoever for the writing and recording of this present Indenture, and also of one other Indenture made or mentioned to be made between the said John Maxwell and William Brown of one part and Messrs Bogle Summerville and Company Merchts in Glasgow North Britain of the other part, and bearing equal date with these presents. And lastly it is covenanted and agreed upon by and between the parties that the said William Steptoe... shall and may at all times untill default shall be made in performance of the provise or condition herein contained peaceably and quietly have hold and enjoy all and singular the premises above mentioned and receive and take the rents... thereof to his and their own proper use and benefit... [Wit:] John Currell, Joseph McAdam Junr, & William Brent. Recorded 18 Feb 1773 by Test Thomas B. Griffin, Cl Cur. [Pages 69a, 70, & 70a]

25 Nov 1772. Deed. ...Between John Maxwell of the county of Northumberland and William Brown of the county of Lancaster in the colony of Virginia of the one part and Messers Bogle Summerville and Company Merchts in Glasgow North Britain of the other part... in and by one Indenture of Bargain and Sale bearing even date with these presents made or mentioned to be made between William Steptoe of the county of Lancaster of the one part and the said John Maxwell and William Brown of the other part, the said William Steptoe for the consideration therein did grant... unto the said John Maxwell and William Brown...that Tenement Messuage Plantation tract or parcel of land situate in the parish of Christ Church and county of Lancaster whereon the said William Steptoe now liveth. To hold unto the said John Maxwell and William Brown... forever in which said Indenture was contained a previse or condition to make the same defearable and void on payment by the said William Steptoe to the said John Maxwell and William Brown of the sum of sixty eight pounds fifteen shillings and eight pence currency with legal interest for the same at a certain day therein particularly mentioned as in and by the said Indenture of Bargain and Sale... the said John Maxwell and William Brown do hereby acknowledge and declare that the sum of five shillings and also the sum of sixty eight pounds fifteen shillings and eight pence... in the said in part recited Indenture of

Mortgage was all the proper money of the said Messers Bogle Summerville and Company and not any part thereof the money of the said John Maxwell and William Brown or any of them that the names of them the said John Maxwell and William Brown were only used in trust, for the said Messers Bogle Summerville and Company... and also for and in consideration of the sum of five shillings to them in hand paid by the said Bogle Summerville and Company at or before the sealing and delivery hereof the receipt whereof is hereby acknowledged. Have granted... unto the said Messers Bogle Summerville and Company... Tenement Plantation tract or parcel of land before mentioned in and by the said part recited Indenture of Mortgage... [Wit:] Robert Gilmour, William Nutt, Isaac Currell, & Eppa Lawson. Recorded 18 Feb 1773 by Test Thomas B. Griffin, Cl Cur. [Pages 70a & 71]

7 Dec 1772. Deed of Bargain and Sale with Receipt. ... Between Rawleigh Carter of the county of Amelia Planter and Sarah his wife of the one part and Burges Ball of the county of Lancaster Gentl of the other part. Whereas Elias Edmonds Sharp late of the said county of Lancaster decd was in his lifetime was seined in fee of and in two separate tracts or parcels of land situate lying and being on Corotoman River in the said county of Lancaster, the one containing two hundred and sixty five acres and the other two hundred and three acres in the whole four hundred and sixty eight acres and being so seined departed this life intestate and without issus, whereupon the two said tracts or parcel of land descended unto his four sisters, to wit, Elizabeth, Thomasine, Ann, and the said Sarah as coheirs... the said Rawleigh Carter and Sarah his wife for and consideration of the sum of one hundred and seventy five pounds ten shillings... paid at or before the sealing and delivery of these presents... sell... unto the said Burges Ball... one full fourth part of both and each of the said two tracts or parcels of land containing one hundred and seventeen acres... clearly and freely discharged of and from all former grants, bargains, mortgages, dowers, title of dowers, or other incumbrances whatsoever (except the Quitrants hereafter becoming due to the Chief Lord of the Fee and also except the dower therein of Sarah Bond Mother of the said Elias Edmonds Sharp and widow of the late Thomas Sharp decd Father of the said Elias Edmonds Sharp during her natural life only)... [Wit:] Wm Chowning, Abraham White, Nicholas George, Henry Carter, Wm Dunaway, & Samuel Mahanes. Received the day of the within Indenture of the within named Burges Ball the sum of one hundred and seventy five pounds ten shillings in full consideration for the within mentioned granted parcel of land. [Wit:] Henry Carter, Abraham White, Wm Chowning, Nicholas George, & Wm Dunaway. Recorded 18 Mar 1773 by Test Thomas B. Griffin, Cl Cur. [Pages 71, 71a, 72, & 72a]

11 Dec 1772. Commission and Certificate. ... To John Winn, Thomas Williams, and Lee Cocks Gent Whereas Rawleigh Carter and Sarah his wife by their

certain Indenture of Bargain and Sale bearing date the seventh day of this instant December have sold... unto Burges Ball one tract of land lying and being in Lancaster County, containing one hundred and seventeen acres and whereas Sarah Carter the wife of the said Rawleigh Carter cannot conveniently travel to our county court of Lancaster to make acknowledgement and Relinquishment of her right in the said land. Therefore we give unto you, or any two or more of you full power to receive the acknowledgement and Relinquishment which the said Sarah Carter shall be willing to make before you of her right in the land contained in the aforesaid Indenture which is hereunto annexed. And we do therefore command you that you personally go to the said Sarah Carter and receive her acknowledgement and Relinquishment of the same, and examine her privily and apart from the said Rawleigh Carter her husband, whether she does the same freely and voluntarily without his persuasion or threats and whether she be willing that the same should be recorded in our said county court of Lancaster, and when you have received her acknowledgement and Relinquishment and examined her as aforesaid, that you distinctly and openly certify us thereof in our said county court under your hands and seals...Witness Thomas B. Griffin clerk of our said court. Pursuant to the within commission to us directed, We the subscribers having examined the within named Sarah Carter privately and apart, from her husband the within named Rawleigh Carter, do hereby certify that she doth freely and voluntarily without the threats or persuasions of her said husband acknowledges the deed and relinquished her right to the land contained in the within mentioned Deed, which is hereunto annexed, and that she is willing the same should be recorded in the county court of Lancaster given unto our hands and seals this 15th day of Dec 1772. [Wit:] John Winn & Lee Cocks. Recorded 18 Mar 1773 by Test Thomas B. Griffin, Cl Cur. [Pages 72a & 73]

12 Jan 1773. Deed of Mortgage. ...Between Edwin Fielding of the county of Fauquier of the one part and William Norris of the county aforesaid and Richard Mitchell and Joseph Norris of the county of Lancaster of the other part... the said Edwin Fielding for and in consideration of the sum of five hundred pounds... [for] the following negroe slaves now in actual possession of the said William Norris, Richard Mitchell, and Joseph Norris, to wit, Anthony, Daniel, Mary, Archer, Violet, Nan, Catoe, Susannah, Solomon, Dick and Dinah, to have and to hold the said slaves and their future increase... Provided nonetheless that whereas the above named William Norris, Richard Mitchell, and Joseph Norris did bind themselves... jointly and severally in a bond with the said Edwin Fielding in the sum of two thousand pounds as sureties for the said Edwin Fielding paying to the Admor of Capt William Dymer, late of the county of Lancaster deceased one moiety of all debts and demands which should be recovered against the administrators of the said William Dymer and also one moiety of all charges attending the same, which bond is now recorded in the

court of Lancaster County and bears date twentieth day of November 1772. It is hereby covenanted and agreed between the said parties that if the said Edwin Fielding... shall and will save and keep harmless the said William Norris, Richard Mitchell and Joseph Norris...from all damages which shall be awarded or recovered against the said William Norris, Richard Mitchell, and Joseph Norris... for or by reason of their entering into the said bond or will give the said William Norris, Richard Mitchell, and Joseph Norris... such further security for their indemnification... shall think fill to demand and require that then it shall and may be lawfull for the said Edwin Fielding... to repossess said hereby granted slaves and their future increase... [Wit:] William Merideth, William Boatman, & Samuel Hunt. Recorded 18 Mar 1773 by Test Thomas B. Griffin, Cl Cur. [Pages 73 & 73a]

9 Jan 1773. Letter of Attorney. Know men by all these presents that I Edwin Fielding of the parish of Leeds and the county of Fauquier have constituted appointed and ordained and by these presents constitute appoint and ordain Joseph Norris of the parish of Christ Church and the county of Lancaster my true and lawful attorney for me and in my name and to my use to ask demand sue for recover and receive all sum or sums of money that now or are or may be hereafter due and owing to me from any person or persons whatsoever and upon receipt or recovery acquittances releases and discharges for the same to grant execute and deliver and to do all lawful acts and things concerning the premises as fully in every respect as if I myself were personally present hereby ratifying and confirming all and every act and acts thing and things which my said attorney shall lawfully do or cause to be done in and concerning the premises... [Wit:] David Boyd. Recorded 18 Mar 1773 by Test Thomas B. Griffin, Cl Cur. [Page 74]

12 Dec 1772. Bill of Sale. Know men by all these presents that I John Wormsley of the county of Lancaster and the parish of Christ Church have bargained sold and delivered to Bailie George of the said county and parish one negroe girl named Hannah for the consideration of sixty five pounds... [Wit:] Nicholas George, & Josiah Harris. Recorded 18 Mar 1773 by Test Thomas B. Griffin, Cl Cur. [Pages 74 & 74a]

14 Nov 1772. Deed from Ann George to Edney Tapscott. ...Deliver unto Edney Tapscott Senr. of the county of Lancaster... all and every part of the land I livd on, situate lying and being in the county of Lancaster during my life, which land the said Edney Tapscott is intituled to the reversion off by Deed of Gift acknowledged and recorded in Northumberland County Court...[Wit:] Test Henry Tapscott & Samuel Dunaway. Recorded 18 Mar 1773 by Test Thomas B. Griffin, Cl Cur. [Page 74a]

16 Oct 1772. Deed of Bargain and Sale with Receipt. ...Between William Lewis
of the county of Northumberland and Anne his wife of the one part and Burges
Ball of the county of Lancaster of the other part. Whereas Elias Edmonds Sharp
decd was in his lifetime seind in Fee of two tracts of land scituate on Corotoman
River in the said county of Lancaster, one tract containing by estimation three
hundred acres, and the other one hundred acres, in the whole four hundred
acres... and being so seined died intestate and without issue, whereupon the said
two tracts or parcels of land descended unto his four sisters Elizabeth,
Thomasine, Sarah and the above said Anne as coheirs, who are seined in equal
portions... Indenture that the said William Lewis and Anne his wife for and in
consideration of the sum of one hundred and thirty pounds... [for] one fourth part
of all the aforesaid two tracts or parcels of land containing by estimation one
hundred acres... to the said Burges Ball... clearly and freely discharged of and
from all former Grants Mortgages Dowers Title of Dowers or other
incumbrances whatsoever, except the Dower thereof of Sarah Bond widow of
Thomas Sharp decd and mother of the said Elias Edmonds Sharp and except the
Quitrants hereafter becoming due unto the chief Lord of the Fee... [Wit:] John
S Woodcock, Jos McAdam Junr, Jos Williams, John Blincoe, Thos Williams
Junr, & Robert Clark Junr. Received the day of the date of the within Indenture
of the within named Burges Ball the sum of one hundred and thirty pounds...
[Wit:] John S. Woodcock, Jos McAdam Junr, Jos Williams, & Thomas
Williams Junr. 19 Nov 1772 ...proved in court by oath of Joseph McAdam
Junr... and at another court held 20th day of May following the same was proved
by oaths of John S. Woodcock and John Blincoe and recorded by Test Thomas
B. Griffin, Cl Cur. [Pages 74a, 75, & 75a]

16 Oct 1772. Commission and Certificate. ...To Lyndsey Opie, Konner Cralls,
and William Eskridge Gent greeting. Whereas William Lewis and Ann his wife
of Northumberland County, by their Indenture of Bargain and Sale bearing date
16 Oct 1772, have bargained and sold unto Burges Ball of the county of
Lancaster a certain Tract of Land lying and being in Lancaster County,
containing one hundred acres m/l whereas the said Ann Lewis cannot
conveniently travel to our court of Lancaster County to acknowledge her right of
Dower in the said land to the said Burges Ball. We command you or any two of
you to take the examination of the said Ann to this said land, privily and apart
from her husband touching her consent thereto and that she will assent to the
said Deed's being recorded in our said court...witness Thomas B. Griffin, clerk
of our said court, at the courthouse aforesaid this 16th day of October 1772.
Pursuant to the within commission to us directed, we have examined the within
named Ann Lewis wife of William Lewis, and she freely and voluntarily
relinquished her right interest in and to the lands and appurtenances in the Deed
made from William Lewis and Ann his wife to the within named Burges Ball
and that she is willing that the said Deed with her privy examination aforesaid

should be recorded in the county court of Lancaster given... 16 Oct 1772. [Wit:] Lyndsey Opie & Konner Cralls. Recorded 20 May 1773 by Thomas B. Griffin, Cl Cur...[Pages 75a & 76]

17 May 1773. Deed of Bargain and Sale with Livery of Seisen. ...Between Thomas Pollard and Mary his wife of the parish of Christ Church in the county of Lancaster ... of one part and Maurice Wheeler of the other part... the said Thomas Pollard and Mary his wife for and in consideration of the sum of two hundred pounds... paid by the said Maurice Wheeler... [for] one piece parcel or tract of land which he [Thomas Pollard] purchased of Mr William Brent containing about the quantity of one hundred acres m/l lying and being in the aforesaid parish of Christ Church and county of Lancaster. Bounded by Glebe Land and the land formerly known by the name of Pricillas... freely and clearly discharged of all Grants Dowers Jointures or other Incumbrances whatsoever except the Quitrant that shall from henceforth grow due to the Lord Proprietor of the Northern Neck of Virginia and the said Thomas Pollard and Mary his wife... shall and will from time to time and at all times hereafter at the request and cost of the said Maurice Wheeler...do execute... conveyances...in the Law for the better and surer conveyances of the said land...forever in absolute Fee Simple as by the said Maurice Wheeler...learned in the law shall be reasonably advised or required and that the said Thomas Pollard and Mary his wife shall and will before some court to be held for the aforesaid county of Lancaster acknowledge these presents with the Livery and Seisen therein endorsed in due form as the law directs... [Wit:] William Griggs, James Pollard, & Jesse George. 17 May 1773 Memorandum peaceable and quiet possession and seisen of land and premises in the within Deed specified was given and delivered unto the within named Maurice Wheeler by the within named Thomas Pollard in name and token of seisen. [Same witnesses as above listed]. Recorded 20 May 1773 by Test Thomas B. Griffin, Cl Cur. [Pages 76 & 76a]

21 May 1773. Deed of Bargain and Sale. Between John Hunton and Frances his wife of the county of Northumberland and Wiccomico Parish of the one part and Aaron Williams of the aforesaid county and parish of the other part... aforesaid John Hunton and Frances his wife for and in consideration of the full and just sum of thirty pounds... to be paid by the above named Aaron Williams...[for] a certain parcel or piece of land scituate and being in the county of Lancaster and Christ Church Parish in Nantepoison Neck containing twenty five acres m/l and bounded by a line of Roger Kelly and also by a cove and creek and known by the name of Black Sows Point it being a piece of land the said John Hunton purchased of John Turberville... [Wit:] Isaac Degge, Bridgar Haynie, & James Tapscott. Recorded 21 May 1773 by Test Thomas B. Griffin, Cl Cur. [Pages 77 & 77a]

11 Dec 1772. Deed of Gift. Know all men by these presents that I Waterman Boatman of the county of Bute in the Province of North Carolina for and in the consideration of the sum of five shillings... paid by Effie Boatman of the county of Lancaster and the colony of Virginia... [for] one Negroe boy slave named Harry...[Wit:] John Miller, James Carter, & Dale Carter. Recorded 20 May 1773 by Test Thomas B. Griffin, Cl Cur. [Page 77a]

11 Dec 1772. Deed of Gift. Know all men by these presents that I Waterman Boatman of the county of Bute in the Province of North Carolina for and in consideration of the sum of five shillings...paid by Abner Palmer of the county of Lancaster and the colony of Virginia... [for] one Negroe boy slave named Tom... [Wit:] John Miller, James Carter, & Dale Carter. Recorded 20 may 1773 by Test Thomas B. Griffin, Cl Cur. [Pages 77a & 78]

11 Dec 1772. Deed of Gift. Apphie Boatman of the county of Lancaster... do give unto myself one Negroe boy named Henry for and during my natural life and after my decease for the natural affection which I have for my son in law Abner Palmer I give the whole right and property of the said Henry... [Wit:] Dale Carter, John Miller, & James Carter. Recorded 20 May 1773 by Test Thomas B. Griffin Cl Cur. [Page 78]

17 Jan 1771. Deed of Gift. ...Mary Percifield of the parish of Wiccomico and the county of Lancaster as well for the natural love and affection which I have to my son Eppeacus Percifield of the parish and county aforesaid... have given... the articles hereafter mentioned, ... one bed and furniture, one young mare, one cow, one iron pott, one iron skillet, and half a dozen pewter plates, only reserving my life in the said articles. To have hold and enjoy said articles, after my decease...[Wit:] Thomas Everitt and Betty Wallace. Recorded 20 May 1773 by Test Thomas B. Griffin, Cl Cur. [Page 78a]

20 May 1773. Deed with Receipt. ...Between William Montague of the county of Essex Gent of the one part, and Robert McTire of the county of Lancaster Planter and Elizabeth his wife and Robert McTire Junr Joiner of the said county of Lancaster of the other part... William Montague for and in the consideration of the sum of two hundred and forty pounds... in hand paid by the said Robert McTire Junr... [to] the said Robert McTire and Elizabeth his wife during their natural lives, and after their decease, unto the said Robert McTire Junr... all that tract or parcel of land formerly held by the said Robert McTire and Elizabeth his wife in Fee Tail in right of the said Elizabeth and by them sold and conveyed unto of the said county of Lancaster Gent containing two hundred and ninety three acres, and also all that part of a tract or parcel of land mentioned in the conveyance to be purchased of Thomas Doggett and Bathsheba his wife, which lyeth to the southward of a line now from the Holly Branch to Mr George

Heale's line taking in a large poplar tree containing about twenty acres more or less in the whole three hundred acres more or less, which said lands are scituate in the said county of Lancaster and purchased by the said William Montague of the said James Ball... belonging to the said Robert McTire and Elizabeth his wife during their natural lives and the longest survivor of them, and after the decease of the survivor, unto the said Robert McTire Junr... Received of the said Robert McTire Junr the sum of two hundred and forty pounds current money in consideration for the within mentioned granted parcels of land and premises. Received the same the day of the sale of the within Indenture. Recorded 20 May 1773 by Test Thomas B Griffin, Cl Cur. [Pages 78a & 79]

21 May 1773. Lease. ...Between George Wale of the county of Lancaster and parish of Christ Church of the one part and William Brent of the same county and parish for the other part... for and in consideration of the Rents Covenants and Agreements herein after reserved and contained he the said George Wale... hath leased... unto said William Brent... all that tract tenement or parcel of land situate lying and being in the county and parish aforesaid, and bounded as followeth. Beginning at a red oak on the road side, called Fleets Bay Road in the line of George Flower, and runing along the said line down to the Indian Creek and down the said creek to the line of George Horton decd thence up the said Horton's line to the said road, and up the said road to the beginning red oak containing by estimation one hundred acres m/l being part or parcel of a tract of land descended to the said George Wale from his father... together with Liberty for the said William Brent... to cut down and clear any part of the aforesaid tract of land for Rail timber and buildings for the use of the said tract of land or plantation, also with the further liberty to cut down and clear Twelve Thousand Tobacco Hills, as the said William Brent thinks most convenient... from and after the first day of January next... unto the end term and expiration of twenty one years...and the said George Wale... doth covenant... with the said William Brent... that in case the said George Wale should over live the said above mentioned term of twenty one years, then the said George Wale doth lease... unto the said William Brent... all the above mentioned... tract of land...yielding and paying yearly and every year during the said first term of twenty one years, also during the last mentioned and intended term of natural life of the said George Wale...the yearly rent and sum of ten pounds...William Brent... agrees with the said George Wale... to plant or cause to be planted three hundred peach trees and seventy five apple trees on the said tract of land... [Wit:] John Stonum and William Hunt. Recorded 17 June 1773 by Test Thomas B. Griffin, Cl Cur. [Pages 79, 79a, & 80]

24 May 1773. Deed of Bargain and Sale. ...Between George Heale of the county of Lancaster Gent and Sarah his wife of the one part and Andrew Robertson of the same county Phasician of the other part... George Heale and Sarah his wife

for and in consideration of the sum of three hundred pounds...[paid by Andrew Robertson for] two tracts or parcels of land scituate on the main branch of Mrs Margaret Balls Mill Pond in the said county of Lancaster containing in the whole by estimation three hundred and seventy four acres to wit, one parcel purchased by said George Heale of William Davenport and Elizabeth his wife, and of George Heale Fauntleroy, scituate on the west side of the said branch and containing by estimation two hundred and seven acres, the other parcel scituated on the east side of the said branch, and decended unto the said George Heale on the decease of his father William Heale Gent decd and joining the other parcel and contains by estimation one hundred and sixty seven acres... [Wit:] Jas Ball, Jesse Ball, Phil Heale, & Wm Sydnor. Received the day of the date of the within Indenture of the within named Andrew Robertson the sum of three hundred pounds in consideration for the within granted land and premises. [Wit:] Jas Ball, Jesse Ball, Phil Heale, & Wm Sydnor. Recorded 17 June 1773 by Test Thomas B. Griffin, Cl Cur. [Pages 80 & 80a]

28 May 1773. Commission and Certificate. ...To James Ball, Jesse Ball, and Burges Smith Gent... Whereas George Heale and Sarah his wife by their certain Indenture of Bargain and Sale bearing date 24 day of May instant have sold and conveyed unto Andrew Robertson one tract of land containing three hundred and seventy four acres... lying and being in Lancaster County, and whereas the said Sarah Heale the wife of the said George Heale cannot conveniently travel to our county court of Lancaster to make acknowledgement and Relinquishment of her right in the said land. Therefore we do give unto you, or any two of you full power to receive the acknowledgement and Relinquishment which the said Sarah shall be willing to make before you... and we do therefore command you, that you personally go to the said Sarah Heale and receive her acknowledgement and Relinquishment of the same and examine her privily and apart from the said George Heale her husband... whether she be willing that the same should be recorded in our said county court of Lancaster... Witness Thomas B. Griffin clerk of our said court... By virtue of the within commission, we the subscribers having examined the within named Sarah Heale privately and apart from her husband the within named George Heale do hereby certify that she doth freely and voluntarily without the threats or persuasions of her said husband acknowledge her right to the land and premises mentioned in a Deed of Bargain and Sale, from the said George Heale and Sarah his wife unto Andrew Robertson bearing date the 24th of this instant May, which is annexed, and that she is willing the same be recorded in the county court of Lancaster...[Wit:] Jas Ball & Jesse Ball. Recorded 17 Jun 1773 by Test Thomas B. Griffin, Cl Cur. [Page 81]

17 May 1773. Bond. Know all men by these presents that we Thomas Pollard, John James, and James Pollard of the county of Lancaster are held and firmly

bound unto Maurice Wheeler in the full and just sum of six hundred pounds...
the condition of the above obligation is such that if the above bound Thomas
Pollard... and Mary Pollard wife of the said Thomas Pollard do and shall in all
things well and truly observe... pay and keep all and singular the covenants...
ought to be... paid and kept... in certain Indentures of Bargain and Sale bearing
even date with the bond or obligation above written... between the said Thomas
Pollard and Mary his wife of the one part, and the above named Maurice
Wheeler of the other part... [Wit:] John McTire, William Griggs, & Bailie
George. Recorded 17 June 1773 by Test Thomas B. Griffin, Cl Cur. [Pages 81
& 81a]

15 Jul 1773. Deed with Livery and Seisen. ...between William Sydnor gent of
the county of Lancaster and Ellen his wife of the one part and Rawleigh
Davenport of the aforesaid county of the other part. Whereas on the death of
George Heale late of the said county gent, a parcel of his land scituate in the
parish of Lunenburg and county of Richmond containing four hundred and eight
acres descended unto his four daughters Elizabeth who intermarried with
William Davenport, Ann who intermarried with Moore Fauntleroy, Sarah and
Catharine as coheirs and upon the death of John Heale late of the said county of
Lancaster his parcel of land scituate in the said county on the main branch of
Capt Jesse Balls Mill containing four hundred and fifty seven acres descended
likewise to the said Elizabeth, Ann, Sarah, & Catharine and whereas it was
agreed between the aforesaid William Davenport and Moore Fauntleroy and
their respective wives upon a division of the said two tracts of land that the said
William Davenport should have the said Moore Fauntleroy's part of the said
tract of land in Lancaster and sixty pounds current money and the said Moor
Fauntleroy should have in lieu of the said William Davenport's part of the said
tract of land in Richmond, Pursuant to which agreement the said William
Davenport and Elizabeth his wife executed a Deed of Conveyance for the same
unto the said Moor Fauntleroy which is recorded in the clerk's office, but the
said Ann departed this life without executing a deed for conveying her part of
the said tract in Lancaster to the said Wm Davenport according to the said
agreement, upon whose death the same descended to the aforesaid Ellen her only
surviving issue, and who is thereof possessed, and whereas the said William
Davenport did by his last Will and Testament give and bequeath all his right and
interest in and to the aforesaid tract of land to his son Rawleigh Davenport... the
said William Sydnor and Ellen his wife being willing that the aforesaid
agreement should be complyed with and for the considerations above mentioned,
have granted... unto the said Rawleigh Davenport... all that tract or parcel of land
scituate in the said county of Lancaster being one fourth part of four hundred
and fifty seven acres which descended to Ann the daughter of Capt George
Heale decd upon the decease of Mr John Heale and allotted to her upon a survey
and division thereof made by William Ball Gent Surveyor of the county of

Lancaster, which descended to Ellen party to these presents... [Wit:] Ja Ewell, Oswald Newby, & James Ewell Junr. Recorded 15 July 1773 by Test Thomas B. Griffin, Cl Cur. [Pages 81a, 82, & 82a]

15 Jul 1773. Deed of Gift. ...Joseph Chinn of the county of Lancaster for and in consideration of the love and affection I have for Kendal Lee of the county of Northumberland and Betty his wife daughter of my late wife Priscilla, and for divers other good causes and considerations me thereunto moving have given... one Negroe girl slave named Sinah and her future increase... [Wit:] Robt McTyre, Richd Mitchell, & Robert Mitchell. Recorded 15 Jul 1773 by Test Thomas B. Griffin, Cl Cur. [Pages 82a & 83]

7 Dec 1772. Lease. ...between Susanna Davis of the county of Lancaster widow of the one part and Willoughby Rout of the county of Northumberland planter of the other part... Susanna Davis for the consideration herein after mentioned hath granted... unto the said Willoughby Rout... all that tract or parcel of land situate in the said county of Lancaster on Corotoman River which formerly belonged to her husband Wm Davis decd containing by estimation two hundred acres... from Christmas Day next ensuing for and during the term of nine years...shall and may peaceably possess... granted parcel of land and premises with its appurtenances during the said term against the lawful claim and demand of all and every person or persons whatsoever, except the Dowers of Margaret Davis and Sarah Mouhon during their natural lives as the same are now laid off. In consideration the said Willoughby Rout doth ... agree to pay the said Susanna Davis or her order or to the guardian for the time being to the Heir at Law of the said Wm Davis yearly and every year during the said term on the first day of January twelve months after the commencement of the said term and the last payment on the first day of January after the end of the said term, and if either or both the said Margaret Davis and Sarah Mouhon should die before the end of the said term that then the said Willoughby Rout... shall pay the further sum of twenty shillings for each of the said Widows Dowers, so dying, to be paid at the times afore mentioned...and the said Willoughby Rout... agree to and with the said Susanna Davis to cover the two dwelling houses on the said land (she the said Susanna Davis finding boards and nails for the same) and to plant out the fruit trees of aple and peach now growing in nurserys on the said plantations in Tenetable repair, and that the said Willoughby Rout... shall not cut or allowed to be cut any wood or timbers on the said land more than sufficient for the use of the said Plantation, except Four Thousand Tobo Hills...[Wit:] Jesse Ball, James Ewell Junr, John Selden, & Peter Conway. Memorandum that on the day of the date of the within Indenture quiet and peaceable possession of Livery and Seisin of the within mentioned land... given by the within named Susanna Davis unto the within named Willoughby Rout by delivering the handle of the door of the Mansion House thereon...[Witnessed by

above witnesses]. Recorded 15 Jul 1773 by Test Thomas B. Griffin, Cl Cur.
[Pages 83 & 83a]

17 Feb 1773. Mortgage. ...Between Nicholas Flood of the parish of
Northfarnham in the county of Richmond of the one part and John Heath of the
parish of Wiccomico in the county of Northumberland of the other part... the
said Nicholas Flood as well for and consideration of the several rents, hires,
covenants, and conditions herein after named on the part of the said John Heath
to be him paid kept and performed, as for and in consideration of the sum of ten
shillings to him the said Flood paid by the said John Heath... during the space of
twelve months to be computed from the eleventh day of December, last past, the
following seventeen negroe slaves known and distinguished by the names of
Kate the Cook wench, Dinah, Nan, Jude and her mulatto daughter Kate, Affy
and her two children Scipio and Nancy, Moll and her two children Dennis and
Nancy, Martha, Milley, Sarah, Simon, Robin, and Tom (all which seventeen said
slaves were purchased from the estate of the said John Heath by the said
Nicholas Flood at Public Sale) and the said Nicholas Flood doth likewise let and
set to hire to the said John Heath the following stocks of cattle and sheep, and
household goods, vizt. one yoke of oxen, one Brindled cow and calf , one cow
with calf, and one yearling, and eighteen head of ewe sheep, and all the
following household goods and furniture, vizl one bed and furniture in the
passage adjoining to Mrs. Heath's chamber, oned [?] bed and furniture in the
room at the head of the stairs, one bed and furniture with white curtains, in the
passage chamber, at the back of Mrs Heaths chamber, and one bed and furniture
with red and white striped curtains in Mrs Heaths chamber, one desk and book
case in the hall, one large square table in the hall, and one double riding chair
and harness, all which said stocks of cattle, sheep, and household goods and
chair were likewise purchased at public sale of the said John Heaths Estate by
the said Nicholas Flood. To have and to hold the said seventeen negroe slaves,
the said stock of cattle and the eighteen ewe sheep and all the said household
goods unto the said John Heath... from the date of these presents untill the
eleventh day of December next ensuing the date hereof (which will compleat
twelve months, he the said John Heath having been put into possession of the
said slaves, on the eleventh day of December last past) he the said John Heath
yielding and paying therefore upon the said eleventh day of December next
ensuing the date hereof unto the said Nicholas Flood... the full and just sum of
sixty pounds... as the rent or hire of the said seventeen slaves stock of cattle and
sheep and household goods and the said John Heath shall and will on the said
eleventh day of December next... deliver unto the said Flood all the above
mentioned seventeen slaves together with all and every of their future issue and
increase and one jacket and breeches or pettycoat of good Virginia cloth or
cotton, one pair of shoes, one pair of stockings and two good Oxnebrig shirts or
shifts for each such slave, and likewise all the stocks of cattle and sheep, and one

moiety or half part of the increase of the said cattle and sheep and all the household goods of every kind, he the said John Heath taking proper care of the said slaves, sheep, cattle, and furniture and maintaining the [same] at his own proper cost and expence...and John Heath doths covenant and agree to and with the said Nicholas Flood, that the said negroe slaves shall not be removed out of the counties of Northumberland, Lancaster or Richmond during the said term, and that they shall not be employed in going by water, during the said term, and that ...the said Flood shall have liberty to take away the negoe boy Simon at any time of the year...allowing to the said John Heath... the rate of eight pounds per year... and as the said John Heath has executed a Bond for one thousand pounds for the performance of all conditions... in this Indenture and as doubts may perhaps arise concerning the title and right of the said John Heath in selling the said slaves... and in consideration of the sum of ten shillings to him the said John Heath by him the said Nicholas Flood at or before the sealing and delivery of these presents...Now this Indenture... the said John Heath hath granted... unto the said Nicholas Flood... tract of land with the appurtanences whereon the said John Heath now dwelleth situate lying and being in the parish of Wiccomico and county of Northumberland... containing by estimation one hundred acres, which was purchased by the said John Heath of George Oldham and Winnifred his wife by deed...in record in county court of Northumberland and also all the Messuage and tract of land with the appurtanences situate lying and being in the said parish of Wiccomico and county of Northumberland aforesaid containing by estimation one hundred acres and adjoining and contiguous to the said first mentioned tract of land and which was purchased by the said John Heath of and from William Garlington and Elizabeth his wife by deed... in county court of Northumberland and likewise all that Messuage and tract of land with the appurtanences situate lying and being in the said parish of Wiccomico and county of Northumberland aforesaid containing by estimation one hundred and forty acres and adjoining and contiguous to the aforesaid tract of land on which the said John Heath now liveth and dwelleth, and which was purchased by the said John Heath of and from William Heath, by deed... in county court of Northumberland, and likewise all that water grist mill with its appurtanences and one acre of land to the said Water Grist Mill appropriated, which said acre of land was purchased by said John Heath of and from Isaac Gaskins and which together with the said mill is situate lying and being in the parish of Wiccomico and county of Northumberland aforesaid, and also all that Messuage and tract of land with the appurtanences situate lying and being in the parish of Wiccomico and county of Northumberland aforesaid, and also all that Messuage and tract of land with the appurtenances situate lying and being in the said parish of Wiccomico and county of Northumberland aforesaid, containing by estimation one hundred acres, and which was purchased by the said John Heath of and from Joseph Kent at two different purchases... of record in the general court, and likewise all that Messuage and tract of land, with the appurtanences situate lying and being in the aforesaid parish of Wiccomico and county of Lancaster, containing by estimation two hundred and forty five acres and which was purchased by said John Heath of and from Edwin Conway Gent by deed... recorded in county court of Lancaster, and all the Messuage and tract of land with the appurtanences situate lying and being in the said parish of Wiccomico and county of Lancaster aforesaid containing by estimation one hundred and sixty acres, and which was purchased by said John Heath of and from John Cundiff by deed... of record in said county court of Lancaster, and also all that Messuage and tract of land with the appurtanences situate lying and being in the parish of Northfarnham and county of Richmond containing by estimation one hundred and forty three acres, and which was purchased by the said John Heath of and from the aforesaid Travers Dowerman by deed...record in the county court of Richmond, and also all that Messuage or tract of land with the appurtanences, situate lying and being in the parish of [blank] and county of Halifax formerly Edgcomb County in the province of North Carolina containing by estimation six hundred and fifty acres, which was purchased by the said John Heath of and from Samuel Huckaby and David Fluker[?] by deed... record in the said county court of Halifax... the true intent and meaning of these presents is that if the said John Heath... paid unto the said Nicholas Flood... the sum of sixty pounds... in and upon the eleventh day of December next and shall deliver up the said slaves stocks of cattle sheep and household furniture at the time mentioned for delivery upon the same, and shall make a sufficient title to the said Flood... [Wit:] Rodham Pritchet, James Lewis, & Alexander Scurlock. Recorded 19 Aug 1773 by Test Thomas B. Griffin, Cl Cur. [Pages 83a, 84, 84a, 85 & 85a]

24 Jun 1773. Bill of Sale. Know all men by these presents. That I John Lawson of Northumberland County Virginia for and in the consideration of the sum of three hundred pounds to me in hand paid by Kendall Lee of the county aforesaid... I do hereby... sold unto him the said Kendall Lee, all my stocks of cattle, sheep and hogs, my two horses known by the name of Lark and Dabster, my mare and colt, and riding chair, one bed and furniture, two square tables and all other my household furniture whatsoever kind or denomination... But it is the true intent and meaning thereof, that if the said John Lawson shall well and truly acquit... the above named Kendall Lee... from his securityship of a bond granted by me and him to Doctor Nicholas Flood for two hundred and seventy pounds seventeen shillings bearing date 15 Jun 1770 against the time of payment in the said bond limited. [Wit:] Charles Lee and Thomas Gaskins Junr. Recorded 16 Jul 1773 by Test Thomas B. Griffin. [Page 86]

23 Jul 1773. Lease with Livery of Seisen. ...Between Burges Ball of the county of Lancaster of the one part and William Wiblin of the said county of the other part... Burges Ball for and in consideration of the yearly rent herein after... the

said Burges Ball... fully... grant... unto the said William Wiblin... all that Plantation whereon the said William Wiblin now dwelleth boundeth as followeth, beginning at a marked red oak by the side of Pritchards Swamp, runing thence south nine degrees east to a markd pine near the corner of the fence between the plantation whereon the said William Wiblin lives and that plantation whereon William Dunaway overseer for the said Burges Ball now dwelleth, from the said markd pine south five degrees west to a bottom near the said Burges Balls Quater [*Quarter*] and where there has been a Layne some years thro the plantation from thence down the said Layne to the main road, thence along the main road to the Church Road [?] from thence to the first mentioned markd tree, containing by estimation one hundred acres... belonging unto the said William Wiblin... for and during his natural lifetime...paying yearly and every year on the first day of February during the said term unto the said Burges Ball... the full and just sum of five pounds... the first payment to be made on the first day of February 1774, and the last payment to be made on the first day of February next ensuing the decease of the said William Wiblin... paid without fraud, and that if the same and any part thereof shall remain unpaid for thirty days after the time the same is hereby covenanted to be paid, that then it shall and may be lawfull for the said Burges Ball... into the said hereby demisd parcel of land and premises to reenter, and to possess... the same and every part thereof in as full and ample manner as if this Indenture had never been made... the said William Wiblin... shall and will during the said term keep the houses and plantation on said premises in Tenantable repair, and that he or they shall before the end of the said term plant orchards of peach apple and other fruit trees, and the same shall be kept inclosed and in good repair during the said term, and further that... [will not] clear any ground nor fall any trees... except such as may be necessary for building or repairing the houses, making and keeping in repair the fences, and for firewood or anything else necessary for improving the plantation...[Wit:] Burges Smith, Henry Towles, & John Bailey. Recorded 19 Aug 1773 by Test Thomas B. Griffin, Cl Cur. [Pages 86, 86a, & 87]

23 Jul 1773. Lease. ...Between William Wale of the county of Lancaster and the parish of Christ Church of the one part and Bartley James of the aforesaid county and parish of the other part... William Wale for and in consideration of the sum of ten pounds... to be paid by the said Bartley James upon the said William Wale's acknowledgement of this lease for the term and time of two years, also the further sum of four pounds five shillings pr year for two years after, then also the further sum of five pounds pr year for three years after, the whole being the term and time of seven years, begining from the first day of January next ensuing from the date thereof and for the said consideration the said William Wale moving hath demised... to the said Bartley James...a certain tract or parcel of land situate lying and being in the aforesaid county of

Lancaster and parish of Christ Church being the plantation whereon the said
Bartley James now lives and whereas for pursuance of this agreement the said
Bartley James is seated as followeth. Begining at a branch known by the name
of Tarkhill from thence to Mr. William Martins line, so along the said Martins
line to Mr. Roger Kelly's land, including the upper part of the said Wales land in
Nantepoison ... [with] free liberty for the said Bartley James... to tend the said
premises with his own force and no otherwise, also to cut down and work any
timber thereon growing for the use of the plantation, doing thereby no manner of
waste... [Wit:] Test Geo Wale. 19 Aug 1773 Recorded by Test Thomas B.
Griffin, Cl Cur. [Pages 87 & 87a]

24 Jul 1773. Deed of Bargain and Sale. ...Between Abraham White of the
county of Lancaster Joiner and Frankey his wife of the one part and Burges Ball
of the same county Gent of the other part... Abraham White and [blank] his wife
for and in consideration of the sum of one hundred and eighty pounds... the said
Abraham White and Frankey his wife do... fully and absolutely grant... unto the
said Burges Ball... forever all that tract or parcel of land situate in the county of
Lancaster, binding on the lands of the said Burges Ball (formerly Mr
Chichesters) Merryman Payne and George Carter which said parcel of land
descended from Judith Payne unto her son Merryman, who sold and conveyed
the same unto his brother William Payne, and by virtue of a power of attorney
from the said William to Merryman Payne and Richard Mitchell Gent the said
parcel of land was sold and conveyed unto Richard Payne, who dying Intestate
and without issues, the same descended unto his brother William Payne Junr
who sold the same unto Abraham White, but died before any conveyance thereof
was made, after whose death the said parcel of land was decreed unto the said
Abraham White by the county court of Lancaster on a suit in Chancery therein
commenced by the said Abraham White, and contains by estimation one
hundred acres... [Wit:] Burges Smith, Henry Towles, John Bailey, & Matt
Myers. Received the day of the date of the within Indenture of the within named
Burges Ball the sum of one hundred and eighty pounds current money in full
consideration for the within mentioned parcel of land and premises. [Same
witnesses as above]. Recorded 16 Sep 1773 by Test Thomas B. Griffin, Cl Cur.
[Pages 87a & 88]

24 Jul 1773. Lease with Livery of Seisen. ...Between Burges Ball of the county
of Lancaster Gent of one part and Abraham White of the same county Joiner of
the other part... the said Burges Ball for and in consideration of the yearly rent
herein after reserved, hath granted... unto the said Abraham White... all that
tract or parcel of land situate in the said county of Lancaster known by the name
of the Hills (except that part thereof heretofore leasd by the said Burges Ball
unto William Wiblin) and is bounded as followeth. Begining on the main road
that leads from the Church to Chaltons Ferry at the mouth or entrance of the lane

64

that divides the said Wiblins part of this tract, and runing thence up the said lane
and along the said Wiblins line to Pritchards Swamp, thence down the said
swamp to George Davis's line thence along the lines of the said Davis, William
Davis, Edward Carter and Elizabeth Towles to the aforesaid main road thence up
the said road to the begining containing by estimation two hundred and fifty
acres... appurtenances thereunto belonging unto the said Abraham White... for
and during the natural lives of the said Burges Ball, Abraham White and
Frankey the now wife of the said Abraham White and the survivor of them, he
the said Abraham White... yielding and paying yearly and every year on the first
day of February during the said term unto the said Burges Ball... the full and
just sum of fifteen hundred pounds of merchantable crop Tobacco clear of cash,
the first payment to be made on the first day of February 1775, and the last
payment to be made on the first day of February next ensuing the decease of the
aforesaid survivor... and that if the same or any part thereof shall be and remain
unpaid for thirty days after the time the same is hereby before covenanted to be
paid, that then it shall and may be lawful for the said Burges Ball... into the said
hereby demised parcel of land and premises to reenter and to possess... in as full
and ample manner as if this Indenture had never been made... [also] the said
Abraham White... shall and will during the said term keep the houses and
plantation on the said premises in Tenatable repair, and that they or one or more
than one of them shall sometime before the end of the said term plant orchards
of peach apple and other fruit trees, and the same shall be kept inclosed and in
good repair during the said term, and further that Abraham White... shall during
the said term clear any ground nor fall any trees on the said hereby demised
premises, except such as may be necessary building or repairing the houses,
making and keeping in repair the fences, and for firewood or anything else
necessary for improving the plantation there... [Wit:] Burges Smith, Henry
Towles, & John Bailey. Recorded 16 Sep 1773 by Test Thomas B. Griffin, Cl
Cur. [Pages 88a & 89]

31 Aug 1773. In obedience to the summons of the sheriff by virtue of an order
of Lancaster County court bearing the date 19th August 1773, We the subscribers
have this day met and viewed valued and awarded the damages in the said order
mentioned, to wit, to Richard Hutchings the sum of three pounds ten shillings
cash, and the John Yerby the sum of two pounds ten shillings cash... [Wit:]
John Longwith, Martin George, William Mason, Benjamin George, Moses
Davis, Thomas Rouand, William Yerby, William Griggs, John Merideth, James
Fendla, Thomas Schofield, and Elmore Dogget, in presence of Bailie George
S.S. Recorded 16 Sep 1773 by Test Thomas B. Griffin, Cl Cur. [Page 89a]

20 Oct 1773. Deed. ...Between Robert McTire of the county of Lancaster
Planter of the one part and James Ball of the same county Gent of the other
part... Robert McTire for and in consideration of the Superior Fortune to his

which he received at his marriage with his present wife Elizabeth and for divers other good causes and considerations him thereunto moving hath given... unto the said James Ball... one negroe girl (and her future increase) called Betty (which the said Robert McTire purchased of Mrs Margaret Ball) in trust for the use and purposes mentioned hereafter, to wit, that the said James Ball... shall when thereunto required, convey and deliver the said negroe girl Betty and her future increase unto such person or persons as the said Elizabeth McTire shall order and direct by Deed Will or otherwise, and in the mean time suffer and permit the said Elizabeth to possess and enjoy the profits or use of the said negroe Betty... [Wit:] Ozwald Newby, John Tapscott, & George Goodridge. Recorded 21 Oct 1773 by Test Thomas B. Griffin, Cl Cur. [Pages 89a & 90]

[Blank] May 1773. Deed of Gift. Know all men by these presents that I Robert McTire of the county of Lancaster for and in consideration of the natural love and affection which I bear unto my son Robert McTire, and for divers other good causes and considerations me thereunto moving hath given... one Molatto boy slave named Solomon... [Wit:] James Ball & Ozwald Newby. Recorded 23 Oct 1773 by Test Thomas B. Griffin, Cl Cur. [Pages 90 & 90a]

22 Feb 1771. Bill of Sale. Know all men by these presents that I John Wormsley of the county of Lancaster hath bargained and sold unto Bushrod Riveer of the said county a Negroe girl named Ann...[Wit:] Edwin Conway & William Norriss. Recorded 18th November 1773 by Test Thomas B Griffin, Cl Cur. [Page 90a]

18 Nov 1773. Certificate. I do hereby certify that Apphia Boatman and William Rain came before me one of his Majesty's Justice's of the Peace for the said county [Lancaster] and made oath upon the Holy Evangelist of Almighty God that the Negroe girl Nanny which Bushrod Riveer purchased of Mr John Wormsley was a Negroe girl belonging to Colo William Tayloe of Lancaster and never lived at any other place than at Colo Tayloe's untill he purchased her. [Wit:] Dale Carter. Recorded 18 Nov 1773 by Test Thomas B Griffin, Cl Cur. [Page 90a]

20 Sep 1773. Certificate. York County. I do hereby certify that Nanny one of the Negroes Mr. John Wormsley, settled with other negroes and land in lieu of the land in York County, was a wailing maid Mrs. Wormsley had in York County and not one of the Negroes belonging to Colo William Tayloe of Lancaster County...by Test Richd Hewitt. [Signed] William Dogges Junr. [Wit:] Bushrod Riveer. Recorded 18 Nov 1773 by Test Thomas B. Griffin, Cl Cur. [Pages 90a & 91]

18 Nov 1773. Deed of Bargain. Between Spencer Dogget of the parish of
Christ Church and county of Lancaster of the one part and Moses George of the
same parish and county of the other part... Spencer Dogget for and in the
consideration of the sum of forty pounds...paid by the said Moses George at or
before the ensealing and delivery of these presents...[for] all these goods and
chattels following (to wit) One Negroe man named Cuffee, one gray mare, a
yoke of oxen, one pair of cart wheels and cart, yoke ring and bolt, one bed and
furniture and bedsted, half a dozen pewter plates, one dish and basin, two chests,
one Petty Augre, one iron pott, one square pine table, one handsaw, a broad ax,
four chizzels, one sett of iron cart wheel boxes, a mans saddle and two bridles,
one sow and five shoats, two small canoes and ten quart bottles, together with all
right title interest claim and demand whatsoever of him the said Spencer Dogget
To have and to hold... provided always and upon this condition, that if the said
Spencer Dogget... shall well and truly pay or cause to be paid to the said Moses
George... the aforesaid sum of forty pounds with Interest for the same at the rate
of five [per] centum [per] annum from the date of these presents on or before the
eighteenth day of May next ensuing...[Wit:] George Galloway & John Miller.
Recorded 19 Nov 1773 by Test Thomas B. Griffin, Cl Cur. Received the day of
the date of the within written Indenture of the within named Moses George the
sum of forty pounds lawful money of Virginia being the consideration money
within mentioned. I say received by me Wit: Spencer Dogget. Recorded
Receipt 19 Nov 1773 by Test Thomas B. Griffin, Cl Cur. [Pages 91 & 91a]

10 Dec 1773. Report of the examination of Clerk's Office. Pursuant to an order
of Lancaster Court we the subscribers have examined the Clerk's office of the
said county and have compared the Minute Books with the several Books of
Record from July 1771(the time said office was last examined and find that the
several orders in the Minute Books are fully and properly recorded, and that the
papers of the several courts are regularly placed including the last court, given
under our hands... [Wit:] James Ball, Burges Smith, & Burges Ball. Recorded
16 Dec 1773 by Test Thomas B Griffin, C Cur. [Page 91a]

14 Dec 1773. Deed of Bargain and Sale. ...Between Thomas Lawson of the
county of Lancaster Gent and Lettice his wife of the one part and Spencer
Hinton of the same county of the other part... Thomas Lawson and Lettice his
wife for and in consideration of the sum of one hundred and seventy
pounds...[for] all that tract or parcel of land on the north side of Muskettoe
Creek in the said county of Lancaster (and is bounded as followeth) beginning at
a pine tree on the said creeks side adjoining the land of Capt Turbervile, and so
running along the said Turberville's line to a corner that divides this land from
the land of Thomas Hunton thence running along the said Huntons line to a
corner stone thence from the said stone to a white gum tree near the North Head
Branch of Muskettoe Creek in a straight line and so down the meanders of the

said creek to the beginning containing by estimation one hundred acres... [Wit:] Robert Clerk, John Robinson, & James Brent. Received the day of the date of the within Indenture of the within named Spencer Hinton the sum of one hundred and seventy pounds current money of Virginia in full consideration for the within mentioned granted parcel of land and premises. [Same witnesses as above]. Recorded 16 Dec 1773 by Test Thomas B. Griffin, C Cur. [Pages 91a, 92, & 92a]

29 Oct 1773. Commission and Certificate. ...To Thomas Pinckard, John Fleet, Edwin Conway and Hugh Brent Gent whereas Thomas Lawson Gent& Lettice his wife by their certain Indenture of Bargain & Sale bearing date 10th of December 1773 have sold and conveyed unto Spencer Hinton one tract of land containing one hundred acres more or less with the appurtenances lying and being in Lancaster County, and whereas the said Lettice cannot conveniently travel to our County Court of Lancaster to make acknowledgement of her rights in the said land, there fore we do give unto you or any two or more of you full power to receive the Acknowledgement which the said Lettice Lawson shall be willing to make before you of her right in the land aforesaid... receive her acknowledgement of the same and examine her privily and apart from the said Thomas Lawson her husband, whether she does the same freely and without persuasions or threats, and whether she be willing that the same shall be recorded in our said County Court of Lancaster... Witness Thomas B. Griffin Clerk of our said court...

10 Dec 1773. Lancaster Sct By virtue of the within Commission to us directed we have examined the within named Lettice Lawson apart from her husband & she doth voluntarily of her own free will acknowledge all her Right Title and Interest of Dower to the said land and premises mentioned in the Deed hereunto annexed without persuasion or threats of her said husband and is willing the same shall be entered upon record... [Wit:] John Fleet & Hugh Brent. Recorded 16 Dec 1773 by Test Thomas B. Griffin, C Cur. [Pages 92a & 93]

10 Dec 1773. Bond. Know all men by these presents that we Thomas Lawson & Hugh Brent of Lancaster County are held and firmly bound unto Spencer Hinton of the said county in the sum of one hundred and seventy pounds of current money of Virginia in case the said Hinton should be dispossesed or molested in a tract of land bought of the said Lawson and convey'd to him by a Deed, and we do hereby further agree to confirm unto the said Hinton... the Warrantee & Appurtenances of the said Deed in Performance of which we bind ourselves... firmly by these presents... [Wit:] Robert Clerk, James Brent, & John Robinson. Recorded 16 Dec 1773 by Test Thomas B. Griffin, C Cur.

29 Sep 1772. Deed of Gift. Know all men by these presents that I Thomas

Rouand of the parish of Christ Church and the county of Lancaster for and in consideration of the love and affection which I have and bear unto my friend Capt Hugh Brent and as well for the sum of five shillings to me in hand paid by the said Hugh Brent at and before the sealing and execution hereof, the Receipt... for diverse other good reasons and causes and consideration me hereunto moving, have given... unto Priscilla Brent a daughter of said Hugh Brent by his present wife Judith one negro girl named Bett... with future increase... for and during the full term & period of her the said Priscilla Brent natural life, and after the death of said Priscilla Brent I do by these presents give... the said Negro together with all her increase to the child or children of the said Priscilla Brent lawfully to be begotten on her body and living at the time of her death... to have and to hold the said Negro Bett and all her increase equally to and among the said children of said Hugh Brent by his present wife Judith... [Wit:] John Maxwell, William Wale, & William Brown-proved in court Deed of Gift from Hugh Brent Gent to his wife Judith... by the oaths of William Brown and William Wale two of the witnesses thereto and ordered to lye for further proof 15th day Oct 1772 by Test Thomas B. Griffin, C Cur. Recorded 16 Dec 1773 by Test Thomas B. Griffin, C Cur. [Pages 93a, 94 & 94a]

29 Sep 1772. Deed of Settlement. ...Between Capt Hugh Brent & Judith his wife of the parish of Christ Church & county of Lancaster of the first part Thomas Rouand & Mary his wife of the parish and county aforesaid of the second part & Capt Edwin Conway of the same parish and county aforesaid guardian to Elizabeth Kinnear (youngest daughter of the said Judith Brent by a former husband, and sister to the said Mary Rouand) of the third part... Hugh Brent and Judith his wife as well for and in consideration of the natural love & affection which they have & bear unto the said Mary Rouand and Elizabeth Kinnear... have given... & forever quit claim unto said Thomas Rouand and Mary his wife, and the said Edwin Conway as guardian unto the said Elizabeth Kinnear all & all manner of Right Title Interest Estate Property Claim & Demand whatsoever which the said Hugh Brent and Judith his wife or any of them by any ways or means... or any the Messuages Lands Tenements and Hereditaments late of Brereton Kenner decd (former husband to the said Judith Brent)... all & every or any of the Negro slaves and all other the personal estate of the said decd Brereton Kenner now being or remaining on that plantation whereon the said Brererton Kennear died either by force or virtue of the Last Will & Testament of the said Brereton Kennear, or by force of any custom or by any other ways or means whatsoever & all actions suits... so that neither Hugh Brent and Judith his wife... have claim challenge or demand or prosecute any action... of the said premises or any part or parcel thereof... and the said Hugh Brent and Judith his wife or any of them shall be utterly excluded & barred forever by these presents, and also all papers... of what nature or kind soever

which were of or belong to the sd Brereton Kennear decd & now in the
possession of Hugh Brent and Judith his wife... and [they] can or may lawfully
get at or come by without any repense or suit in law or equity, to have and to
hold all & singular the aforesaid premises with the appurtenances unto the said
Thomas Rouand... & the said Edwin Conway... in consideration of the premises
have given... unto the said Hugh Brent one Negro woman slave named Joan
now in possession of the said Hugh Brent together with all the future increase of
the said Negro... and the said Edwin Conway & the said Thomas Rouand for &
in consideration of the aforesaid premises have given... unto the said Hugh
Brent one full Moiety of all the corn & Tobo [tobacco] that was made on the
lands & by the slaves of the sd decd Brereton Kennear in Northumberland
County in the year of our Lord 1771... and lastly this Indenture witnesseth that
whereas the said Brereton Kennear decd late of Northumberland County did in
and by his Last Will & Testament in writing nominate & appoint his wife now
the aforesaid Judith Brent party to these presents Executrix of his said Will, and
whereas the said Judith Brent hath since taken it upon herself the Burthen of the
Execution thereof and equally fully & honesly divided & distributed the goods
& chattels of the sd Brereton Kenner amongst the said Mary Rouand &
Elizabeth Kennear children & legatees of the said Brereton Kennear . Now the
said Thomas Rouand & the said Edwin Conway... covenant with the said Hugh
Brent and Judith his wife... shall & will from time to time and at all times
hereafter fully acquit... the said Hugh Brent and Judith his wife... their & every
of their goods & chattels of & from all sum & sums of money ... which shall or
may at any time or times hereafter happen to be demanded or recovered from the
said Hugh Brent and Judith his wife... for or by reason of the Executors Life of
the said last Will & Testament of the said Brereton Kennear decd & of & from
all actions... whatsoever which shall or may happen arise or be for or by reason
of the same premises...[Wit:] John Maxwell, William Brown, & William Wale.
Deed of Settlement acknowledged by Edwin Conway & Recorded 15 Oct 1772
by Test Thomas B. Griffin, C Cur. Deed of Settlement from Hugh Brent &
others to Rouand & Kenner & recorded 16 Dec 1773 by Test Thomas B. Griffin,
C Cur. [Pages 94a, 95, 95a, & 96]

24 Dec 1773. Deed with Receipt. ...Between James Ewell of the county of
Lancaster Gent and Mary his wife of the one part and Burges Ball of the same
county Gent of the other part... James Ewell and Mary his wife for & in
consideration of the sum of fifteen hundred pounds... [for] all that tract or parcel
of land scituate on Fairweather's Creek in the said county of Lancaster formerly
granted to Anthony Stephens by patent bearing date 26th day of March anno
domini 1651, and purchased by the said James Ewell of Richard Chichester Gent
containing by estimation five hundred acres... and is bounded on the said creek
and the lands of the said Burges Ball... [Wit:] James Ball, Burges Smith, Ann
Ball, & James Ball Junr. Received the day of the date of the within Indenture of

70

the within named Burges Ball the sum of fifteen hundred pounds current money
of Virginia in full consideration for the within mentioned granted parcel of land
& premises. [same witnesses as listed above] Recorded 20 Jan 1774 by Test
Thomas B. Griffin, C Cur. [Pages 96 & 96a]

28 Jan 1774. Commission. ...To Burges Smith, James Gordon, & John Taylor
– Gent whereas James Ewell Gent and Mary his wife by their certain Indenture
of Bargain & Sale bearing date 24 December 1773 have sold & conveyed unto
Burges Ball one tract of land containing five hundred acres more or less with the
appurtenances lying and being in Lancaster County and whereas the said Mary
cannot conveniently travel to our county court of Lancaster to make
acknowledgement of her right in the said land, therefore we do give unto unto
you or any two or more of you full power to receive the acknowledgement ...go
to the said Mary Ewell and receive her acknowledgement of the same and
examine her privily and apart from the said James Ewell her husband whether
she does the same freely and voluntarily without his persuasions or threats &
whether she be willing that the same should be recorded in our said county court
of Lancaster... Thomas B. Griffin Clerk of our said court... `signed] Thomas B.
Griffin, Cl Cur. [Page 97]

22 Feb 1774. Commission and Certificate. ...By virtue of the within
Commission to us directed we have examined the within named Mary Ewell
apart from her husband James Ewell & she doth voluntarily of her own free will
acknowledge her right title & Interest of Dower to the said land & premises in
the Deed hereto annexed without persuasion or threats of her said husband & is
willing the same shall be entred upon record... [Wit:] John Taylor & James
Gordon. Recorded 15 Sep 1774 by Test Thomas B. Griffin, Cl Cur. [Page 97]

1 Dec 1773. Deed of Feoffment with Livery and Seisin ...between George
Davis of the county of Lancaster & Maryann his wife of the one part & Abraham
White of the same county of the other part... George Davis and Maryann his
wife for & in consideration of the sum of eighty pounds... fully bargain... &
sell... unto the said Abraham White... forever all that tract or parcel of land
scituate in the said county of Lancaster whereon the said George Davis now
dwelleth, and which was devised by the Last Will & Testament of Richard Davis
Great Grand Father of the said George unto his son Richard from whom it
descended by several descents unto the said George Davis in Fee Simple and is
bounded on the lands of Burges Ball Gent Edward Carter William Davis
Corotomon River and Pritchard's Swamp containing by estimation one hundred
acres... [Wit:] James Ball, Richard Cundiff, & George Rowtt [?]
Memorandum: that on the day of the date of the within Indenture quiet and
peaceable possession and Livery with Seisin of the within mentioned granted
parcel of land & premises was had & given by the within named George Davis

unto the within named Abraham White... [same witnesses as listed above].
Recorded 20 Jan 1774 by Test Thomas B. Griffin, Cl Cur. [Pages 97, 97a, &
98]

15 Jan 1774. Deed of Feoffment with Livery and Seisin. ...between Elias
Edmonds of the Lower Precinct of the parish of Christ Church in the county of
Lancaster & colony of Virginia of the one part, and the Reverend James Waddell
of the same parish & county in the colony of Virginia aforesaid of the other
part... Elias Edmonds for and in consideration of the sum of one hundred and
seventy five pounds... paid by the said James Waddell before the date of these
presents... do grant bargain & sell to the said James Waddell... a certain tract or
parcell of land with the appurtenances scituate lying and being in the aforesaid
parish of Christ Church and county of Lancaster aforesaid between the branches
of the Corotoman River & is bounded as followeth, vizt by the land of the said
James Waddell James Gordon Gent and James Robb decd containing by
estimation the quantity of two hundred & fifty acres... [Wit:] James Gordon,
John Yerby, & James Tapscot.   Memorandum-that this day to wit, 15 January
1774 peaceable and quiet possession & Seizen of the land & premises in the
within Deed specified was given & delivered unto the within named James
Waddell by the within named Elias Edmonds by the delivery of Turf & Twigg
upon the premises in the name & token of Seizen in the presence of us John
Yerby, James Gordon, & James Tapscot. Recorded 20 Jan 1774 by Test
Thomas B. Griffin, Cl Cur. [Pages 98, 98a, & 99]

7 Jan 1774. Deed. Know all men by these presents that we Jesse Robinson &
James Robinson Ann Robinson & Sarah Robinson for & in the consideration of
the natural love & affection which we the parties bear to our sister Winny
Robinson the wife of Eleazer Robinson & for & towards her future support &
maintenance, have given & granted... one Negro woman commonly called &
known by the name of Dinah together with her future increase... lawfully
begotten forever, which said Negro Dinah was given to the use of the said
Winny Robinson with her future increase by the will of James Robinson of the
county of Lancaster... for & during her natural life... [Wit:] James Norris,
George Norris & Elizabeth Robinson. Recorded 17 Feb 1774 by Test Thomas
B. Griffin, Cl Cur. [Page 99]

15 Jul 1773. Deed of Bargain and Sale with Interest. Know all men by these
presents that I Joseph Sullivant of the county of Lancaster and the parish of
Wiccomico for & in consideration of the sum of one hundred and six pounds,
one shilling & four pence three farthings... paid... by Thomas Reid Merchant of
said county ... do bargain and sell unto the said Thomas Reid one Negro
woman named Jean about thirty years of age, four negro girls vizt Nell about
thirteen years of age, Violet about seven years of age, Dark about four years of

age, & Feme about two years of age, also one Negro boy named Jack about eleven years of age... the said Joseph Sullivant... doth covenant... with the said James Reid... now at the making & delivery of these presents hath full right & lawful authority to bargain & sell the above Negro slaves & every of them in manner & form... the said Joseph Sullivant shall well & truly pay him the said Thomas Reid the said sum of one hundred and six pounds one shilling & four pence three farthings... on or before the first day of July next ensuing with legal interest on twenty three pounds seventeen shillings & one penny half penny part thereof from the fifth day of March 1768. And on eighty two pounds five shillings & three pence one farthing other part thereof from the date of these presents and that in case any of the slaves herein named shall die before the said Thomas Reid shall get actual possession of and sell the same that then & in such a case the said Joseph Sullivant shall bear the loss... [Wit:] Robert Dennistoun & Thomas Wallace.

15 Jul 1773. Provision. Provided always and it is the true intent and meaning of these presents that if the said Joseph Sullivant... shall well and truly pay or cause to be paid to the said Thomas Reid... the sum of one hundred and six pounds one shilling and four pence three farthings... on or before the first day of July next ensuing after the date of the above Bargain and Sale with Interest on twenty three pounds seventeen shillings and one penny half penny thereof at the rate of five [per] centum [per] annum from the fifth day of March .... 1768, and on the sum of eighty two pounds five shillings and three pence one farthing other part thereof at the rate aforesaid from the date of these presents... by Thomas Reid. Recorded 17 Feb 1774 by Test Thomas B. Griffin, Cl Cur. [Pages 99a & 100]

12 Jul 1773. Indenture and Bond. ...between Thomas Pollard of the county of Lancaster and the colony of Virginia of the one part, and John James of the county & colony aforesaid, of the other part... Thomas Pollard for and in consideration of the sum of two hundred and eighty pounds current money of Virginia, to him in hand paid by the said John James, the receipt whereof the said Thomas Pollard doth hereby acknowledge himself to be fully satisfied and paid, hath granted... unto said John James... whole right and title to three Negroes to wit, Bristol, Seipis, & Winny. Also one blacksmith named John Hutchinson or the Tobo [tobacco] he the said Hutchinson is now sold for to Bailie being thirteen thousand pounds of crop Tobo [tobacco], and casks, four feather beds & furniture, one desk, one oval table, one bay mare, one cart and oxen, one Tumbler and wheels, two tables, four cows and three calves, one looking glass, two chests, four iron potts, two pr and irons, two coffe potts, and one large Tumbler... [Wit:] Thomas Hubbard.

Know all men by these presents that I Thomas Pollard of the county of Lancaster & colony of Virginia am held and stand firmly bound unto John James of the county and colony aforesaid in the full and just sum of two hundred and eighty

pounds current money of Virginia to be paid unto the said John James...
The condition of the above Obligation is such that if the above bounden Thomas
shall pay or cause to be paid unto the aforesaid John James all damage that may
accrue to him on account of being security for the said Thomas Pollard to Mr.
James Gordon for a considerable sum of money as is specified in Bonds given
by the said Pollard to the aforesaid James Gordon in which Bonds the aforesaid
John James stands bound as security, as also for a Bond given by the said
Pollard to John Heath then the above to be void, or else to remain in full force
and virtue. Recorded 17 Feb 1774 by Test Thomas B. Griffin, Cl Cur. [Pages
100 & 100a]

17 Feb 1774. Deed with Receipt. ...between Thomas Pollard of the county of
Lancaster of the one part and Charles Lee of the same county of the other part...
Charles Lee for and in consideration of the sum of ten pounds... in hand paid at
or before the sealing and delivery of these presents the Receipt whereof said
Charles Lee doth hereby acknowledge and ... have granted, bargain'd and
sold... unto said Thomas Pollard... for ever one acre of land situate in the said
county of Lancaster, bounded as followeth, beginning at a pursimon stump on
the northwest side of a place now dug for a mill, and running across a point to a
stake and thence to the creek, be the same more or less the said acre of land...
[Wit:] James Maxwell, Henry Lawson, & Thomas Lawson. Receiv'd the day of
the date of the within Indenture of the within named Thomas Pollard the sum of
ten pounds current money in full consideration for the within acre of land.
[signed] Charles Lee. Recorded 17 Mar 1774 by Test Thomas B. Griffin, Cl
Cur.   [Pages 100a & 101]

17 Mar 1774. Agreement. I do hereby oblige myself my heirs & C to build a
mill on the acre of land as purchased of Mr. Charles Lee, if not to return the land
to the said Lee again, also to pay unto said Lee ten pounds current money or
credit in Mr. Gilmour's Store before I go to work on the said Mill also that the
sd acre of land is still the property of the said Lee untill the said sum of ten
pounds is paid as above... [signed] Thomas Pollard. N.B. I do further agree
that if the Mill is not compleated by the first of March 1777 that the acre of land
purchased as above shall likewise be the property of the said Lee. [Wit:] Test
Thomas Lawson & John Maxwell. Recorded 17 Mar 1774 by Test Thomas B.
Griffin, Cl Cur. [Pages 101 & 101a]

27 Jan 1774. Deed with Livery & Seisen. ...between James Pinckard of the
lower precinct of the parish of Christ Church in the county of Lancaster and the
colony of Virginia of the one part and James Gordon of the same parish and
county in the colony of Virginia aforesaid Gent of the other part... James
Pinckard for and in consideration of the sum of sixty pounds... to him in hand
paid by the said James Gordon before the date of these presents... [for] a certain

tract or parcel of land with the appurtenances situate lying and being in the aforesaid parish of Christ Church and county of Lancaster aforesaid and is bounded by the land of the said James Gordon, Peter Conway, James Pinckard Junr, Thomas Pinckard, William Edwards & James Robb decd containing by estimation the quantity of one hundred acres... whereon Mary Pinckard now lives, the mother of the said James Pinckard... [Wit:] James Tapscot, John Davis, James Pinckard Junr, & William Boatman. Memorandum: that this day to wit the twenty seventh day of January anno domini 1774. Peaceable and quiet possession & Seisin of the land & premises in the within Deed specified was given & delivered unto the within named James Gordon by the within mentioned James Pinckard by the delivery of Turf & Twig upon the premises in the name & token of Seizen. In prescense of James Tapscot, James Pinckard Junr & John Davis. Recorded 17 Mar 1774 by Test Thomas B. Griffin, Cl Cur. [Pages 101a & 102]

12 Mar 1774. Deed. ... between Benjamin George of the county of Lancaster & Catherine his wife of the one part & Jesse George of the county of Lancaster of the other part... Benjamin George and Catherine his wife for & in consideration of the sum of forty five pounds current money in hand paid at or before the sealing & delivery of these presents... [for] one moiety of all that tract & parcel of land situate in the said county of Lancaster which Nicholas Lawson purchased of William Dymer by Deed of Feoffment bearing date twelth of October in the nineteenth year of the reign of his late Majesty King George the second containing one hundred acres & bounded as mentioned in the said Deed, which said parcel of land on the decease of the said Nicholas Lawson descended unto his two daughters the aforesaid Catherine and Sarah the now wife of the said Jesse George & who are thereof now possessed as coheirs in Fee Simple... [Wit:] Edwin Conway, James Patrick, John Nichols, & Bailie George. Received the day of the date of the within Indenture of the within named Jesse George the sum of forty five pounds current money in full consideration the within mentioned granted parcel of land & premises. [Wit:] James Gordon, Edwin Conway, James Patrick, John Nichols, & Bailie George. Recorded 17 Mar 1774 by Test Thomas B. Griffin, Cl Cur. [Pages 102a & 103]

12 Mar 1774. Commission & Certificate . ...To Edwin Conway, Hugh Brent, & James Gordon Gent... Benjamin George and Katherine George his wife by their Deed of Bargain & Sale bearing date the 12th of March 1774 have sold & conveyed unto Jesse George one tract of land containing one hundred acres more or less with appurtenances lying and being in Lancaster County & whereas the said Catherine George wife of the said Benjamin George cannot conveniently travel to our county court of Lancaster to make acknowledgement of her right in the said land, therefore we do give unto you or any two or more of you, full power to receive the acknowledgement which the said Katherine George shall be

willing to make before you of her right... we do therefore command you that
you personally go to the said Katherine George & receive her acknowledgement
of the same & examine her privily & apart from the said Benjamin George her
husband whether she does the same freely and voluntarily without his
persuasions or threats, & whether she be willing that the same shall be recorded
in our said county court of Lancaster... [Wit:] Edwin Conway & James Gordon.
Recorded 17 Mar 1774 by Test Thomas B. Griffin, Cl Cur. [Page 103 & 103a]

22 Mar 1774. Lease. ...between William Nutt & Martha his wife of the parish
of Wiccomico & county of Northumberland of the one part & Thomas Rouand
of the parish of Christ Church & county of Lancaster of the other part... William
Nutt & Martha his wife for & in the consideration of the sum of five shillings
lawful money of Virginia to them in hand paid by the said Thomas Rouand at &
before the sealing & delivery of these presents. The receipt whereof hereby
acknowledged have granted... bargain & sell unto the said Thomas Rouand all
those two Messuages two tracts of land & two plantations of which William
Dymer late of the parish of Christ Church & county of Lancaster aforesaid
Gentleman died seized one of which said tracts of land being the dwelling
plantation of said William Dymer at the time of his death with the appurtenances
containing by estimation five hundred acres be the same more or less & being all
the lands which the said William Dymer held in the said county of Lancaster
situate lying & being in the parish of Christ Church & the county of Lancaster
aforesaid... from the first day of this instant [blank] for & during & unto the full
end & term of one whole year thence next ensuing & fully to be complete &
ended yielding & paying therefore at the expiration of the said year one ear of
Indian corn... Recorded 21 Apr 1774 by Test Thomas B. Griffin, Cl Cur. [Pages
103a & 104]

23 Mar 1774. Release with Receipt. ...between William Nutt & Martha his wife
of the parish of Wiccomico & county of Northumberland of the one part &
Thomas Rouand of the parish of Christ Church & county of Lancaster of the
other part... William Nutt & Martha his wife for & in consideration of the sum
of eight hundred pounds lawful money of Virginia to them in hand paid by the
said Thomas Rouand at & before the ensealing & delivery the receipt whereof is
hereby acknowledged... of every part & parcel thereof do hereby acquit release
& discharge the sd Thomas Rouand... (in his actual possession now being by
virtue of a Bargain & Sale to him thereof made for one whole year by Indenture
bearing date the day next before the day of the date of these presents & by force
the statute for transferring uses into possession)... for ever all those two
Messuages two tracts of land & two plantations of which William Dymer late of
the parish of Christ Church & the county of Lancaster aforesaid gentleman died
seized (one of which said tracts of land being the dwelling plantation of the said
William Dymer at the time of his death) with the appurtenances containing by

estimation five hundred acres be the same more or less & being all the lands the said William Dymer held in the said county of Lancaster situate lying and being in the said county of Lancaster & said parish of Christ Church aforesaid... Received the day of the date of the within written Indenture of the within named Thomas Rouand the sum of eight hundred pounds lawfull money of Virginia being the consideration money within mentioned. I say received by me-William Nutt. Recorded 21 Apr 1774 by Test Thomas B. Griffin, Cl Cur. [Pages 104, 104a, & 105]

21 Apr 1774. Deed with Livery and Seisen. ...between Charles Barrett of the county of Lancaster Waterman of the one part & Peter Williams of the county of Northumberland Waterman of the other part... Charles for & in consideration of the sum of sixty pounds current money of Virginia to him in hand paid, or secured to be paid, the receipt whereof he doth hereby confess & acknowledge & him the said Peter doth hereby exhonerate & discharge, hath bargained sold on feoffed & confirmed & by these presents doth bargain sell on feoff and confirm unto the said Peter... all that tract of land scituate lying and being in the parish of Christ Church & county of Lancaster, containing by estimation thirty acres... bounded by Hugh Brents land & George Hortons Indian Creek & a small cove commonly called the Back Cove... [Wit:] Onesephorus Harvey, Thomas Hubbard, & John Bar. Memorandum that on the 21st day of April 1774 Livery & Seisen of the premises within was made unto the said Peter Williams by the said Charles Barrett by delivery of Turf & Twig in presents of us. This Deed with Livery and Seisen thereon indorsed from Charles Barrett to Peter Williams were acknowledged in court by the said Charles & Ann his wife, she being first privily examined according to law. Recorded 21 Apr 1774 by Test Thomas B. Griffin, Cl Cur. [Pages 105 & 105a]

21 Apr 1774. Deed of Bargain & Sale. ...between Matthew Myars of the county of Lancaster of the one part and Jeremiah Dogget & Molly his wife of the same county of the other part... Matthew Myars for and in consideration of the sum of one hundred & twenty pounds current money in hand paid at or before the sealing & delivery of these presents... for ever all that tract or parcel of land scituate on Rappahannock River in the said county of Lancaster which was devised by the last Will & Testament of Walter Arms late of the sd county of Lancaster decd unto his daughter Hannah & afterwards conveyed & confirmed unto her by her brother Walter Arms by Deed bearing date the thirteenth day of September 1720, and by Jesse Light son & heir at law of the said Hannah sold & conveyed unto the said Matthew Myars by Indenture bearing date the thirteenth day of December 1768 containing eighty eight acres, be it more or less, & is bounded on the lands of William Arms & Francis Stephens & Rappahannock River... may at all times hereafter peaceably & quietly possess occupy & enjoy the said hereby granted parcel of land and premises with all & singular its

appurtenances & the same shall & will warrant & defend unto the said Jeremiah Dogget & Molly his wife... & every of them against the lawfull claim & demand of all & every person or persons whatsoever, except a certain part thereof formerly conveyed by George Light & John Light unto Solomon Ewell by Indenture bearing date the nineteenth day of April 1760 containing by estimation twenty five acres, which said part the said Matthew Myars doth hereby warrant & defend against the claim & demand of him & all persons whatsoever claiming by for or under him... [Wit:] James Ball, John Harris, & Nichs George. Received the day of the date of the within Indenture of the within named Jeremiah Dogget & Molly his wife the sum of one hundred and twenty pounds current money in full consideration for the within mentioned granted parcel of land & premises. [same witnesses as listed above]. Recorded 21 Apr 1774 by Test Thomas B. Griffin, Cl Cur. [Pages 105a & 106]

3 Nov 1773. Lease with Memorandum. Between William West of the parish of Christ Church in the county of Lancaster of the one part & Thomas Pollard of the parish & county aforesaid of the other part... William West for & in consideration of the sum of eighteen pounds current money of Virginia to him in hand paid by the said Thomas Pollard the receipt whereof he doth hereby acknowledge himself to be fully satisfied, doth by these presents bargain & sell unto the said Thomas Pollard... a peice or parcel of land lying & being in the county aforesaid containing by estimation fifty acres... bounded as followeth beginning at a hickery at the corner of said Wests fence & from thence running down the said fence [blank] the head of a branch, and down sd branch to the main swamp & bounded round by the said swamp to Mr. Elmore Doggets line & up the said line to the aforesaid hickory... from the twenty first day of December next ensuing for & during the term of nine years from thence next ensuing to the Intent whereof the said Thomas Pollard shall & may be in actual possession of the said land & premises & the said West doth agree to & with the said Pollard to execute any other instrument of writing for the more safe conveyance of the said land, when thereunto required... [Wit:] James Pollard, Thomas Hathaway, Lawson Hathaway, & William Swillivan. The true intent & meaning of the within Instrument of Writing is that the said William West doth give & grant unto the said Thomas Pollard the same previledge by the within Lease that he now enjoys under a Lease he has from William Steptoe & no other. [Wit:] Lawson Hathaway, Thomas Hathaway, & James Pollard. Recorded 21 Apr 1774 by Test Thomas B. Griffin, Cl Cur. [Pages 106 & 106a]

21 Apr 1774. Deed of Bargain and Sale with Receipt. ...between Meredith Mahanes John Selden James Selden & Mary Selden of the county of Lancaster of the one part and Lott Palmer of the same county of the other part... Merideth Mahanes John Selden James Selden & Mary Selden for & in consideration of the sum of twenty five pounds to them in hand paid the receipt whereof they doth

hereby acknowledge & confess hath granted bargained & sold unto the said Lott Palmer... for ever a tract or parcel of land containing thirty acres... situate lying & being in Lancaster County & part of the tract whereon John & Mary Selden now lives & bounded by the main swamp side that makes to Everetts Mill & the land of William Taylor & land of Thomas Yerby including thirty acres... [Wit:] William Davenport, James Tapscot, & John James. N.B. The said Lott Palmer nor his heirs hath no rite to the swamp ground, but have prevaledge of the timbers out of the said swamp for the use of his plantation. Received the 21st day of April 1774. Full satisfaction for the purposes within contained. I say received by me-Meredeth Mahanes, James Selden, & John Selden. [Wit:] William Davenport. Recorded 21 Apr 1774 by Test Thomas B. Griffin, Cl Cur. [Pages 106a, 107, & 107a]

17 Mar 1774. Report of Allotment. We the subscribers met & laid off John Pasquett 25 acres of land be the same more or less beginning at a corner hickory in branch on the south side of the house where John Pasquit now lives from thence running a straight line of marked trees to the Spring Branch on the north side of the said house from thence down the branch to the creek running round the creek side & up the branch to the beginning... [Wit:] John Marideth, Will Marideth, & John Yerby. Recorded 21 Apr 1774 by Test Thomas B. Griffin, Cl Cur. [Page 107a]

1 Nov 1773. Deed of Mortgage. ...between John Rogers of the county of Lancaster of the one part & Henry Tapscot of the county aforesaid of the other part... John Rogers for & in consideration of the sum of sixty nine pounds seven shillings current money to him... paid by the said Henry Tapscot, at or before the sealing & delivery of these presents... [for] all that tract or parcel of land situate in the county of Lancaster which descended unto him the said John Rogers on the death of his brother William Rogers, bounded on the lands of Richard Rogers decd Mr. Joseph Chinn & Thomas Mott containing one hundred and ninety five acres... said parcel of land is hereby acknowledged to be now in the actual possession of the said Henry Tapscot... the said John Rogers... shall pay or caused to be paid unto the said Henry Tapscot... the sd sum of sixty nine pounds seven shillings current money on or before the first day of January next ensuing that then it shall and may be lawfull for the said John Rogers... into the hereby granted & mortgaged parcel of land & premises to reenter & enjoy the same as in his former estate. [Wit:] John Tapscot, Jos Shearman, John Bailey, Wm Perciful, & Lawry Oliver. Recorded 19 May 1774 by Test Thomas B. Griffin, Cl L Cur. [Pages 108 & 108a]

24 Mar 1774. Lease. ...between Thomas Rouand and Mary his wife of the parish of Christ Church & county of Lancaster of the one part and John Berryman of the aforesaid parish & county of the other part... Thomas Rouand

and Mary his wife for and in consideration of the sum of five shillings lawful
money of Virginia to them in hand paid by the said John Berryman at and before
the sealing & delivery of these presents... & sell unto the said John Berryman all
those two Messuages two tracts of land and two plantations of which William
Dymer late of the parish of Christ Church and county of Lancaster aforesaid
Gent died seized one of which said tracts of land being the dwelling plantation
of the said William Dymer at the time of his death, with the appurtanences
containing by estimation five hundred acres... and being all the lands which the
said William Dymer held in the said county of Lancaster aforesaid... [Wit:]
Hugh Brent, James Brent, Maurice Brent, & Newton Brent. Received the day of
the date of the within five shillings being full consideration of the within
contents. Recorded 19 May 1774 by Test Thomas B. Griffin, Cl Cur. [Pages
108a & 109]

5 Mar 1774. Deed of Release. ...between Thomas Rouand and Mary his wife
of the parish of Christ Church and the county of Lancaster of the one part &
John Berryman of the said county & parish aforesaid of the other part... Thomas
Rouand and Mary his wife for & in consideration of the sum of nine hundred
pounds lawful money of Virginia to them in hand paid by the said John
Berryman at & before the ensealing & delivery hereof the Receipt whereof is
hereby acknowledged & thereof, & of every part thereof & parcel thereof... unto
the said John Berryman (in his actual possession now being by virtue of a
Bargain & Sale to him thereof made for one whole year by Indenture bearing
date with the day next before the day of the date of these presents and by force
of the statute for transferring User into Possession)... all those two Messuages,
two tracts of land & two plantations of which William Dymer late of the parish
of Christ Church & county of Lancaster aforesaid Gentlem died seized (one of
which said tracts of land being the dwelling plantation of the said William
Dymer at the time of his death) with the appurtenances containing by estimation
five hundred acres... and being all the land the said William Dymer held in the
said county of Lancaster situate lying & being in the said county of Lancaster &
parish of Christ Church aforesaid... [Wit:] Hugh Brent, James Brent, Maurice
Brent & Newton Brent. Received the day of the date of the within presents the
sum of nine hundred pounds current money being the full consideration of the
within contents. Recorded 19 May 1774 by Test Thomas B. Griffin, Cl Cur.
[Pages 109,109a, 110,& 110a]

21 Apr 1774. Commission. ...to Hugh Brent Thomas Lawson & John Fleet
Gent whereas Thomas Rouand & Mary his wife by their Deed of Release
bearing date 25 Mar 1774 have sold and conveyed unto John Berryman two
tracts of land containing five hundred acres more or less with the appurtenances
lying & being in Lancaster County & whereas the said Mary Rouand the wife of
said Thomas Rouand cannot conveniently travel to our county court of Lancaster

to make acknowledgement of her right in the said land, therefore we do give unto you or any two or more of you, full power to receive the acknowledgement which the sd Mary shall be willing to make before you... we do therefore command you that you personally go to the said Mary Rouand & receive her acknowledgement of the same & examine her privily & apart from the said Thomas Rouand her husband whether she does the same freely & voluntarily without his persuasions or threats, & whether she be willing that the same should be recorded in our said county court of Lancaster... [Wit:] Thomas B. Griffin. [Pages 109a & 110]

10 May 1774. Certificate. ... By virtue of the within Commission to us directed we have examined the within Mary Rouand apart from her said husband & she doth voluntarily of her own free will acknowledge all her right title & Interest of Dower to the said lands & premises mentioned in the said Deed hereto annexed without the persuasions or threats of her said husband & is willing the same should be recorded in our county court of Lancaster... [Wit:] Hugh Brent & Thomas Lawson. [Pages 110 & 110a]

19 May 1774. Report. Pursuant to an order of Lancaster Court dated the 21 Apr 1774 we the subscribers have viewed the road in the sd order mentioned and find the road antiently used over the bridge cross the head of Mud Creek cuts of about 45 acres of Mr. Thomas B. Griffin's land and about 35 acres of Mr. Rawleigh Downman's land & where said Downman has turned said road is about six hundred yards further, that the road proposed by William Stotts is as near as the said antient road, but cannot be made so dry & passable without a great deal of work, & will cut off about 20 acres of Mr. James Tapscot's land & as much of Mr. Henry Newby's land, & that the new road which runs altogether on a line to the main road is near a mile further to Moratico Neck than the said antient road... [Wit:] Jesse Ball, Burges Smith, & Burges Ball. Recorded 19 May 1774 by Test Thomas B. Griffin, Cl Cur. [Page 110a]

10 Jun 1774. Deed. ...between Burges Ball of the county of Lancaster Gentl of the one part & LeRoy Griffin of the county of Richmond & Jesse Ball of the county of Lancaster Gent Trustees for Mary the wife of Thomas Glascock & her two children Thomas and Mary Glascock of the other part... Burges Ball for & in consideration of the love and affection that he hath for the said Mary Glascock & her two said children Thomas & Mary & for divers other good causes & considerations him thereunto moving hath given... unto the said LeRoy Griffin & Jesse Ball... in trust for the said Mary Glascock & her two children, Thomas & Mary Glascock, the following negro slaves to wit, Bess, James, Hannah, and her young child [blank] being part of the slaves purchased by the said Burges Ball of the said Thomas Glascock as per Bill of Sale bearing date the 27th day of August last past, to have & to hold the said hereby granted

Bess, James, Hannah & her child [blank] and their future increase unto the said
LeRoy Griffin & Jesse Ball... or either of them take and apply the profits of all
& every of the said hereby granted slaves to and for the support & maintenance
of the said Mary Glascock & her two children Thomas & Mary Glascock in such
proportion as they shall think proper during the natural life of the said Mary
Glascock the elder & at her decease to divide the said hereby granted slaves &
their increase, or such of them that shall be living equally between the said two
children Thomas & Mary Glascock... and in case either of the said two children
Thomas & Mary should dye without issue in the life time of their mother, then
all the said slaves & their increase to be & remain to the survivor of the said
children, & if both the said two children Thomas & Mary Glascock should die
without issue in the life time of their mother, then all the said hereby granted
slaves & their increase to return to the said Burges Ball... [Wit:] James Ball,
Peter Conway, & Burges Smith. Recorded 16 Jun 1774 by Test Thomas B.
Griffin, Cl Cur. [Pages 111 & 111a]

11 Dec 1773. Deed of Mortgage. Whereas the within named John Heath... did
farm & take on hire from the within mentioned Nicholas Flood for the term of
one year from the said eleventh day of December in the year aforesaid & from
thence next ensuing all the within named slaves except Simon being sixteen in
number & also the within mentioned household furniture & stocks of cattle
sheep & C [chattel?] for the yearly rent or hire of sixty pounds lawful money of
Virginia to be paid by the said John Heath ... to the said Nicholas Flood... on
the eleventh day of December next ensuing the date of these presents... [all
above listed presents along with] the sum of ten shillings lawful money of
Virginia to the said John Heath in hand well & truly paid by the said Nicholas
Flood at or before the ensealing & delivery of these presents the receipt whereof
the said John Heath doth... acquit release and discharge the said Nicholas
Flood... that all & singular the lands tenements & hereditaments mentioned &
comprised in the within recited Indenture of Bargain & Sale bearing date 17 Feb
1773 & every of them with their & every of their respective appurtenances shall
from henceforth stand, remain & be charged & chargeable with & be a security
to the said Nicholas Flood... for payment of the said further sum of sixty pounds
on the aforesaid eleventh day of December next ensuing after the date of these
presents, for the rent & hire of the said sixteen slaves household furniture stocks
of cattle & sheep & C [chattel] together with the lawful interest for the same
from the said eleventh day of December last as above mentioned untill the same
shall be paid & shall not be redeemed or redeemable untill as well the said sum
of sixty pounds for the rent aforesaid with interest for the same as aforesaid as
also the sum of sixty pounds recurred by the said Indenture of Bargain & Sale
dated 17 Feb 1773 & all interest due for the same sums respectfully shall be
fully paid & satisfied unto the said Nicholas Flood... if it shall happen that the
said two annual rents or hires of sixty pounds, or any part thereof shall be behind

& unpaid in part or in the whole on the day on which it ought to be paid as aforesaid... the said Nicholas Flood... shall have the same power & authority and the same liberty to distrain & make distress for the aforesaid rent or hire...as if the said Nicholas Flood was a landlord, and the slaves household furniture stocks & C were lands & shall have to all intents & purposes the same power & previledge for the recovery of the said rent of sixty pounds, as the act or acts of the General Assembly of Virginia gives to land lords for the recovery of the rents of lands, and the said John Heath doth covenant... with the said Nicholas Flood... shall & will well truly pay or cause to be paid unto the said Nicholas Flood... the sum of sixty pounds... on the aforesaid eleventh day of December next ensuing with lawful interest for the same from the said last mentioned day untill payment thereof without any deduction or abatement of the same for Levies or cloathing or other things on any account or pretext whatsoever... signed by John Heath 21 Jan 1774. [Wit:] William Nelms, James Crain, William Haynie, Samuel Peachey Junr, John C. Coche, Samuel Williams, & William Mishelle. Recorded 21 July 1774 by Test Thomas B. Griffin. [Pages 111a, 112, & 112a]

26 Jul 1774. Election Poles in Lancaster County for Mr. James Selden.
Column 1: William Mountague, William Schofield, James Waddell, John Arms, Edwin Conway, James Currell, William Mason, James Mahone, Aaron Williams, Thomas Schofield, Jacob Currell, Henry Carter, John Nichols, Ben. George, William Yerby, John Yerby, William Galloway, William Griggs, Charles Lee, Roger Kelly, John James, Benj. Gaston, Richard Hutchings, John Riveer, George Brent, Thomas Brent, Edney Tapscot, Richd Cundiff, Ozwell Newby, John Rogers, John Goodridge, Moses Chilton, Thomas Chilton, Richd Ball, Richd Goodridge, John Williams, Richd Mitchell Junr, & Patrick Connally.
Column 2: John Longwith, Moses George, Stephen Shelton, William Wale, Richard Payne, Jesse Robinson, John McTire, John Davis, John Campbell, Samuel Yopp, Thomas Edwards, Richard Lock, Joshua Hubbard, Thomas Percifull, James Pinckard, John Miller, John Merideth, Jeremiah Dogget, William Mott, Thomas Robb, William Martin, Bushrod Riveer, James Wallace, Bartlet James, Lawson Hathaway, Elijah Percifull, Travis Webb, George Davis, William Riveer, Peter Riveer, John Merryman, William Dogget, William Riveer Junr, James Fendla, George Norris, William Edwards, William Chilton, & Charles Hammonds.
Column 3: Bailie George, Jesse Robinson, Thomas Dunaway, Richd Mitchell, Hugh Brent, Spencer George, William Mitchell, Thomas Rouand, Joseph Norris, Thomas Flint, Thomas Garner, Jos Sullivant, Henry Mase, Benj. Cundiff, Eleazar Robinson, Thomas Stott, Raw Davenport, James Webb, Thomas Bell, Merideth Maines, Moses Davis, Thomas Pitman, William Yopp, Elmore Dogget, Thos Hammonds, Martin George, Spencer Dogget, Thomas George, Henry M. Horn, John Bean, Maurice Wheeler, William Graham, William

Sullivant, Stephen Chilton, Johnson Riveer, Richd Overstreet, James Norris, & William Wiblen.

Column 4: Elias Edmonds, James Kirk, John Yerby, Thos Lawson, John Connally, George Yerby, Jona Pullen, John Baylie, James Simmons, John Pope, Robert McTire, John Fleet, George Edwards, Thomas Haydon, Raw Stott, John Hunton, Fleet Hinton, William Hubbard, William Bean, John Cundiff, George Bean, Robert Pinckard, John Carter, Lott Palmer, Saml Brumley, William Stott, John Payne, John Wormsley, Jesse Ball, John Norris, John Taylor, John Boyd, John Harris, John Chowning, James Brent, William Sanders, & James Tapscot. Per James Tapscot. Copy John Chinn Sheriff. [Pages 112a & 113]

26 Jul 1774. [Election Poles in Lancaster County] for Charles Carter Esqr.
Column 1: William Montague, Charles Rogers, William Schofield, James Waddell, Edwin Conway, Nicholas Currell, James Currell, Antho. Garton, William Mason, James Moughon, Aaron Williams, Thomas Schofield, Jacob Currell, Harry Carter, John Nichols, Thomas Carter, Gavin Lowry, Benj. George, William Yerby, John Yerby, William Galloway, William Griggs, Charles Lee, Roger Kelly, John James, Benj. Garton, Thomas Carter Junr, Richd Hutchings, John Riveer, John Leland Clk[?], John Eustace, Eppa Lawson, James Newby, John Wormsley, & Thomas Hunton.

Column 2: George Brent, Thomas Brent, Henry Lawson, Merryman Payne, Jesse Chilton, Edney Tapscot, John Longwith, Moses George, Will. Chowning, Thomas West, William Wale, Jesse Robinson, John Campbell, Samuel Yopp, Richd Lock, Joshua Hubbard, Coleman Dogget, James Pinckard Junr, John Miller, John Meredith, William Arms, Augustine Rice, George Carter, William Mott, Thomas Robb, Will. Martin, Bushrod Riveer, Bartlet James, Lawson Hathaway, James Ball, John Yerby, Dale Carter, John Norris, Peter Conway, & Andrew Robertson.

Column 3: Bailie George, Lazarus George, Thomas Garner, Jos. Sullivant, Rawleigh Shearman, William Yopp, Elmore Dogget, Thomas Hammonds, Martin George, Henry Currell, James Kirk, Thomas Myars, John Payne, Henry Carter, Elias Edmonds, James Kirk Junr, John Yerby, John Connally, Robert Chinn, George Yerby, Jona. Pullen, John Bailey, James Simmons, John Pope, John Fleet, George Edwards, Thomas Haydon, John Hunton, Fleet Hinton, Jesse George, James Gordon, William Sydnor, Raw. Downman, Fort Sydnor, & David Galloway.

Column 4: Benj. Waddy, Antho. Sydnor, Robert Pinckard, John Carter, Lott Palmer, Will. Stott, Rhodam Lundsford, Richd Hinton, Peter Riveer, Will. Chilton, Will. Dogget, Will. Brumley, Thad. McCarty, Edward Carter, James Fendla, George Norris, Will. Edwards, Will. Chilton, Charles Hammonds, Henry M. Horn, John Bean, John Clutton, Will. Sullivant, Stephen Chilton, Abraham White, Thomas B. Griffin, Thomas Pinckard, Richd Hall, David Currie Clk,

Mungo Harvey, Will. Landers, Burges Smith, & James Tapscot. Per Thomas Shearman Copy John Chinn Sheriff. [Pages 113 & 113a]

26 Jul 1774. [Election Poles in Lancaster County]for Mr. Burges Ball.
Column 1: Charles Rogers, John Arms, Nicho. Currell, Antho. Garton, Thomas Carter, Garvin Lowry, Thomas Carter Junr, Henry Lawson, Merryman Payne, Jesse Chilton, Moses George, Stephen Chilton, Will Chowning, Thomas West, Richard Payne, John McTyre, John Davis, Thomas Edwards, Thomas Percifull, Coleman Dogget, Thomas Myars, Will. Arms, Augustine Rice, George Carter, John Payne, Henry Carter, Jeremiah Dogget, James Wallace, & Elijah Percifull.
Column 2: Travis Webb, Will. Pasquet, Jesse Robinson, Lazarus George, Thomas Dunaway, Richd Mitchell, Hugh Brent, Spencer George, Will Mitchell, Thomas Rouand, Jos. Norris, Thomas Flint, Henry Mayes, Ben. Cundiff, Eleaz. Robinson, Thomas Stott, Raw. Davenport, James Webb, Thomas Bell, Merideth Maine, Moses Davis, Thomas Pitman, Raw Shearman, Spencer Dogget, Harry Currell, James Kirk, Thomas Lawson, Robert Chinn, & Robert McTire.
Column 3: Raw. Stott, Will Hubbard, Will. Bean, John Cundiff, George Bean, Ben Waddy, Samuel Brumley, John Payne, Richd Cundiff, Ozwell Newby, John Rogers, John Goodridge, Moses Chilton, Rhodam Lundsford, Thomas Chilton, Richd Ball, Richd Hinton, Richd Goodridge, John Williams, Richd Mitchell Junr, Patrick Connally, George Davis, William Riveer, Will. Chilton, John Merryman, Will. Brumley, Will. Riveer, Edward Carter, & Thomas George.
Column 4: Morris Wheeler, John Clutton, Will. Graham, Abraham White, Johnson Riveer, Richd Overstreet, James Norris, Will. Wiblin, Burges Smith, James Newby, Andrew Robertson, Jesse George, John Taylor, James Gordon, Edward Blackmore, Henry Towles, George Chitwood, John Boyd, John Harris, John Chowning, Will. Sydnor, James Brent, Nicho. George, David Galloway, Mungo Harvey, Richard Hall, Thomas B. Griffin, & Jesse Ball. Per Bridgar Haynie Copy John Chinn Sheriff. The above polls taken for the Election of Burgesses ... recorded 26 Jul 1774 by Test Thomas B. Griffin. [Page 113a]

12 Aug 1774. Power of Attorney. Know all men by these presents the whereas Richard Chichester Esquire of Lancaster County & Colony of Virginia by his Last Will & Testament bearing date 17 May 1743 did devise give & bequeath unto his eldest son John Chichester of the same county & colony of Virginia all his estate real & personal (except certain Legacies therein specified) being & lying in the counties of Devonshire & Dorset, the town of Exeter or elsewhere in England, which he the said Richard Chichester was possessed of or any ways entitled by virtue of the Last Will & Testament of Chilcot Symes his uncle which said Will bears date 24 Jun 1742, and whereas the said John Chichester died before his age of twenty one years leaving a widow Jane Chichester some time since married to John Payne Esqr of Goochland County & the colony of Virginia which said widow (now Payne) is entitled to a third or some other part

of the said real estate no settlement or jointure having been made upon her, previous or subsequent to her marriage with the said John Chichester, and leaving also an infant daughter Mary Chichester his only child & heir some few years ago married to Burges Ball Esquire of the county of Lancaster & the aforesaid colony of Virginia (all of which said parties have duly signed... & delivered these presents and whereas the said real & personal estates & the profits & emoluments thereof have been under the controul direction & management of the High Court of Chancery in London & many proceedings have thereupon been had, & whereas the said court of Chancery appointed John Blackburn Merchant in London as guardian to said Mary Chichester (now Ball) the infant untill she arrives to a proper age, and whereas the said Mary has now come to the age of twenty one years & is very desirous together with the aforesaid Burges Ball the husband & aforementioned John Payne & Jane his wife to have all matters relative to the said estates fully settled & adjusted in every respect whatsoever. Know ye that the said Burges Ball & Mary his wife, John Payne & Jane his wife have made ordained... & by these presents do make ordain... & appoint Cyrus Griffin Esquire our true just & lawful attorney... to settle with demand & receive of & from the said High Court of Chancery, the Lord Chancellor or any of the officers thereof & also of & from the aforesaid John Blackburn the guardian...whatever ballance or other interest, profits or emoluments may be accruing to us or any of us... & to take all lawful ways & means or otherwise for the recovery and adjustment thereof... to make seal & deliver for us & in our names all acquittances or sufficient discharges for the same & to do all lawful acts & things whatsoever concerning the premisses as fully in every respect as we ourselves might or could do if we were personally present. And also we constitute and appoint the said Cyrus Griffin our true & lawful attorney to grant bargain sell... in any manner the aforesd estate or estates lying & being in the counties of Devonshire, Dorset, the Town of Exeter or elsewhere in England belonging to us or any of us the said parties by the Right of Inheritance or by virtue of the devices, bequests or marriages before mentioned ... & as our proper acts & deeds to execute sign seal & deliver such conveyances & assurances of the said premises whether a fine or fines, lease & release, bargain & sale or whatever writing or writings instrument or instruments of writing may be thought necessary unto any purchaser or purchasers, lessee or leessees, mortgage or mortgages... according to the Tenor & Design of the respective agreements whether in Fee Simple for Live or years giving & by these presents granting unto our said attorney full power & absolute authority to do execute & perform any act or acts.. that shall be needful & necessary... as we the said Burges Ball, Mary Ball, John Payne & Jane Payne might or could do if we were then & there personally... and things our attorney shall do or cause to be done by virtue & according to the true intent & meaning of these presents, hereby revoking all other letters or powers of attorney or other instruments of writing whatever... [Wit:] James Ball Judge of the court of Lancaster, Dale

Carter one of the Justices of the county of Lancaster, Richard Mitchell one of the Justices of Lancaster County, Thomas B. Griffin Clerk of the Court of Lancaster County, & LeRoy Griffin one of the Justices of Richmond County. [When signatures listed for parties involved listed as: Burges Ball, Mary Ball, John Payne, & Jean Payne]. Recorded 15 Sep 1774 by Test Thomas B. Griffin. [Pages 114, 114a, & 115]

12 Aug 1774. Certificate. We certify & make oath that Burges Ball, Mary Ball, John Payne & Jean Payne have duly signed sealed acknowledged & delivered the above Letter of Attorney being first read & clearly understood. We certify further that Burges Ball the first subscriber in the above power or Letter of Attorney is lawfull husband to Mary Ball the second subscriber & that the said Burges Ball was more than twenty one years old at the execution of the said power or Letter of Attorney, that the said Mary Ball is the only child to John Chichester Esquire deceased of Lancaster County of the colony of Virginia & that the said Mary Ball was also more than twenty one years of age at the execution of the aforesaid Letter or Power of Attorney, that the above mentioned John Chichester was the eldest son... of Richard Chichester Esquire of the aforesaid county & colony of Virginia which Richard Chichester was nephew & devise of his uncle Chilcot Symes who left him estates both real & personal in England by his Last Will & Testament bearing date 4 Jun 1742, entitled the last Will & Testament of me Chilcot Symes of Poorstock in the county of Dorset. We further certify & make oath that John Payne the third subscriber to the Letter of Attorney is lawfull husband to Jane Payne the last subscriber in the said Letter of Attorney & that the said John Payne was also at the execution of the said Power of Attorney, more than twenty one years old & that the aforesaid Jean Payne was formerly the widow of the aforesaid John Chichester Esquire & the mother of the above mentioned Mary Ball... [Wit:] James Ball, Dale Carter, Richd Mitchell, & James Gordon- Justice of the Peace for the county court of Lancaster. Recorded 15 Sep 1774 by Test Thomas B. Griffin, Cl Cur. [Page 115]

12 Aug 1774. Commission. ...to James Ball, Dale Carter, & Richard Mitchell Gentlemen Justices of the county court of Lancaster, whereas Burges Ball & Mary Ball his wife of the county of Lancaster & John Payne & Jane his wife of the county of Goochland at present residing in the county of Lancaster by their Letter of Attorney bearing date 12 Aug 1774 have made... Cyrus Griffin Esquire of the county of Lancaster & colony of Virginia to be their just true & lawful attorney to manage... & grant... all their right to lands tenements estates real & personal lying & being in the counties of Devonshire & Dorset, the town of Exeter or elsewhere in England , & whereas the said Mary Ball and Jean Payne cannot conveniently travel to our court of Lancaster to acknowledge personally the said Power or Letter of Attorney, we therefore give unto you or any two or

more of you full power & authority to receive the acknowledgement and take the examination of the said Mary Ball & Jean Payne to the aforesaid Power or Letter of Attorney privily & apart from their said husbands touching their consent thereto, & whether they freely & voluntarily give up & relinquish their rights & interests to the lands, tenements, or other estates in the aforesaid Power or Letter of Attorney... & whether they do the same & freely & voluntarily without the persuasions or threats of their respective husbands & whether they be willing that the same should be recorded in our said county court of Lancaster... [signed] Thomas B. Griffin, Cl Lan Curt. [Page 115a]

13 Aug 1774. Certificate. Pursuant to the above Commission to us directed three of his Majesties Justices of the county court of Lancaster, we having examined Mary Ball the wife of Burges Ball & Jane Payne the wife of John Payne in the said commission privately & apart from their said husbands, do hereby certify... each of them freely & voluntarily without the threats or persuasions of their respective husbands appoint Cyrus Griffin Esquire in the said Commission & Letter or Power of Attorney mentioned their just true & lawful attorney & each of them do freely & voluntarily relinquish their rights & interests to the sd lands tenements & estates with their appurtenances as are mentioned in the sd Power or Letter of Attorney... and are willing their said attorney should sell... all their rights & interests in the aforesaid land tenements or estates... & they are willing that the said Letter or Power of Attorney with their privy examination should be recorded in the county court of Lancaster... [Wit:] James Ball, Dale Carter & Richd Mitchell. Recorded 15 Sep 1774 by Test Thomas B. Griffin, Cl Lan Cur. [Pages 115a & 116]

18 Aug 1774. Deed of Bargain & Sale with Receipt. ...between Philip Smith of the county of Westmoreland Gent of the one part & William Montague of the county of Lancaster late of the county of Essex of the other part... Philip Smith for & in consideration of the sum of two hundred & thirty pounds current money in hand paid at or before the sealing   of these presents... unto the said William Montague... for ever all that tract or parcel of land scituate in the county of Lancaster bounded as followeth beginning at a marked oak on the west side of the road that leads from Capt Selden's Mill to Cundiffs, thence S85 W102 poles, thence S25 E69 poles to the road that leads from Mrs Margaret Ball's Mill to Cundiffs, thence down the said road till it intersects the line between the said Selden & Mrs Martha Miller thence S26 W177 P to Mr Ball's Mill Swamp, thence up the said swamp the several meanders thereof to a branch that divides this land from the land of Mr Richard Ball, thence up the said branch & along the line or bounds of the said Richard Balls land to the first mentioned road, thence up the said road to John Boyd's line, thence along said line S45 E103 P thence S33 45W to the beginning, containing four hundred and seventy acres, which said parcel of land was (pursuant to a Decree of the general

court) purchased of the said William Montague by John Smith of the county of Middlesex Gent with the approbation of James Ball & Kendal Lee Gent in Trust for Lucy the widow of Baldwin Matthews Smith Gent decd & her assigns during her natural life, remainder to the aforesaid Philip Smith son of the said Baldwin Matthews Smith in Fee Simple, as by the said Decree bearing date 11 Apr 1762 & by Indenture bearing date 13 Nov 1762 made between the said William Montague & Hannah his wife of the one part & the said John Smith of the other part... [Wit:] David Boyd, LeRoy Peachey, Burges Smith, John Warden, & James Waddell. Received the day of the date of the within Indenture of the within named William Montague the sum of two hundred and thirty pounds current money in full consideration for the within mentioned granted parcel of land & premises. [Wit:] David Boyd, John Warden, LeRoy Peachey, James Waddell, & Burges Smith.   Recorded 15 Sep 1774 by Test Thomas B. Griffin, Cl Cur. [Pages 116, 116a, & 117]

18 Aug 1774. Deed, Receipt & Bond. Know all men by these presents that I Philip Smith of the county of Westmoreland am held & stand bound unto William Montague of the county of Lancaster in the sum of five hundred pounds current money which payment well & truly to be made unto the said William Montague.... I bind myself... firmly by these presents... The condition of the above obligation is such that if the above bounded Philip Smith... shall & will at all times hereafter well & truly abide by... the articles... mentioned & contained in a certain Indenture of Bargain & Sale made & entred into between the said Philip Smith of the one part & the said William Montague of the other part bearing even date with these presents... [Wit:] LeRoy Peachey, David Boyd, Burges Smith, John Warden, & James Waddell. Recorded 20 Oct 1774 by Test Thomas B. Griffin, Cl Cur. [Pages 117 & 117a]

3 Nov 1774 Surveyed by Jesse Ball. Agreeable to an order of Lancaster Court dated the 20th Oct 1774 we the subscribers have met on the land mentioned in the said order & divided it agreeable to the above Plat. [Wit:] Richard Mitchell, John Chinn, & Jesse Ball. Contents 107 acres 1R 8P by a scale of 20 poles to an inch. At a court held for Lancaster County on 7 Nov 1774 A Report of the Survey and Division of the land belonging to Richard Rogers decd was returned & ordered to be recorded. [by] Test Thomas B. Griffin, Cl Cur. [Pages 117a & 118]

17 Nov 1774. Deed of Bargain and Sale with Receipt.   ...between Hannah Rogers of the county of Lancaster Spinster of the one part & Richard Stott of the same county Planter of the other part... Hannah Rogers for & in consideration of the sum of twenty pounds current money in hand paid at or before the sealing & delivery of these presents... & confirm unto the said Richard Stott ... for ever all that tract or piece or parcel of land scituate in the fork of Colo James Ball's Mill

Pond in the aforesaid county bounded as followeth beginning at a small red oak
on the side of the south branch of the said mill pond, & running thence N38 E99
pole to Susanna Stonum's line, thence along her line N55 ½ W47 pole, thence
S24 ½ W to the said branch thence up the meanders of the said to the beginning
containing twenty one & a half acres more or less, being part of a parcel of land
descended unto the said Hannah as co heiress of her father Richard Rogers
decd... [Wit:] James Newby, William Stonum, & Thomas Stott. Received the
day of the date of the within Indenture of the within named Richard Stott the
sum of twenty pounds current money in full consideration for the within
mentioned granted parcel of land & premises. [same witnesses as above].
Recorded 17 Nov 1774 by Test Thomas B. Griffin, Cl Cur. [Pages 118 & 118a]

30 Jul 1774. Deed. Know all men by these presents that I William Steptoe of
the county of Lancaster for & in consideration of the sum of five shillings to me
in hand paid by William Broun of the said county as well as for divers other
good causes & considerations me hereunto moving have given... unto the said
William Brown two negro slaves named Jenny & her son Harry & the future
increase of the said slave Jenny... Provided always and it is the true intent and
meaning hereof that the said William Steptoe... do & shall at all time & times
for ever hereafter indemnify... the said William Broun... of & from all & all
manner of action or actions suits troubles controversies molestation costs and
demands whatsoever which shall or may at any time hereafter be had made sued
prosecuted brought or done by any person or persons whatsoever upon or against
the said William Broun ... for or by reason or on account of a negro boy slave
named Willoughby this day purchased by the said William Broun of me the said
William Steptoe for the price of twenty nine pounds current money of
Virginia... [Wit:] Harry Carter & Betty Carter. Recorded 15 Dec 1774 by oath
of Harry Carter & ordered to lye for further proof. 16 Feb 1775 Deed
acknowledged by William Steptoe & ordered to be recorded by Test Thomas B.
Griffin, Cl Cur. [Pages 118a & 119]

15 Dec 1774. Sheriff Bond. Know all men by these presents that we Richard
Mitchell Henry Tapscot & Joseph Norris are held & firmly bound unto our
Sovereign Lord King George the Third in the sum of one thousand pounds to be
paid to our said Lord the King... to which payment well & truly to be made we
bind ourselves... jointly & severally firmly by these presents... The condition
of the above obligation is such that whereas the above bound Richard Mitchell is
constituted & appointed Sheriff of the county of Lancaster during pleasure by
commission from his Excellency the Governor of this colony under the seal of
the said colony this day 25th October last, if therefore the said Richard Mitchell
shall well & truly collect & receive all officers fees & duties put into his hands
to collect & duly account for & pay the same to the officers to whom such fees
are due respectively, at such times as are prescribed & limited by law, & shall

well & truly execute & due return make of all process & precepts to him directed & pay & satisfy all sums of money & tob[o] by him received by virtue of any such process to the person or persons whom the same shall be due his or their Exers Admors or Assigns, & in all other things shall truly & faithfully execute & perform the said office of sheriff during the time of his continuance therein then the above obligation... [Wit:] George Scurlock & James B. Booth.   Recorded 15 Dec 1774 by Test Thomas B. Griffin, Cl Cur. [Pages 119a & 120]

15 Dec 1774. Sheriff Bond. Know all men by these presents that we Richard Mitchell Henry Tapscot & Joseph Norris are held & firmly bound unto our Sovereign Lord King George the Third in the sum of five hundred pounds to be paid to our said Lord the King ... to which payment well & truly to be made we bind ourselves... jointly & severally firmly by these presents... The condition of the above obligation is such that whereas the above bound Richard Mitchell is constituted & appointed Sheriff of the county of Lancaster during pleasure by commission from his Excellency the Governor of this colony under the seal of the said colony this day 25th October last, if therefore the said Richard Mitchell shall well & truly collect all Quitrents, Fines Forfeitures & Amerciaments accruing or becoming due to his Majesty in the said county & shall duly account for & pay the same to the officers of his Majesty's Revenue for the time being on or before the second Tuesday in June annually & shall in all other things truly & faithfully execute the said office of sheriff... [Wit:] George Scurlock, James B. Booth, & Robert Chinn. Recorded 15 Dec 1774 by Test Thomas B. Griffin, Cl Cur. [Pages 119a & 120]

1 Feb 1775. Deed with Receipt.   ...between John Rogers of the county of Lancaster and Ann his wife of the one part & John Chinn of the same county Gent of the other part... John Rogers and Ann his wife for & in consideration of the sum of eighty five pounds current money in hand paid at or before the sealing & delivery of these presents...confirm unto the said John Chinn... for ever all that tract peice or parcel of land scituate in the said county of Lancaster being part of a parcel of land whereon the said John Rogers now dwelleth & which descended unto him on the death of his father John & brother William Rogers, bounded as followeth, beginning at a large ash tree in the mouth of a small branch, that issueth out of the main Northward Branch of Colo James Ball's Mill Pond, & running thence up the said small branch S52 E27 ½ pole, thence S12 pole , thence S5 W25 P, thence S46 E119 P to an old dead Hickory, thence N89 W54 P, to a large sassafras, thence N79 W45, thence N79 W45 P to a large pine in an old field near the said Rogers's house, thence W113 P to a stone near a large black oak, thence N2 ½ E to the aforesaid main branch thence the said branch to the beginning containing one hundred & four acres... [Wit:] John Smither, John Stonum, George Newby, Holland Haynie, & James Warwick. Received the day of the date of the within Indenture of the within

named John Chinn the sum of eighty five pounds current money in full consideration for the within mentioned granted land & premises. [Wit:] John Smither, George Newby, & James Warwick. Recorded 16 Feb 1775 by Test Thomas B. Griffin, Cl Cur. [Pages 120 & 120a]

14 Feb 1775. Deed with Receipt. ...between John Rogers of the county of Lancaster and Ann his wife of the one part and Richard Stott of the same county of the other part... John Rogers & Ann his wife for & in consideration of the sum of nineteen pounds seven shillings current money in hand paid at or before the sealing & delivery of these presents... confirm unto the said Richard Stott... all that tract or parcel of land, being part of a parcel of land, whereon the said John Rogers now dwelleth & which descended to him by the death of his father John, & brother William Rogers, & is bounded as followeth, beginning in the main swamp of Colo James Ball's Mill, where Mr John Chinn's line intersects the same, which he lately purchased of the said John Rogers & running thence S2 ½ W along the said line of Mr Chinn to a corner stone, thence due west to the line formerly Richard Rogers's, thence along said line to the said Mill Swamp, thence up the said swamp to the beginning containing eighteen acres... [Wit:] Thomas Stott, William Newton, & James Luckam. Received the day of the date of the within Indenture of the within named Richard Stott the sum of nineteen pounds seven shillings current money in full consideration for the within granted land and premises. [same witnesses as listed above.]. Recorded 16 Feb 1775 by Test Thomas B. Griffin, Cl Cur. [Pages 121 & 121a]

20 Oct 1774. Deed of Gift. ...Between Sarah Overstreet of the county of Lancaster & the colony of Virginia of the one part & Elizabeth Lynton Arms & Mary Arms of the other part... Sarah Overstreet for & in consideration of the natural love & affection which she doth bear to the said Elizabeth Lynton Arms & Mary Arms daughters of my brother William Arms & for their better preferment in marriage, & diverse other good causes & considerations me thereunto moving, have given... unto the said Elizabeth Lynton Arms my negro boy James, & to Mary Arms, my negro girl Judith... & further I the said Sarah Overstreet have put the sd Elizabeth Lynton Arms in possession of the said negro James (except the use of the said James I reserve for myself during my natural life) & have put the said Mary Arms in full possession of the said Judith by a delivery unto them... [Wit:] Henry Towles, William Chowning, & Matt Myars. Recorded 16 Feb 1775 by Test Thomas B. Griffin, Cl Cur. [Pages 121a & 122]

19 Jan 1775. Deed with Receipt. ...between John Hunton of the parish of Christ Church in the county of Lancaster of the one part & Jeremiah Ashburn of the said parish & county of the other part... John Hunton for & in consideration of the sum of thirty one pounds ten shillings current money to him in hand paid

by the said Jeremiah Ashburn... [for] ten acres & a half, scituate in the parish & county aforesaid, & bounded as follows, to wit, beginning at a blown up pine on Cool Spring Cove from thence running along the line of Thomas Hunton SW to two sweet gums at the head of Peach Orchard Cove, thence running SE along a line of marked trees to a corner pine, thence running NE along a line of marked trees to a stooping pine standing on a point in the fork of Cool Spring Cove, from thence to the beginning... [Wit:] Charles Hunton, James Blackerby, & William Hunton. Received of the within named Jeremiah Ashburn the sum of thirty one pounds ten shillings current money, the consideration within mentioned....[John Hunton]. Recorded 16 Feb 1775 by Test Thomas B. Griffin, Cl Cur. [Pages 122 & 122a]

20 Apr 1775. Deed of Bargain & Sale. ...between Thomas Rouand & Mary his wife of the county of Lancaster in the colony & Dominion of Virginia of the one part which said Thomas is the eldest son & heir at law to the late Hugh Rouand second son of Samuel Rouand of Greenhead in the shire of Lanerk both decd & John Rouand brother to the said Thomas Rouand of the colony & county aforesaid of the other part... whereas by contract of marriage dated 11 Apr 1743 made & past betwixt Jean Graham daughter of John Graham decd late deacon of the Taylors in the city of Glasglow in North Britain & Lilias Weir his wife & Robert Smith Hammerman in the sd city of Glasgow. To which contract the said Lilias Weir the mother, was also a party, the said Lilias Weir became bound to make the said Jean Graham & the said Robert Smith her husband for his interest & the children of the said marriage a Bairn of her house   & half shearer of her hail goods & gear debts & sums of money & all other her effects heretable or moveable whatsoever after her decease after the said Lilias Weir had set aside two thousand merks to be disposed of as she pleased as by the said contract of marriage relation thereunto being had among the Sheriffs Court Books of Lanerk in North Britain 6 Jun 1757 will more fully appear, did give... to & in favor of her other daughter Grizzel Graham in life rent for her life rent use allernaly during all the days & years of her lifetime & to the children to be procreate of the said Grizzel Graham her body either of her present or any subsequent marriage, whom failling to James & Silas Smiths her grand children equally betwixt them & the heirs of their body whom also failing to Hugh Rouand aforesaid nephew of the said Silas Weir... in Fee all & haill that southmost half belonging to the said Silas Weir of all & haill that tenement of land high & Laigh with the yeard at the back thereof rebuilt after the great fire lying within the burgh of Glasgow beyond the Gallow Gate Bridge on the north side of the said street & in that part thereof called Spoutmouth bounded by the lands of the deceased Hugh Corbett of Hardgray on the south & west parts the lands sometime belonging to Andrew Ker thereafter to Allan Corbett then to Patrick Maxwell Cordiner on the north the common passage leading to the Spouts on the east parts & consisting the said hail Ticklike [Sicklike?] all & hail that first

storey or changehouse two collars at the stair foot high back in the second
storey, high loft above the same back house top house southernmost of the two
fore Merchants Shops Brew House Midden Stead & Fulzia or Dung Class &
Houses therein   which are all parts & portions of that tenement of land high &
laigh back & fore with closs yeard & pertinents lying on the east side of the Salt
Market Street of Glasgow which belonged to John Simpson Armourer bounded
betwixt the lands of old belonging to Adam Scott thereafter to James Garmourlie
& to George Black on the north the lands now of John Mclae on the south the
Burn Molindinar on the east and the Kings High Street on the west parts &
unlike manner all & hail these houses Malt Kiln Barn & yeards with one acre
three roods & thirty four falls of ground in South Croft of Meikle in Meikle
Govan all lying within the parish of Govan regality of Glasgow & Sheriffdom of
Lanerk as the same were lately possest by James King late Heretor thereof and
last by [blank] bounded as follows, vizt the said one acre three rood & thirty four
falls of ground by the lands of Robert Wallace Surgeon on the west William
Shiell's lands on the east the Burndyhe & the said Robert Wallace's lands on the
south & the common road on the north parts & the said houses malt kiln & yeard
by the said road on the south parts the High Street of Meikle Govan on the north
Stephen Rowan's yard & barn on the west Robert Rowan of Broom Loan his
house & yard on the east parts together   with all right heretable title of right
claim interest property prosession or other right or title whatsoever which the
said Lilias Weir her authors or predecessors had have might or could claim or
pretend thereto or to any part or portion thereof in time coming burdened always
with the obligations presentable by the said Lilias Weir in consequence of the
contract of marriage aforesaid. Now this Indenture witnesseth that the aforesaid
Thomas Rouand & Mary his wife for & in consideration of the natural love &
affection which they & each of them have and bear unto the aforesaid John
Rouand party to these presents & as well for & in consideration of the sum of
five shillings current money of Virginia to them in hand paid well & truly, by
the said John Rouand at & before the sealing & delivery of these presents... by
these presents as well as for diverse other good causes & considerations them
thereunto moving have given... unto the said John Rouand... which the said
Thomas Rouand & Mary his wife or either of them now have or hath or ever had
or may wrought to have of in to or out of all & singular the houses outhouses
barns yards lands buildings tenements & hereditaments whatsoever with their &
every of their appurtenances mentioned or intended to be mentioned in the
aforesaid Deed... of the aforesaid Lilias Weir and also the Reversion &
Reversions... to the said John Rouand... for ever by the said John Rouand... or
his or their counsel learned either in the laws of Scotland or Virginia shall be
reasonably advised... written at the parish of Christ Church in the county of
Lancaster in the colony & dominion of Virginia aforesaid where stamped paper
is not used nor can the same conveniently be had... [Wit:] Hugh Brent, Thomas
Lawson & John Maxwell. Received 20 Apr 1775 of the within named John

Rouand five shillings currt money of Virginia being the full consideration money within mentioned to be paid to me & my wife Mary Isay. [Wit:] Henry Towles & John Berryman. [Pages 123, 123a & 124]

Commission. ...To John Fleet, Thomas Lawson, & Hugh Brent Gent Justices of the county court of Lancaster in the colony of Virginia whereas Thomas Rouand & Mary his wife by their certain Indenture of Bargain & Sale for land & houses bearing date 20 Apr 1775 have sold & conveyed unto John Rouand one tract of land containing houses. tenements, closses, lots & parcels of land & appurtenances as by the above annexed Indenture is fully & clearly expressed lying & being in Great Britain, otherwise called Scotland & in the city of Glasgow & whereas the said Mary Rouand cannot conveniently travel unto our county court of Lancaster to make her acknowledgment of her right in the said land & houses therefore we do give unto you or any two or more of you full power to receive the acknowledgmt of her right in the said land & houses aforesaid... we do therefore command you that you personally go to the said Mary Rouand & receive her acknowledgement of the same & examine her privily & apart from the said Thomas Rouand her husband whether she does the same freely and voluntarily without his persuasions or threats, & whether she be willing that the same should be recorded in our said county court of Lancaster... on 20 Apr 1775. ...by virtue of the within commission to us directed we have examined the within named Mary Rouand apart from her husband & she doth voluntarily of her own free will acknowledge her right title & interest of dower to the said lands & premises mentioned in the Deed hereto annexed without the persuasions or threats of her said husband & is willing the same shall be entered upon record certified 20 Apr 1775. [Wit:] John Fleet & Thomas Lawson. Deed of Bargain & Sale from Thomas Rouand & Mary his wife to John Rouand with the Receipt thereon endorsed were acknowledged in court by the said Thomas Rouand & also the annexed Commission of Relinquishment with a Certificate of Examination were returned in court... recorded by Test Thomas B. Griffin, Cl Lan Cur. [Pages 123, 123a, 124, 124a, & 125]

12 Dec 1774. Deed. ...between John Heath & Judith his wife of the parish of Wiccomico in the county of Northumberland of the one part & Nicholas Flood of the parish of North Farnham in the county of Richmond of the other part... John Heath did on 21 Nov 1771, did make and execute a certain Deed of Bargain and Sale to Nicholas Flood in the nature of a Mortgage as security to the said Nicholas Flood for several sums of money advanced and lent by the said Nicholas Flood to the said John Heath in which sd Deed of Bargain & Sale were included several Messuages Tenements Tracts or Parcels of land situate lying & being in the counties of Northumberland Lancaster & Richmond & among others one certain Messuage... said therein to have been purchased by said John Heath of and from John Cundiff, containing one hundred and sixty acres, situate

lying & being in the said parish of Wiccomico & county of Lancaster as by the
above mentioned Deed of Mortgage of record in the counties of Northumberland
Lancaster & Richmond, & as by Deed from the said John Cundiff to the said
John Heath may more fully & at large appear & whereas the said John Heath not
being able to satisfy pay & discharge the several sums of money due to the said
Nicholas Flood as well as on account of the above mentioned Deed of Mortgage
as on account of several subsequent Deeds of Mortgages, vizt by one Deed
bearing date February 17th, 1773 & by one Memorandum in the nature of a new
mortgage on the back of the said last mentioned Deed of Mortgage & dated
January 21st in this current year... 1774, all which Deeds of Mortgage &
Memorandums in the nature of new mortgages are of record in the offices of the
counties of Lancaster Northumberland & Richmond as by recourse being thereto
had may more fully and at large appear) did on 25 Apr 1774 set up to publick
sale at Northumberland Court House one hundred acres of the said land which
had been purchased by the said John Heath of and from John Cundiff it being all
the remainder of that said tract of land, the other sixty acres thereof (as
mentioned above) having been before, vizt on the sd 25 Apr set up to publick
sale by Colo James Ball as agent or Attorney in Fact for Richard Clay & the
Exers of Thomas Midgley by virtue of a decree of the county court of
Northumberland dated [blank] & which was purchased together with other lands
on this sd day of sale by the above mentioned Nicholas Flood... as by an
account of the said sales delivered to the said Nicholas Flood by Onesiphorus
Harvey Deputy Sheriff of the said county of Northumberland & who was
appointed by the said James Ball as Cryer or Auctioneer to sell & dispose of the
said lands... remaining one hundred acres of land so set up to publick sale by
John Heath, the said Nicholas Flood did then purchase at a price of thirty pounds
sterling, for which said sum of thirty pounds reduced into current money at the
rate of thirty percent exchange the said John Heath did agree to take credit in his
Bonds & Mortgages to the said Nicholas Flood for & in consideration of which
said sum of thirty pounds sterling settled for... & for & in consideration of the
further sum of ten shillings sterling to him the said John Heath in hand paid by
the said Nicholas Flood before the ensealing & delivery of these presents... the
above mentioned thirty pounds sterling is hereby acknowledged by the said John
Heath & himself therewith fully contented satisfied & paid & thereof & of every
part & parcel doth by these presents forever acquit... said Nicholas Flood...
forever he the said John Heath hath granted... unto the aforesaid Nicholas
Flood... for ever all the aforesaid one hundred acres of land it being the
remainder of that messuage or tenement which the said John Heath purchased
from John Cundiff... [Wit:] Henry Tapscot, James Tapscot, Robert McCleay,
Joseph Pope, & Samuel Peachey Junr. Recorded 20 Apr 1775 by Test Thomas
B. Griffin, Cl Cur. Court held June 15, 1775 Deed from John Heath to Nicholas
Flood was further proved in court by the oath of Joseph Pope. Recorded by Test
Thomas B. Griffin, Cl Cur. [Pages 125, 125a, & 126]

29 Sep 1774. Deed with Receipt. ...between James Ewell of the county of Lancaster & Mary his wife of the one part & Nicholas George of the same county of the other part... James Ewell & Mary his wife for & in consideration of the sum of one hundred pounds current money of Virginia to the said James Ewell in hand paid by the said Nicholas George at or before the sealing & delivery of these presents... [for] one hundred acres of land be it more or less situate in the county of Lancaster (and being the land which the said James Ewell purchased of Richard Chichester who purchased the same of Captain Merryman Payne & Richard Mitchell attorneys for Capt William Payne as appears by Indenture bearing date 18 Jun 1764 & is bounded as particularly mentioned in one certain Deed of Conveyance for the said land from one John Seayres and Catherine his wife, bearing date 16 Oct 1736 unto Judith Payne mother of the said William Payne & Merryman Payne)... [Wit:] Burges Ball, Richard Glascock, Henry Armistead, Mary Ball, & Jane Payne. Received the day of the date of the within named Nicholas George the sum of one hundred pounds current money being the consideration within mentioned for the within granted land & premises. [Wit:] Richard Glascock, Burges Ball, & Henry Armistead.

29 Sep 1774. Commission...to Burges Smith, James Selden, John Taylor, Burges Ball & James Gordon Gent greeting, whereas James Ewell & Mary his wife have by Indenture of Bargain & Sale bearing equal date herewith conveyed unto Nicholas George of the county of Lancaster one hundred acres of land situate in the said county of Lancaster & whereas the said Mary Ewell wife of the above named James Ewell cannot conveniently travel to our county court of Lancaster to make her personal acknowledgement of the said Indenture hereto annexed we do hereby authorize & require you or any two or more of you to go to the said Mary Ewell & her examine separate & apart from her said husband whether she doth freely & voluntarily acknowledge & relinquish her Dower to the lands in the said Deed... [Wit:] Thomas B. Griffin. By virtue of the within commission to us directed taken the examination of Mary the wife of James Ewell privily & apart from her said husband, who saith she doth freely & voluntarily relinquish her Right of Dower in the land contained in the Deed hereunto annexed without the threats or persuasions of the said James Ewell & that she is willing the same should be recorded 1 Sep 1774. [Wit:] James Selden & John Taylor. Recorded 20 Apr 1775 by Test Thomas B. Griffin, Cl Cur. [Pages 126a, 127, & 127a]

28 Mar 1775. Deed of Bargain and Sale with Receipt. ...between Susannah Stonum of the county of Lancaster widow of the one part & Richard Stott of the same county planter of the other part... Susannah Stonum for & in consideration of the sum of twenty pounds current money in hand paid, at or before the sealing & delivery of these presents...sell... unto the said Richard Stott... all that peice parcel or tract of land which descended to her on the death of her father Richard

Rogers scituate on the main branch of Colo James Balls Mill Pond in the said
county of Lancaster bounded according to a Plat of Division among the coheirs
of the said Richard Rogers & recorded in the county court of Lancaster,
containing twenty one acres, be it more or less... [Wit:] Thomas Stott, George
Cammell, & Thomas Kern. Received the day of the date of the within Indenture
of the within named Richard Stott the sum of twenty pounds current money in
full consideration for the within granted land & premises. [same witnesses as
listed above]. Recorded 15 Jun 1775 by Test Thomas B. Griffin, Cl Cur. [Pages
127a & 128]

16 Aug 1775. Deed of Bargain and Sale with Seisin. ...between Mungo Harvey
of the county of Lancaster of the one part & John Mason of the same county of
the other part... Mungo Harvey for & in consideration of the sum of seventy
pounds current money... at or before the sealing & delivery of these
presents...unto the said John Mason... for ever all that tract peice or parcel of
land which the said Mungo Harvey purchased of James Hill & Eliza his wife&
whereon Leanna Purcell now lives or dwelleth the same being situate in the said
county of Lancaster binding on the land of Jonathan Pullen commonly called
Thatchers the land of Charles Carter Esq & on the eastern branch of Corotomon
River containing by estimation one hundred acres... clearly & freely discharged
of & from all former & other grants mortgages dowers or other incumbrances
whatsoever (except the Incumbrance of Leanna Purcell, who is to occupy &
enjoy the said granted parcel of land for and during her natural life as allotted to
her in consequence & consideration of a Relinquishment of her Dower in the
land the said Mungo Harvey purchased of her son William Thatcher, & also the
Quitrents hereafter becoming due to the Chief Lord Proprietor thereof)... [Wit:]
William Dogget, Jesse Donnellan, & John Yopp. Received the day of the date
of the within named Indenture of the within named John Mason the sum of
twenty pounds current money in full consideration of the within granted parcel
of land & premises. [Same witnesses as listed above]. Memorandum. That
quiet & peaceable possession & seisin of the tract or parcel of land within
mentioned to be granted, was given & delivered by the within named Mungo
Harvey unto the within mentioned John Mason, to hold to him... for ever
according to the Tenor, Purport, Form & Effect of this Deed of Bargain & Sale
within written... [Same witnesses as listed above]. Recorded 17 Aug 1775 by
Test Thomas B. Griffin, Cl Cur. [Pages 128a, 129, & 129a]

20 Jan 1775. Indenture of Livery with Seisin or Deed in Trust with
Memorandum and Commission with Certificate. ...between Burges Ball of the
county of Lancaster Gent & Mary his wife of the one part & Henry Armistead of
the same county of the other part... Burgess Ball & Mary his wife for & in
consideration of the sum of five shillings current money in hand paid (the
receipt of which the said Burges Ball & Mary his wife doth hereby

acknowledge) as for divers good causes & considerations them thereunto
moving have given... unto the said Henry Armistead ... all that tract or parcel of
land situate in the said county of Lancaster which descended unto the said Mary
in Fee Simple on the death of her father John Chichester late of the said county
of Lancaster Gent decd and is bounded on Rapahannock River, Fairwethrs &
Brice's Creeks & the land formerly belonging to Sharp containing by estimation
five hundred acres... [Wit:] James Gordon, Ann Gordon, Winnefred Armistead,
Eliza Gordon, Sally Payne, & Jane Payne. Memorandum. That quiet and
peaceable possession & livery & seisin of the above mentioned parcel of land
was had & given unto the above named Henry Armistead by the above named
Burges Ball and Mary his wife by commission by delivery of Turf & Twig...
[Wit:] Winnefred Armistead, Ann Gordon, Elizabeth Gordon, Sally Payne &
Jane Payne. ...To James Ball, Jesse Ball, & James Gordon Gent Justices of the
county court of Lancaster ... whereas Burges Ball Gent & Mary his wife have
by Indenture bearing date 20 Jan 1775... conveyed unto Henry Armistead... a
tract or parcel of land situate in the said county of Lancaster containing by
estimation five hundred acres... whereas the said Mary Ball wife of the above
named Burges Ball cannot conveniently travel to our county court of Lancaster
to make her personal acknowledgement of the said Indenture we do hereby
authorize & require you or any two or more of you to go to the said Mary & her
examine privily & apart from her said husband whether she doth freely and
voluntarily acknowledge the said Indenture... & without persuasions or threats
of her said husband & such acknowledgement as she shall be willing to make
you are required to send certified... witness Thomas B. Griffin clerk of our said
county court of Lancaster... 20 Jan 1775. By virtue of the within commission to
us directed, We the subscribers having examined the within named Mary Ball
privily & apart from her husband the within named Burges Ball do hereby
certify that she doth freely & voluntarily without the persuasions of her said
husband acknowledge her right to the land and premises mentioned & contained
in a certain Indenture between the said Burges Ball and Mary his wife of the one
part & Henry Armistead of the other part, which is hereunto annexed, & that she
is willing the said Indenture may be recorded in the county court of Lancaster...
21 Jan 1775. [Wit:] James Ball & James Gordon. Proved in court by oaths of
Winnefred Armistead & Elizabeth Gordon, witness thereto & ordered to lye for
further proof...Recorded 17 Aug 1775 by Test Thomas B. Griffin, Cl Cur. 18
Aug 1775, Indenture further proved by oath of Winnefred Armistead a witness
thereto that she saw James Gordon, Ann Gordon, Jane Payne & Sally Payne sign
& witness this Indenture before sd Burges Ball & Mary his wife, & it is ordered
to lye for further proof. 21 Sep 1775 Deed in Trust with the Memorandum
thereon endorsed by Burges Ball and Mary his wife to Henry Armistead was
acknowledged in court by the said Burges, and also further and fully proved by
the oaths of James Gordon & Ann Gordon... recorded by Thomas B. Griffin, Cl
Cur. [Pages 129a, 130 & 130a]

24 Jan 1775. Deed of Bargain and Sale with Receipt. ...between Burges Ball Gent & Mary his wife of the county of Lancaster and colony of Virginia of the one part & Henry Armistead of the same county and colony of the other part... Burges Ball & Mary his wife for & in consideration of the sum of two thousand pounds lawful money of Great Britain to them in hand paid by the said Henry Armistead at or before the sealing & delivery of these presents... [for] certain lands & tenements in the counties of Dorset Devonshire & such estate as may be in the town of Exeter, & all such other estate or estates as may be in the kingdom of England, which descended to the said Mary by the death of her father John Chichester late of the county of Lancaster & colony of Virginia Gent deceased... [Wit:] James Gordon, Ann Gordon, Jesse Ball, & Margaret Bailey. Received the day of the date of this Indenture of the within mentioned Henry Armistead the sum of two thousand pounds lawful money of Great Britain being the consideration within mentioned. [same witnesses as listed above]. [Pages 131 & 131a]

24 Jan 1775. Commission. ...To Jesse Ball & James Gordon Gent Justices of the county court of Lancaster greeting, whereas Burges Ball Gent & Mary his wife of the county of Lancaster have by Indenture of Bargain and Sale bearing equal date herewith conveyed unto Henry Armistead of the same county, all their right title interest claim & demand in & to certain lands & tenements in the counties of Dorset Devonshire & such estate as may be in the town of Exeter and all such other estate or estates as may be in the kingdom of England mentioned in the said Indenture hereunto annexed & whereas the said Mary wife of above named Burges Ball cannot conveniently travel to our county court of Lancaster to make her personal acknowledgement of the said Indenture, we do therefore hereby authorize & require you to go to the said Mary Ball & her examine separate & apart from her said husband whether she doth freely & voluntarily acknowledge the said Indenture hereto annexed & that without persuasions or threats of her said husband & such acknowledgement as she shall be willing to make you are required to send certified... to the Justices of our said county court of Lancaster... Witness Thomas B. Griffin clerk of our said court... 24 Jan 1775. [Page 131a]

Certificate. By virtue of the above commission to us directed we this day examined Mary Ball wife of Burges Ball Gent privily & apart from her said husband & she the said Mary Ball freely & voluntarily acknowledged the said Indenture hereto annexed to Henry Armistead & declared she did the same without persuasions or threats of her said husband & that she was willing the same be recorded in our county court of Lancaster... [Wit:] Jesse Ball & James Gordon. 17 Aug 1775 proved by oaths of Jesse Ball & Margaret Bailey... & ordered to lye for further proof... [Indenture] further & fully proved by the oaths of James Gordon and Ann Gordon...recorded 21 Sep 1775 by Test Thomas B. Griffin, Cl Cur. [Pages 131a & 132]

8 Aug 1775. Deed with Receipt with Livery & Seisin. ...Between Le Roy Edwards of the parish of Washington & county of Westmoreland of the one part, and Merideth Mahanes of the parish of Wiccomico & county of Lancaster of the other part... Le Roy Edwards for & in consideration of the sum of fifty five pounds lawful money of Virginia to him in hand paid by the said Merideth Mahanes at & before the sealing & delivery of these presents... Le Roy Edwards doth hereby acknowledge & for divers other good causes & considerations him thereunto moving... hath granted... unto the said Merideth Mahanes... for ever all that plantation tract or parcel of land situate lying & being in the parish of Wiccomico & county of Lancaster containing one hundred and ten acres & is bounded as follows, Beginning at a marked locust post, a corner to this land & John Crowders and in the line between this & Thomas Edward's land thence running S33 degrees E 92 ½ Poles by a marked slooping hiccory to a marked chestnut in the line between this land & that of John Carter thence along the said line S27 degrees 30 minutes 28 Poles to a marked chestnut standing on the side of a branch thence S39 degrees 50 minutes E 12 ½ Poles to a marked chestnut a corner to William Pasquet's land thence S25 degrees E15 Poles to a marked tree, thence S29 degrees E6 Poles to another marked tree thence still along William Pasquet's line S39 E 11 Poles to a marked red oak a corner to this land & the land of said Merideth Mahanes, thence N85 E20 Poles to a marked red oak, thence N85 50E P along the line between this & Merideth Mahanes land 72 poles to a marked chestnutt, thence N65E20 Poles to a marked oak a corner to this land & the lands of the said Merideth Mahanes & Robert Pinckard, thence N20 W124 along a line of marked trees between this & Robert Pinckard's land to a marked oak standing on the north side of the road leading to a dividing creek a corner to this land & the lands of Robert Pinckard and John Crowder, thence west 112 poles along a line of marked trees between this & John Crowder's land across a branch to a marked Spanish Oak, thence N88 W48 P to the beginning post containing one hundred and ten acres... [Wit:] William Brown, John Bean, Craven Everit, & Thomas Edwards. Received 8 Aug 1775 of the within named Meredith Mahanes fifty five pounds lawful money of Virginia being the full consideration money within mentioned to be paid to me, I say received by me...LeRoy Edwards [Same witnesses as listed above.] Be it remembered that 8 Aug 1775 peaceable & quiet possession of the land & other the premises in this Deed contained was delivered by the within named LeRoy Edwards to the within named Meredith Mahanes by the delivery of Turf & Twig on the premises according to the Form & Effect of this Deed... [Wit: same as listed above]. Recorded 17 Aug 1775 by Test Thomas B. Griffin, Cl Cur. [Pages 132, 132a, 133, & 133a]

8 Aug 1775. Bond. Know all men by these presents I LeRoy Edwards of the parish of Washington in the county of Westmoreland am held & firmly bound unto Meredith Mahanes of the parish of Wiccomico in the county of Lancaster in the full & just sum of one hundred pounds lawful money of Virginia to be paid to the said Meredith Mahanes... to which payment well & truly to be made & done I bind myself... firmly... The condition of the above obligation is such that if the above bound LeRoy Edwards... do & shall in all things well & truly observe... all and singular the covenants... whatsoever which on the part & behalf of the said LeRoy Edwards... ought to be observed... in a certain Indenture bearing even date with the above written obligation... [Wit:] John Bean, William Brown, Thomas Edwards, & Craven Everitt. Recorded 17 Aug 1775 by Test Thomas B. Griffin, Cl Cur. [Page 134]

17 Nov 1774. Bond. Know all men by these presents that I John Hathaway of Fauquier County am held & firmly bound unto Thomas Hathaway of Lancaster County in the just & full sum of one thousand pounds current money of Virginia to be paid unto the said Thomas Hathaway... to which payment well & truly to be made I bind myself... firmly... The condition of the above obligation is such that if the above bounded John Hathaway... do warrant & make good all his & their whole right & title to a tract of land in Lancaster County now in possession of Sarah Hathaway for her life unto Thomas Hathaway of Lancaster County... [Wit:] James Hathaway, Dolley Currell, William Lawson, & Lawson Hathaway. Recorded 17 Aug 1775 by Test Thomas B. Griffin, Cl Cur. [Page 134a]

17 Nov 1774. Bond. Know all men by these presents that I John Hathaway of the parish of Leeds & the county of Fauquier am held & firmly bound unto Lawson Hathaway of the county of Lancaster in the just & full sum of five hundred pound current money of Virginia to which payment well & truly to be made unto said Lawson Hathaway... The condition of the above obligation is such that if the above bounded John Hathaway... do warrant & make good his & their whole right & title unto a tract of land called Andrews in Lancaster County now in possession of said Lawson Hathaway unto the said Lawson Hathaway... [Wit:] William Lawson & Thomas Hathaway. Recorded 17 Aug 1775 by Test Thomas B. Griffin, Cl Cur. [Pages 134z & 135]

5 Jan 1775. Deed of Bargain and Sale with Receipt. ...between Henry Armistead & Winnefred his wife of the county of Lancaster & colony of Virginia of the one part & Burges Ball Gent of the same county & colony of the other part... Henry Armistead & Winnifred his wife for & in consideration of the sum of two thousand pounds lawful money of Great Britain to them in hand paid by the said Burges Ball at or before the sealing & delivery of these presents...[for] all their right title interest claim & demand in & to certain lands & tenements in the counties of Dorset Devonshire & such estate as may be in the

town of Exeter & all such other estate or estates as may be in the kingdom of
England, being the estate or estates which the said Henry Armistead purchased
of the said Burges Ball and Mary his wife which may more fully appear relation
being had to the Deed executed by the said Burges Ball & Mary his wife bearing
date 24 Jan 1775 together with all... & singular the appurtenances to the said
lands and tenements together with the profits & emolaments of such estates
which be in the kingdom of England unto the said Burges Ball... [Wit:] Jesse
Ball, James Gordon, Ann Gordon, & Margaret Bailey. Received the day of the
date of this Indenture of the within mentioned Burges Ball the sum of two
thousand pounds current money of Great Britain being the consideration within
mentioned. [same witnesses as listed above]. Recorded 18 Aug 1775 by Test
Thomas B. Griffin, Cl Cur. [Pages 135 & 135a]

25 Jan 1775. Commission. ...To Jesse Ball & James Gordon Gent Justices of
the county of Lancaster greeting whereas Henry Armistead & Winnefred his
wife of the county of Lancaster have by Indenture of Bargain & Sale bearing
equal date herewith conveyed unto Burges Ball of the same county all their right
title interest claim & demand in & to certain lands & tenements in the counties
of Dorset Devonshire & such estate as may be in the town of Exeter & all such
other estate or estates as may be in the kingdom of England, which the said
Henry Armistead purchased of the said Burges Ball mentioned in the Indenture
hereto annexed, and whereas the said Winefred Armistead wife of the within
named Henry Armistead cannot conveniently travel to our county court of
Lancaster to make her personal acknowledgement of the said Indenture, we do
therefore hereby authorize & require you to go to the said Winefred Armistead
& her examine separate and apart from her said husband whether she doth freely
& voluntarily acknowledge the said Indenture hereto annexed and that without
the persuasions or threats of her said husband and such acknowledgement as she
shall be willing to make...[Wit:] Thomas B. Griffin clerk of our said court...
Recorded 19 Aug 1775.[Pages 135a & 136]

25 Jan 1775. Certificate. By virtue of the above Commission to us directed we
this day examined Mrs Winefred Armistead wife of Henry Armistead privily and
apart from her said husband and she the said Winefred Armistead freely and
voluntarily acknowledged the said Indenture hereto annexed to Burges Ball Gent
and declared that she did the same without persuasions or threats of her said
husband, and that she was willing the same should be recorded in our county
court of Lancaster... [Wit:] Jesse Ball & James Gordon. Recorded 19 Aug
1775 by Test Thomas B. Griffin, Cl Cur. [Pages 135a & 136]

21 Sep 1775. Deed of Bargain and Sale with Receipt. ...Between Peter
Conway of the county of Lancaster Gent and Frances his wife of the one part
and Edwin Conway of the same county Gent of the other part... Peter Conway

and Frances his wife for and in consideration of the sum of one hundred pounds current money in hand paid by the said Edwin Conway at or before the sealing and delivery of these presents... for ever all that tract or parcel of land scituate in the said county of Lancaster, which was purchased of Edward Sanders Porter by Peter Conway late of the said county Gent decd & father of the aforesaid Peter & by him devised by his last Will and Testament unto his said son in Fee Simple, & is bounded as followeth, Beginning at a side marked white oak in the line between this and William Schofield's land and running thence N55 #179 ½ Pole to a marked gum, corner of this land, the said Edwin Conway's & Mrs. Owens's thence N20 W172 pole to several marked young chestnuts corner of William Yopp & near his house thence S87 W20 P to an old dead marked oak in a swamp, thence along the meanders of the swamp 9 pole to a side marked white oak standing on the side of the hill, thence S15.20 W182 pole to a stake near the road, thence along the meaders of a branch to where two runs meet in the line of this land said Edwin Conways & William Schofields, thence N65 E to the beginning, containing one hundred & ninety one acres... [Wit:] James Selden, James Gordon, & John Hall. Received the day of the date of the within Indenture of the within named Edwin Conway the sum of one hundred pounds current money in full consideration for the within granted parcel of land and premises. [same witnesses as listed above]. Recorded 21 Sep 1775 by Test Thomas B. Griffin, Cl Cur. [Pages 136a, 137 & 137a]

21 Sep 1775. Commission. ...To James Selden, James Gordon, & John Taylor Gent. Whereas Peter Conway and Frances Conway his wife by their certain Indenture of Bargain & Sale bearing date 21 Sep 1775 have sold & conveyed unto Edwin Conway one tract of land containing one hundred & ninety one acres... lying & being in Lancaster County, & whereas the said Frances Conway cannot conveniently travel to our county court of Lancaster to make acknowledgement of her right in the said land therefore, we do give unto you or any two or more of you full power to receive the acknowledgement of her right in the land aforesaid, contained in the aforesaid Indenture which is hereunto annexed, which the said Frances Conway shall be willing to make before you, & we do therefore command you that you personally go to the said Frances Conway & receive her acknowledgement of the same & examine her privily & apart from the said Peter Conway her husband whether she does the same freely & voluntarily without his persuasions & threats & whether she be willing that the same should be recorded in our said county court of Lancaster... Witness Thomas B. Griffin clerk of our said court... [Pages 137 & 137a]

21 Sep 1775. Certificate. Pursuant to the above directed to we the subscribers two of his Majesty's Justices of the peace for the county of Lancaster have examined Frances Conway privily and apart from her husband Peter Conway & the said Frances Conway freely & voluntarily without any fear force threats or

persuasions of her said husband Peter Conway and relinquishes & gives up all her Right of Dower of in to & out of the tract or parcel of land & appurtenances in the annexed Indenture, to the said Edwin Conway, & in the same manner acknowledges her full & free approbation & consent thereto... [Wit:] James Selden & James Gordon. Recorded 21 Sep 1775 by Test Thomas B. Griffin, Cl Cur [Page 137a]

20 Sep 1775. Bond or Deed of Gift. Know all men by these presents that I Epaphroditus Lawson of the county of Lancaster and parish of Christ Church & colony of Virginia for & in consideration of the natural love & affection, which I have & do bear unto my daughter Elizabeth Hunt, have given & granted & by these presents do give... two Negroes to wit, on negro boy named George, & one negro girl named Silvia & her increase but in case my said daughter Elizabeth Hunt should die without heir and before John Hunt who intermarried with the said Elizabeth, that then the said negroes & their increase should vest and continue in the possession of the said John Hunt during his natural life & after his death to return to me if living if not to my children & their heirs to be equally divided amongst them... [Wit:] Henry Lawson & William Lawson. Recorded 21 Sep 1775 by Test Thomas B. Griffin, Cl Cur. [Page 138]

24 Jan 1775. Deed of Bargain and Sale with Receipt. ... Between Burges Ball and Mary his wife of the county of Lancaster & the colony of Virginia of the one part and Henry Armistead of the same county of the other part... Burges Ball and Mary his wife for & in consideration of the sum of five pounds current money of Virginia to them in hand paid by the said Henry Armistead at or before the sealing & delivery of these presents... [for] all that tract or parcel of land containing five hundred acres more or less situate in the said county of Lancaster which descended unto the said Mary in Fee Simple on the death of her father John Chichester late of the said county of Lancaster Gent decd and is bounded on Rappahannock River, Fearweather's Creek, the creek that divides this land from Paynes formerly called Brice's Creek, and the land formerly belonging to Sharp... [Wit:] James Gordon, Jesse Ball, Ann Gordon, & Margaret Bailey. Received the day of the date within mentioned of the said Henry Armistead the consideration money within mentioned being five pounds. [Wit:] James Gordon, Ann Gordon, & Jesse Ball. Recorded 21 Sep 1775 by Test Thomas B. Griffin, Cl Cur. [Pages 138, 138a, 139, & 139a]

24 Jan 1775. Commission. ... To Jesse Ball and James Gordon Gent Justices of the county court of Lancaster, greeting, whereas Burges Ball Gent and Mary his wife of the county of Lancaster have by Indenture of Bargain and Sale bearing equal date herewith conveyed unto Henry Armistead a tract or parcel of land situate in the said county of Lancaster containing by estimation five hundred acres... & bounded as specified in the said Indenture, and whereas the said Mary

Ball wife of the above named Burges Ball cannot conveniently travel to our county court of Lancaster to make her personal acknowledgement of the said Indenture we do hereby authorize and require you to go to the said Mary and her examine separate and apart from her said husband whether she doth freely and voluntarily acknowledge the said Indenture hereto annexed and that with out the persuasions or threats of her said husband, and such acknowledgement as she shall be willing to make... [Wit:] Thomas B. Griffin, Cl Cur. [Page 139]

24 Jan 1775. Certificate. By virtue of this commission to us directed we this day examined Mrs Mary Ball wife of the above named Burges Ball Gent and she the said Mary did freely and voluntarily acknowledge the said Indenture hereto annexed to Henry Armistead and declared she did the same without the persuasions or threats of her said husband, and that she was willing the same should be recorded in our county court of Lancaster ... [Wit:] Jesse Ball & James Gordon. [Page 139]

25 Jan 1775. Deed of Bargain and Sale with Receipt. ...Between Henry Armistead and Winnifred his wife of the county of Lancaster and colony of Virginia of the one part and Burges Ball of the same county of the other part... Henry Armistead and Winnifred his wife for & in consideration of the sum of five pounds current money of Virginia to them in hand paid by the said Burges Ball at or before the sealing and delivery of these presents... [for] all that tract or parcel of land containing five hundred acres... situate in the county of Lancaster aforesaid which said tract of land the said Henry Armistead purchased of the said Burges Ball and Mary his wife as by deed executed 24 Jan 1775... [Wit:] Jesse Ball, James Gordon, Ann Gordon, & Margaret Bailey. Received the day of the date of the within mentioned Burges Ball the sum of five pounds current money being the consideration within mentioned for the within granted land & premises. [same witnesses as listed above]. Recorded 21 Sep 1775 by Test Thomas B. Griffin, Cl Cur. [Pages 139a, 140, & 140a]

25 Jan 1775. Commission. ...To Jesse Ball & James Gordon Gent Justices of the county court of Lancaster greeting whereas Henry Armistead and Winnefred his wife have by Indenture of Bargain and Sale bearing equal date with these presents conveyed unto Burges Ball a tract or parcel of land situate in the said county of Lancaster containing by estimation five hundred acres be the same more or less and bounded as is specified by the said Indenture hereto annexed, and whereas the said Winefred Armistead cannot conveniently travel to our county court of Lancaster to make her personal acknowledgement of the said Indenture, we do hereby authorize and require you or any two or more of you to go to the said Winefred and her examine privily and apart from her said husband whether she doth freely and voluntarily acknowledge the said Indenture hereunto annexed and that without the persuasions or threats of her said husband and such

acknowledgement as she shall be willing to make... Witness Thomas B. Griffin, Clerk of our said county court of Lancaster... Recorded 21 Sep 1775 by Test Thomas B. Griffin, Cl Cur. [Pages 140 & 140a]

25 Jan 1775. Certificate. By virtue of the above Commission to us directed we this day examined Winefred Armistead wife of Henry Armistead privily and apart from her said husband and she the said Winefred Armistead freely & voluntarily acknowledged the said Indenture hereinto annexed to Burges Ball and declared that she did the same without the persuasions or threats of her said husband, & that she was willing the same should be recorded in the county court of Lancaster... [Wit:] Jesse Ball & James Gordon. Recorded 21 Sep 1775 by Test Thomas B. Griffin, Cl Cur. [Page 140a]

18 May 1775. Report. In obedience to an order of Lancaster County court... We the subscribers have viewed the road leading to Taylor's Landing and find that Mrs Martha Miller have (for the distance of about one hundred & fifty yards) turned the road over the line upon Mrs Margaret Ball instead of continuing it upon her own land where it formerly was, & that the advantages or disadvantages on either side we look upon to be very trifling, given under our hands this 19th day of September 1775. [Wit:] Edwin Conway, Peter Conway & James Gordon. Recorded 21 Sep 1775 on the motion of Richard Ball &[entered by] Test Thomas B. Griffin, Cl Cur. [Pages 140a & 141]

21 Jun 1775. Power of Attorney. Know all men by these presents that I Henry Parry Mariner am impowered by Elizabeth Clay Admtrice of Richard Clay late of the Bourough of Liverpoole decd who was Exor of Thomas Midgley late of the said bourough decd & copartner with the said Richard Clay to appoint an attorney or attorneys to demand sue for and receive all debts dues & demands from all & every person or persons whatsoever in Virginia unto the copartnership of the said Richard Clay & Thomas Midgley and to give releases... for the same, & to convey all lands Messuages and Tenements recovered or received for said debts as by the said Power, recorded in the county court of Essex may more fully appear... I the said Henry Parry by virtue of the said power, do hereby nominate constitute and appoint James Ball of the county of Lancaster in the said colony of Virginia Gentleman, to ask demand sue for & receive all debts dues claims & demands whatsoever due from all & every person or persons in the said colony of Virginia unto the copartnership of the said Richard Clay & Thomas Midgley decd, and to give releases & discharges for the same, & also to convey by Deeds of Bargain & Sale or other conveyance all lands tenements messuages or other real estate he shall receive or may have received in discharges of such debts unto such person... as he shall think proper hereby ratifying & confirming all & every act or acts as he the said James Ball shall act do or perform in the said premises, in as full & ample manner as if the

same were done personally by the said Elizabeth Clay... [Wit:] Richard
Mitchell, John Chinn, & Thads McCarty. Recorded 19 Oct 1775 by Test
Thomas B. Griffin, Cl Cur. [Page 141]

21 Dec 1775. Deed of Bargain and Sale with Memorandum and Receipt.
...Between Peter Conway of the parish of Christ Church in the county of
Lancaster & colony of Virginia Gent of the one part & Thomas Griggs eldest
son & heir at law of Lee Griggs late of the county of Lancaster decd... Peter
Conway for & in consideration of the sum of one hundred & fifty pounds current
money to him by the said Thomas Griggs in hand paid before the ensealing &
delivery of these presents... for ever one hundred & fifty acres of land situate in
the parish of Wiccomico in the county of Lancaster & lieth adjacent to the lands
of Mrs Hanna Owen, William Yopp & binding on a swamp commonly known
by the name of the Horse Head Swamp also joining the land of John Carter &
John Bean... [Wit:] Thomas Brent Senr, John Bean, Jesse Denny, Edwin
Conway, & James Gordon. Memorandum: that this day to wit, the 21 day of
December 1775, peaceable and quiet possession & seizen of the lands and
premises in the within mentioned Deed was given & delivered unto the within
named Thomas Griggs by the within mentioned Peter Conway by the delivery of
Turf & Twig in the name of Seizen of the whole. [Wit:] Thomas Brent Senr,
John Bean, & Jesse Denny. Received this 21 Dec 1775 the full & just sum of
one hundred and fifty pounds current money of Virginia being the full value for
the within tract or parcel of land... [Wit:] Thomas Brent Senr, John Bean, &
Jesse Denny. Recorded 21 Dec 1775 by Test Thomas B. Griffin, Cl Cur. [Pages
141a, 142, & 142a]

12 Dec 1775. Commission. ...To Edwin Conway Jesse Ball & James Gordon
Gent. Whereas Peter Conway & Frances his wife by their certain Indenture of
Bargain & Sale bearing date 21 Dec 1775 sold & conveyed unto Thomas Griggs
one tract of land containing one hundred & fifty acres more or less with all the
appurtenances lying & being in Lancaster County & whereas the said Frances
Conway cannot conveniently travel to our county court of Lancaster to make
acknowledgement of her right in the said land therefore we do give unto you or
any two or more of you full power to receive the acknowledgement which the
said Frances Conway shall be willing to make before you of her right in the land
aforesaid contained in the aforesaid Indenture which is hereunto annexed, & we
do therefore command that you personally go to the said Frances Conway &
receive her acknowledgement of the same & examine her privily & apart from
the said Peter Conway her husband whether she does the same freely &
voluntarily without his persuasion or threats & whether she be willing that the
same shall be recorded in our said county court of Lancaster... Witness Thomas
B. Griffin Clerk of our said court at the courthouse of the said county...
Recorded 21 Dec 1775 by Test Thomas B. Griffin, Cl Cur. [Page 142a]

21 Dec 1775. Certificate. We the subscribers having by virtue of the within Commission examined the within named Frances Conway privily & apart from the within named Peter Conway her husband, do certify hereby that she doth freely & voluntarily without the threats or persuasions of her husband acknowledge her right to the parcel of land & appurtenances contained in the Deed within mentioned, which is hereunto annexed, & that she is willing the said Deed may be recorded in the county court of Lancaster... [Wit:] Edwin Conway, Jesse Ball, & James Gordon. Recorded 21 Dec 1775 by Test Thomas B. Griffin, Cl Cur. [Page 142a]

16 Jan 1776. Deed of Feoffment with Memorandum. ...between Henry Tapscot of the county of Lancaster of the one part & Lowry Oliver of the same county of the other part, whereas John Oliver of the parish of Saint Sepulchris London Iron Monger and Elenora his wife by a certain instrument of writing under their hands & seals bearing date [blank] February 1775 hath thereby impowered the said Henry Tapscot to make sign seal & execute any act or deed necessary for effectually conveying unto the said Lowry Oliver... a certain tract of land & premises scituate in the said county of Lancaster which formerly belonged to William Oliver late of the said county of Lancaster decd and now in the Tenure & Occupation of the said Lowry Oliver containing one hundred acres more or less by the said Instrument of Writing recorded in the county court of Essex... Henry Tapscot by virtue of the aforesaid power & in consideration of the sum of thirty five pounds current money & the said John Oliver's part of his father's personal estate as mentioned in a letter of instructions from the said John Oliver to the said Henry Tapscot, to be paid by the said Lowry Oliver at or before the sealing & delivery of these presents (as by the said letter accorded in the county court of Lancaster appear)... [for] all that tract or parcel of land scituate in the said county of Lancaster which formerly belonged to William Oliver father of the said John & Lowry, & from him descended unto his son John, & is bounded on the lands of Rawleigh Downman, Samuel Brumley, Mary Newby, and William Brumley containing one hundred and fifty acres... [Wit:] William Brumley, Henry Hazard, Robert McCleay, & John Tapscot. Memorandum: that on the day of the date of the within Indenture quiet & peaceable possession and Livery of Seisin of the within mentioned parcel of land and premises was had & given by the within named Henry Tapscot unto the within named Lowry Oliver, by delivery of the handle of the door of the chief mansion... [Wit] William Brumley, Henry Hazard, Robert McCleay, & John Tapscot. Recorded 18 Jan 1776 by Test Thomas B. Griffin, Cl Cur. [Pages 143 & 143a]

2 Oct 1775. Deed of Feoffment with Memorandum. ...between Henry Overstreet of the county of Lancaster of the one part & Nicholas George of the said county of the other part... for & in consideration of the sum of three hundred pounds lawfull money of Virginia to the said Henry Overstreet in hand

paid, at or before the sealing & delivery of these presents by the said Nicholas George... [for] all that parcel of land, being a part of a parcel of land granted to George Heale by Patent bearing date 12 Jul 1692 bounded as followeth, beginning at a cedar post standing near the Island Road & running thence E20 poles to an old red oak standing on Corotoman Road, thence S25 E46 poles, thence S28 E38 poles, thence S37 E68 poles, thence S23 E42 poles, thence WSW 121 poles to a red oak, thence N35 W to intersect the line of the said Patent, thence the course of the said Patent to the beginning cedar post containing one hundred & thirty acres scituate & being in the county of Lancaster being part of a parcel or tract of land purchased by James Ball Gent of William Ball Gent of the said county, & since purchased of the sd James Ball Gent by George Tuning, & since that time purchased of the said George Tuning by Richard Overstreet, all which sales & conveyances may more fully appear relation being had to the records of Lancaster County... [Wit:] Jeremiah Dogget, George Connelly, Richard Overstreet, & Elizabeth Wibblin. Memorandum: That on the day of the date of the within Indenture peaceable & quiet possession & Livery of Seisin of the within land & premises was made & given unto the within named Nicholas George by the within named Henry Overstreet, by delivery of Turf & Twig thereon unto the said Nicholas George in full token of Livery & Seisin...[Wit:] Jeremiah Dogget, George Connelly, & Richard Overstreet. Recorded 18 Jan 1776 by Test Thomas B. Griffin...proved in court by oaths of Jeremiah Dogget & George Connelly... & ordered to lye for further proof. Recorded 21 Mar 1776... Deed... further proved in court by oath of Elizabeth Wiblin... by Test Thomas B. Griffin, Cl Cur. [Pages 144 & 144a]

18 Jan 1776. Deed of Feoffment with Memorandum. ...Between Moses George and Wilmouth his wife of the county of Lancaster of the one part & Patrick Connelly of the same county of the other part... Moses George and Wilmouth his wife for & in consideration of the sum of twelve pounds ten shillings current money of Virginia to them paid by the said Patrick Connelly... for ever a certain tract or parcel of land situate lying and being between the branches of Corotoman in the said county of Lancaster & is part of a tract of land which descended to the said Moses George by the death of his father containing by estimation ten acres... & bounded as followeth, beginning at a corner stone near the said Connellys Barn & running close on the main road leading to the hollowing point till it comes to a red oak which divides between Lazarus George & the said Moses George which said oak is a corner line & from thence north to a sassafras tree & from thence to a persimmon tree & from thence to a hickory tree which is a corner line & then to the stone first mentioned... [Wit:] Colon Dogget, Wm Schofield, Charles Purcell, & John Dogget. Memorandum: [blank] day of [blank] 1776 Livery of Seisin was made this day made & given unto the within named Patrick Connelly by the within mentioned Moses & Wilmouth George of the within compromised ten acres of land & premises by the delivery

of Turf & Twig on the said land... [same witnesses as listed above]. Recorded 18 Jan 1776 by Test Thomas B. Griffin, Cl Cur. [Pages 144a, 145, & 145a]

18 Aug 1772. Deed or Agreement. ... between Sarah Wale Widow & Relict of George Wale decd of the county of Lancaster of the one part & George Wale son of the said Sarah School Master of the aforesd count of Lancaster of the other part... Sarah Wale for diverse good causes & valuable considerations her thereunto especially moving, hath given... unto the said George Wale one equal Moiety of all that tract or parcel of land situate lying & being in the aforesaid county of Lancaster whereon she the said Sarah Wale now lives which George Wale aforesaid decd devised unto her... by his last Will & Testament bearing date 23 Mar 1767 in these words (to wit) It is my will & desire that my loving wife Sarah Wale may live & enjoy herself with every part & parcel of my estate of what nature & kind soever during her widowhood... and the said George Wale doth by these presents covenant... with the said Sarah Wale that she... shall live & enjoy herself with the other Moiety of the aforesaid tract of land on which said Moiety all the houses & orchards are to be included & taken in for & during the term & period of her natural life & no longer... now it is the intent & meaning of this Instrument of Writing, that the said Sarah Wale shall not cut down or cause or suffer to be cut down sold made use of or destroyed any more or other wood or timber now growing whatsoever on the aforesaid tract of land or Moiety of land than what shall be necessary to support the aforesaid tract of land in fence rails & firewood & to repair & keep in repair the houses thereon already built, also that the said Sarah Wale shall pay or cause to be paid unto the said George Wale when demanded by him the sum of thirty pounds current money of Virginia & also to pay unto the said George Wale for every year hereafter on the first day of January next ensuing from the date hereof the sum of ten pounds current money as long as the said George Wale shall think proper to rent his aforesaid Moiety of land unto the said Sarah Wale & lastly for the due performance of all & singular the matters... herein already mentioned both parties to these presents do hereby bind themselves... each to the other in the sum of thirty pounds current money of Virginia to be paid by the party failing to the party observing or willing to observe... [Wit:] Maurice Brent, James Brent, & William Wale. Recorded 15 Jul 1773 ... by oath of William Wale... & ordered to lye for further proof by Test Thomas B. Griffin, Cl Cur. Recorded 18 Apr 1776 This Agreement between Sarah Wale & George Wale further proved in court by the oaths of James Brent & Maurice Brent... by Test Thomas B. Griffin, Cl Cur. [Pages 145a & 146]

18 Jan 1776. Deed with Receipt. ...Between John Hunton & Frances his wife of the parish of Wiccomico & in the county of Northumberland of the one part & William Boatman of the parish of Christ Church in the county of Lancaster of the other part... John Hunton and Frances his wife, for & in consideration of the

sum of one hundred and forty two pounds seven shillings & six pence lawful money of Virginia to the said John Hunton by the said William Boatman in hand well & truly paid at & before the sealing & delivery of these presents... [for] a tract or parcel of land situate lying & being between the creeks of Musketoe & Nantepoison in the county of Lancaster, being part of a larger tract which the said John Hunton a few years ago purchased of John Turberville Gent of Westmoreland County & whereon the sd John Hunton lately lived containing seventy one acres & thirty perches including the Cool Spring Cove & the marshes to the said land adjoining & also another cove known by the name of Walnut Cove & is bounded as follows, beginning at a point on the east side of the Cool Spring Cove, from thence running up the side of the same to a marked pine in the line between this & John Edwards' land, thence S 5[degrees] W 21 P to a marked post in the same line, thence along the said line S22 ½ E to a spreading gum standing on Musketoe shore, thence along Musketoe Creek to a point at the mouth of a creek a corner to this land & that of Thomas Lawson's thence along the said Lawson's line N10[degrees] E58 P to an old dead marked pine, thence N37[degrees] E46 P to a marked pine in the line of this & Thomas Hunton's land thence N50 E57 P to an old stump standing on the head of a branch near two gum trees a corner to this and Jere Ashburn's land, thence by marked trees S53 E30 P to a marked pine in Ashburne's line, thence S67 E8 P to a marked pine another corner to this & Ashburn's land, thence N20 E to a marked pine on the head of the Cool Spring Cove, thence N10 ¾ P to a marked pine on the mouth of the cove, and from thence across the cove to the beginning... [Wit:] Martin Shearman, George Hunt, Thomas Norris & Colon Dogget. Received this [blank] day of [blank] 1766 of the within named William Boatman one hundred & forty two pounds seven shillings & six pence lawful money of Virginia being the full consideration money within mentioned to be paid to me. I say received by me-John Hunton. Recorded 21 Mar 1776 by Test Thomas B. Griffin, Cl Cur. [Pages 146a, 147, 147a, & 148]

21 Mar 1776. Deed of Bargain and Sale with Receipt. ...between John Hunton & Frances his wife of the parish of Wiccomico & county of Northumberland of the one part & John Edwards of the parish of Christ Church in the county of Lancaster of the other part... John Hunton & Frances his wife for & in consideration of the sum of two hundred & seventy nine pounds eight shillings & one penny half penny lawful money of Virginia to the said John Hunton in hand well & truly paid at or before the sealing & delivery of these presents... for ever a tract or parcel of land situate lying & being between Musketoe & Nantepoison Creeks in Lancaster County being part of a larger tract which the said John Hunton lately bought of John Turberville Gent of Westmoreland County & whereon the said John Hunton lately lived containing one hundred & thirty four acres three roods & nine perches including several smaller coves of water with the marshes adjoining to the said land & also a large cove or creek

that makes out from the main spring nigh the dwelling house... which said tract or parcel of land is bounded as followeth beginning at a marked persimmon standing on Musketoe Shore in the line of this and Richard Hinton's formerly John Hunton's land thence along Musketoe Creek including the marshes to a marked spreading gum in the line of this & William Boatman's land thence N22 ½ W to a marked post in Boatman's line thence along the said line N5 E21 P to a marked pine nigh the head of the Cool Spring Cove thence by the last side of the Cool Spring Cove & the south side of Nantepoison Creek including several small coves & ponds of water & the large Spring Cove or Creek to a marked post fixed on the beach at a corner to this & Richard Hintons formerly John Hunton's land & from thence S10 E to the beginning on Musketoe Creek... [Wit] William Brown, John McAdam, & William Boatman. Received 6 Mar 1776 of the within named John Edwards the sum of two hundred & seventy nine pounds eight shillings & one penny half penny lawful money of Virginia being the full consideration money within mentioned to be paid to me, I say received by me John Hunton. [Wit:] William Brown & John McAdam. Recorded 21 Mar 1776 by Test Thomas B. Griffin, Cl Cur. [Pages 148, 148a, 149, & 149a]

20 Mar 1776. Deed of Feoffment with Receipt and Livery & Seisin. ...between Mary ann Dogget of the parish of Christ Church in the county of Lancaster of the one part & William Dogget of the same parish & county aforesaid of the other part... Maryann Dogget for & in consideration of the sum of fifty pounds current money of Virginia by the said William Dogget to her in hand well & truly paid at or before the sealing & delivery of these presents... and also for diverse other good causes and considerations her thereunto moving she the said Maryann Dogget hath granted... unto the said William Dogget... for ever a certain peice or parcel of land situate lying and being in the parish of Christ Church & county of Lancaster being part or parcell of that tract of land whereon the said William Dogget now lives & which descended & came to the said Maryann from her mother Ann daughter of John Emerson formerly of Lancaster County decd & who afterwards intermarried with Benjamin Dogget decd uncle to the said William Dogget which said peice or parcel of land contains forty acres... [Wit:] William Brown, John Nichols, William Steptoe, & William West. Received 20 Mar 1776 of the within named William Dogget the sum of fifty pounds lawful money of Virginia being the full consideration money to be paid to me. I say received by me Maryann Dogget. [same witnesses as listed above]. Be it remembered, 20 Mar 1776 full quiet & peaceable possession & Seisin of the within mentioned peice or parcel of land & other the premises in this Deed contained was had given & delivered by the within named Maryann Dogget to the within named William Dogget by the delivery of Turf & Twig...[same witnesses as listed above]. Recorded 21 Mar 1776 by Test Thomas B. Griffin, Cl L Cur. [Pages 149a, 150, & 150a]

20 Mar 1776. Deed of Feoffment with Receipt and Livery and Seisin.
...between John Edwards & Margaret his wife of the parish of Christ Church in
the county of Lancaster of the one part & William Dogget of the same parish &
county aforesaid of the other part... John Edwards & Margaret his wife for & in
consideration of the sum of fifty pounds lawful money of Virginia by the said
William Dogget to the said John Edwards in hand well & truly paid at & before
the sealing & delivery of these presents... for ever a certain peice or parcel of
land situate lying and being in the parish of Christ Church & county of Lancaster
being part & parcel of that tract whereon the said William Dogget now lives &
which descended & came to the said Margaret wife of the said John Edwards
from her mother Ann who intermarried with Benjamin Dogget decd Uncle to the
said William Dogget, which said which said Ann the mother of the said
Margaret Edwards was daughter of John Emerson formerly of the county of
Lancaster decd which said peice or parcel of land contains forty five acres...
[Wit:] William Brown, John Nichols, William Steptoe, & William West.
Received 20 Mar 1776 of the within named William Dogget the sum of fifty
pounds lawful money of Virginia being the full consideration money within
mentioned to be paid to me, I say received by me John Edwards. [same
witnesses as listed above]. Be it remembered that 20 Mar 1776 full quiet &
peaceable possession & Seisin of the within mentioned peice or parcel of land &
other the premises in the Deed contained was had given & delivered by the
within named John Edwards to the within named William Dogget by the
delivery of Turf & Twig on the premises... [same witnesses as listed above].
Recorded 21 Mar 1776 by Test Thomas B. Griffin, Cl Cur. [Pages 151, 151a,
152, & 152a]

13 Feb 1776. Division of Land. We the subscribers at the desire of William
Dogget & Betty his wife, Maryann Dogget & John Edwards & Margaret his wife
did divide the land whereon the said William Dogget now lives between the said
William Dogget & Betty his wife, John Edwards & Margaret his wife, &
Maryann Dogget dividing the same into three parcels & allowing one double
share thereof to the said William Dogget for what he bought of his brother &
sister in law Richard Hutchings & Leanna his wife, the parties above said, to
wit, William Dogget & Betty his wife, John Edwards & Margaret his wife, &
Maryann Dogget are of full age & agreed to this division. In witness whereof
we the dividers John Nichols, William Steptoe, & William West... [witnesses as
listed above]. Recorded 21 Mar 1776 by Test Thomas B. Griffin, Cl Cur. [Page
152a]

16 May 1776. Report of a View of a Road. In obedience to an order of
Lancaster court we the subscribers being first served before one of his Majesty's
Justices Peace to view the road petition for by James Bush against William
Riveer junr have met & viewed the road & find the way very sufficient & the sd

114

Bush met any damage thereby...[Wit:] James Norris, John Payne, & Jesse
Robinson. Recorded 16 May 1776 by Test Thomas B. Griffin, Cl Cur. [Pages
152a & 153]

18 Apr 1776. Power of Attorney. Know all men by these presents that I
Thomas Pollard of the county of Lancaster & parish of Christ Church have
constituted & appointed & by these presents do make constitute & appoint
James Kirk & William Yerby or either of them jointly & severally my true &
lawful attorney & attorneys, for me & in any name place or stead to enter into
have & take quiet & peaceable possession & Seizen of a certain tract or parcel of
land, situate lying & being in the county of Lancaster containing by estimation
one acre... it being a part of a tract of land purchased of William Steptoe of the
county aforesaid, which in one Indenture bearing date 18 Apr [blank] and made
or mentioned to be made between the said Thomas Pollard of the one part and
Rawleigh Hazard of the county aforesaid of the other part & granted or
mentioned to be granted by me unto the said Rawleigh Hazard... or into any part
or parcel thereof in the name of the whole... [Wit:] Richard E. Lee & Thomas
Carter. Recorded 16 May 1776 by Test Thomas B. Griffin, Cl Cur. [Page 153]

13 Apr 1776. Deed of Feoffment with Livery and Seisin. Between James Ball
of the county of Lancaster Gent of the one part & James Ball Junr son of the said
James Ball of the other part... James Ball for & in consideration of the natural
love and affection which he hath for his said son, & for diverse other good
causes and considerations him thereunto moving hath given... unto James Ball
Junr... all that Messuage tenement tract or parcel of land situate in the said
county of Lancaster which the said James Ball purchased of Chattin Dogget &
John Chattin bounded on the lands of Mr John Chinn Thomas Dunaway John
Mason Johnson Riveer the Presbyterian Glebe & Thomas Flint containing by
estimation three hundred & sixty three acres... [Wit:] Richard Goodridge, James
Bush, & Derby Dunaway. Memorandum: on the day of the date of the within
Indenture quiet & peaceable possession & Livery of Seisin of the within
mentioned lands & premises were had & given by the within named James Ball
unto the within named James Ball Junr by delivery of Turf & Twig of the said
lands... [same witnesses as listed above]. Recorded 16 May 1776 by Test
Thomas B. Griffin, Cl Cur. [Pages 153a & 154]

18 Jan 1776. Report. In obedience to an order of Lancaster County Court... We
the subscribers did meet & view the road petitioned for by Joseph Norris & do
report, that the turning the said road will not be of any prejudice to the publick
but of great advantage to the petitioner. Witness this 29 Mar 1776. [Wit:]
Richard Mitchell & John Chinn. Recorded 20 June 1776 by Test Thomas B.
Griffin, Cl Cur. [Page 154]

1 May 1776. Deed with Livery and Seisin. ...Between William Graham & Judith Swan his wife, Ann Taite, William Keene, & John Graham all of the parish of St Stephen in the county of Northumberland of the one part & William Mountague Gent of the parish of Christ Church in the county of Lancaster of the other part... William Graham, Ann Taite, William Keene, & John Graham for & in consideration of the sum of three hundred & ten pounds eight shillings lawfull money of Virginia to William Graham one of the parties to these presents in hand well & truly paid at & before the ensealing & delivery... by these presents & for diverse other good causes & considerations them thereunto moving...have granted... unto the said William Mountague... for ever all that plantation tract or parcel of land situate lying & being in the parish of Christ Church & county of Lancaster commonly known & distinguished by the name of Taites Quarter containing three hundred & eighty eight acres & bounded as followeth, beginning at a marked poplar standing on the side of a hill a little above the mouth of a branch that runs into the head of Cap. James Selden's Mill Pond from thence running N48 degrees W355 ½ P. along a line of marked trees to an old rotten stump of a hiccory tree said to be formerly marked & standing by the side of the road or path leading from Selden's Mill to Wiccomico thence N87 degrees W83 ½ P along a hedge row of trees & underwood in the old field into the woods thence S29 degrees E60 P to the road leading from Cap James Selden's Mill to Mrs Margaret Ball's Mill, thence along the said road S88 degrees W& S71 degrees W50 P thence S31 degrees E by a line of marked trees dividing this from James Selden's land 176 P to a marked oak in the same line standing by the road side, thence along the said line of marked trees S30 degrees E256 P to a water fence running into Cap James Selden's Mill Pond, from thence up the said Mill Pond to the beginning which said tract or parcel of land is a parcel of a larger tract of eight hundred & fifty acres formerly belonging to William Therriot who by his last Will gave the same to his daughter Ann mother of the said Ann Taite, after whose death the said eight hundred & fifty acres came to her son William Keene a brother in law of the said Ann Taite, who by his certain Deeds of Lease & Release bearing date 10 & 11 Sep 1723, recorded among the records of Lancaster County Court did grant two hundred & ninety nine part thereof unto the said Ann Taite in Tail & afterwards by his last Will recorded as aforesaid did give unto the said Ann Taite one Moiety of another third part of the said tract, afterwards the said Ann Taite on the 11th day of June [blank] sued out a writ of ad quod domnum whereby she docked the Intail of the said 299 acres of land & by her Deed of Bargain & Sale bearing date the 21 Sep 1767 sold the same to Newton Keene which said Writ & Inquisition thereupon had & Deed of Bargain & Sale are recorded among the records of the Secretary's office, the said Newton Keene afterwards on 13 Mar 1769 by his certain Deed recorded among the records of Lancaster County Court sold & released the same to William Graham one of the parties to these presents... lastly the said William Graham & Judith Swan his wife, Ann Taite, William

Keene & John Graham... have made ordained constituted & appointed Richard
Ball & James Selden Gent of the county of Lancaster their true & lawful
attorneys jointly & either of them severally for them William Graham & Judith
Swan his wife, Ann Taite, William Keene & John Graham... [Wit:] John
Sinclair, Sarah Quille, Margt Sinclair, Geo H. Opie, William Kenner, & Bushrod
FauntLeroy. Be it remembered that 1 May 1776 peaceable & quiet possession &
Seisin of all & singular the lands & premises in this Deed mentioned to be
granted & conveyed was taken & had by the within named Richard Ball [blank]
for & in the names of William Graham, Ann Taite William Keene & John
Graham & every of them & afterwards was for & in the names of the said
William Graham Ann Taite William Keene & John Graham & every of them
was delivered by the said Richard Ball [blank] unto the within named William
Mountague... according to the Form & Effect of this present Deed... [Wit:]
William Ball, John Lawson, & James W Ball. Received 1 May 1776 of the
within named William Mountague [blank] being the full consideration money
within mentioned to be paid to me I say received by me John Graham. ... Proved
in court by John Sinclair & ordered to lye for further proof... Recorded 16 May
1776 by Test Thomas B. Griffin, Cl Cur. 20 June 1776 further & fully proved in
court by oaths of George Opie, William Kenner, & Bushrod Fauntleroy,
recorded by Test Thomas B. Griffin, Cl Cur. [Pages 154, 154a, 155, 155a, 156,
156a, & 157]
10 Jun 1776. Commission. To Kenner Cralle Joseph Ball & William Eskridge
Gent Whereas William Graham & Judith Swan his wife by their Indenture of
Feoffment bearing date 1 May 1776 have sold & conveyed unto William
Mountague one tract of land containing three hundred & eighty eight acres more
or less with appurtenances lying & being in Lancaster County & whereas the
said Judith Swan Graham cannot conveniently travel to our county court of
Lancaster to make acknowledgement of her right in the said land, therefore we
do give unto you or any two of you full power to receive the acknowledgement
which the said Judith Swan Graham shall be willing to make before you of her
right in the land aforesaid contained in the aforesaid Indenture which is hereunto
annexed & we do therefore command you that you personally go to the said
Judith Swan Graham & receive her acknowledgement of the same & examine
her privily & apart from the said William Graham her husband whether she does
the same freely and voluntarily without his persuasions or threats & whether she
be willing that the same shall be recorded in our said county court of
Lancaster... Witness Thomas B. Griffin Clerk of our sd court... Recorded 16
May 1776 by Test Thomas B. Griffin, Cl Cur. 20 June 1776 further & fully
proved in court by oaths of George Opie, William Kenner, & Bushrod
Fauntleroy, recorded by Test Thomas B. Griffin, Cl Cur. [Page 156a]

11 Jun 1776. Certificate. Northumberland court. By virtue of the annexed
Commission & in the obedience thereto we the subscribers personally went to

the within named Judith Swan Graham & received her acknowledgement for the
land in the Deed mentioned having privily & apart from the said William
Graham her husband she having declared that she was willing the same should
be recorded in the county court of Lancaster... [Wit:] Kenner Cralle & William
Eskridge. Recorded 16 May 1776 by Test Thomas B. Griffin, Cl Cur. 20 June
1776 further & fully proved in court by oaths of George Opie, William Kenner,
& Bushrod Fauntleroy, recorded by Test Thomas B. Griffin, Cl Cur. [Page 157]

17 Apr 1776. Deed of Bargain and Sale with Receipt. Between John Eustace
Gent & Alice Corbin his wife of Northumberland County of the one part &
William Gibson of the county of Lancaster of the other part... John Eustace &
Alice Corbin his wife for & in consideration of the sum of one hundred & fifty
pounds to them in hand paid by the said William Gibson... [for] a certain tract or
parcel of land situate lying and being in the parish of Christ Church & county of
Lancaster containing one hundred & forty five acres of land purchased by the
said John Eustace of Col Charles Carter of the county of King George & known
by the name of the Brick House, beginning by a survey & Plat made by Griffin
Garland dated 17 Mar 1769, begins at O. where the main road crosses Dick's
Branch thence down the road to P at Sequmore tree planted, thence N70 W170 P
to Q a possimon bush in a bottom at the head of a branch thence N25 E to Dick's
Branch which line divides this land from the land Mr John Yerby bought of Col
Carter in the year 1767, thence down Dick's Branch the several meanders
thereof to the beginning... [Wit] John Yerby, Michael Wilder, Hugh Brent, &
Thomas Lawson. Received the day of the date of the within written Indenture of
the within named William Gibson the full consideration within mentioned.
[Wit:] John Yerby & Michael Wilder. Recorded 18 Jul 1776 by Test Thomas B.
Griffin, Cl Cur. [Pages 157, 157a, & 158]

29 Jun 1776. Commission. ...To Hugh Brent, Thomas Lawson Gent whereas
John Eustace & Alice Corbin his wife by their certain Indenture of Bargain and
Sale bearing date 17 Mar 1776 have sold & conveyed unto William Gibson one
tract of land containing one hundred and forty five acres more or less with
appurtenances lying & being in Lancaster County & whereas the said Alice
Corbin cannot conveniently travel to our county court of Lancaster to make
acknowlegement of her right in the said land, therefore we do give unto you or
any two or more of you full power to receive the acknowledgement which the
said Alice Corbin shall be willing to make before you of her right in the land
aforesaid contained in the aforesaid Indenture which is hereto annexed & we do
therefore command you that you personally go to the said Alice Corbin &
receive her acknowledgement of the same & examine her privily & apart from
the said John Eustace her husband whether she does the same freely &
voluntarily without his persuasions or threats & whether she be willing that the

118

same should be recorded in our said county court of Lancaster... Thomas B. Griffin. Recorded 18 Jul 1776 by Test Thomas B. Griffin, Cl Cur. [Page 158]

29 Jun 1776. Certificate. By virtue of the within Commission to us directed we the subscribers did personally examine the within mentioned Alice Corbin Eustace touching her acknowledgement of the within mentioned Indenture privily & apart from the within named John Eustace her husband, that she does the same freely & voluntarily without his persuasions or threats & that she is willing the same shall be recorded in our county court of Lancaster... [Wit:] Hugh Brent & Thomas Lawson. Recorded 18 Jul 1776 by Test Thomas B. Griffin, Cl Cur. [Page 158]

18 Apr 1776. Deed with Livery and Seisen with Receipt. ...Between Thomas Pollard & Mary his wife of the county of Lancaster of the one part & Rawleigh Hazard of the county aforesaid of the other part... Thomas Pollard for & in consideration of the sum of forty pounds current money of Virginia to him the said Thomas Pollard in hand well & truly paid, at or before the sealing & delivery of these presents... [for] a tract or parcel of land, scituate, lying & being in the county of Lancaster containing one acre more & less & is part of a tract of land purchased by the said Thomas Pollard of William Steptoe by Deed recorded in the county court of Lancaster... bounded as follows, beginning at the main Church Road & running streight with the east end of the dwelling house to a ditch near John Eustace's line & up the said line to the road & up the said road to the beginning... [Wit:] William Yerby, James Kirk, Bailie George, Richd E. Lee, & Michael Wilder. Be it remembered that on 18 Apr 1776 full quiet & peaceable possession & Seizen was had & taken of the within mentioned acre of land & premises by James Kirk & William Yerby attornies for the within mentioned Thomas Pollard & by them delivered over to the within mentioned Rawleigh Hazard... in the presence of Thomas Lawson, Hugh Brent, & John Hall. Received the day of the date of the within written Indenture from the within named Rawleigh Hazard the sum of forty pounds the consideration within mentioned. [Wit:] Hugh Brent. Recorded 18 Jul 1776 by Test Thomas B. Griffin, Cl Cur. [Pages 158a, 159, & 159a]

30 May 1776. Deed of Bargain and Sale. Between James Waddel & his wife Mary Waddel of the county of Lancaster of the one part & Elisha Hall of the same county Phisician of the other part.. James Waddel & his wife Mary Waddel for & in consideration of the sum of seven hundred & fifty pounds current money of Virginia to him by the said Elisha Hall in hand paid before the ensealing & delivery of these presents... [for] all that tract or parcel of land situate lying & being in the county of Lancaster containing three hundred & ninety five acres of land more or less, eighty acres part of the said tract or parcel of land was formerly granted to a certain Henry Boatman by a Proprietor's Deed

dated 30 Sep 1695 & by the said Henry Boatman by his Deed dated 5 Oct 1695 sold & conveyed unto a certain Joseph Tayloe) (& by the said Joseph Tayloe by his Deed dated 20 Dec 1711. Sold & conveyed unto a certain William Olivit) Deed (& by the said William Olivit by his Deed dated 9 Feb 1719 sold & conveyed unto a certain John Bell Cl R decd father to the said Charles Bell/party to these presents/ & three hundred & fifteen acres the other part thereof was purchased by the said John Bell decd of a certain Damerson Pasquet by Deed bearing 9 Feb 1719 which said two tracts of land was by the said John Bell in his last Will & Testament & given & bequeathed unto the said Charles Bell & his heirs forever as by the said Deeds & Will may appear & is bounded on the lands of John Yerby, Robert Edmonds & the land of John Edwards decd together with all houses... & appurtenances... [Wit:] Richard Hall & John Hunton. Recorded 21 Nov 1776 by Test Thomas B. Griffin, Cl Cur & ordered to lye for further proof. Recorded 19 Dec 1776 proved by oath of Richard Hall & recorded by Test Thomas B. Griffin, Cl L Cur. [Pages 160, 160a, 161, & 161a]]

31 May 1776. Commission. ...To Dale Carter, James Selden, & Edwin Conway Gent whereas the Revd Mr James Waddel & Mary Waddel his wife by their certain Indenture of Bargain & Sale bearing date 30 May 1776 have sold & conveyed unto Elisha Hall one tract of land containing three hundred & ninety five acres more or less, with the appurtenances lying & being in Lancaster County & whereas the said Mary Waddel cannot conveniently travel to our county court of Lancaster to make acknowledgement of her right in the said land, therefore we do give unto you or any two or more of you full power to receive the acknowledgement which the said Mary Waddel shall be willing to make before you of her right in the land aforesaid contained in the aforesaid Indenture which is hereunto annexed, & we do therefore command you that you personally go to the said Mary Waddel & receive her acknowledgement of the same & examine her privily & apart the said Revd James Waddel her husband, whether she does the same freely & voluntarily without the persuasions or threats of her said husband & whether she be willing that the same should be recorded in our said county court of Lancaster... witness Thomas B. Griffin clerk of our said court... Recorded 19 Dec 1776 proved by oath of Richard Hall & recorded by Test Thomas B. Griffin, Cl L Cur. [Page161]]

17 May 1776. Certificate. By virtue of the annexed Commission to us directed & in obedience thereto we the subscribers did personally go to the said Mary Waddell in the Commission named & examined her privily & apart from her said husband James Waddell touching & concerning her relinquishment of her right in the said lands in the annexed Deed mentioned to be sold by her said husband to Elisha Hall & she saith that she doth freely & voluntarily of her own accord and without threats or persuasions of her said husband relinquish all her right & title whatsoever of in & to the said tract or parcel of land in the said

120

Deed mentioned & contained & is willing that this her acknowledgement be
recorded. [Wit:] Dale Carter & Edwin Conway. Recorded 19 Dec 1776 proved
by oath of Richard Hall & recorded by Test Thomas B. Griffin, Cl L Cur. [Pages
161 & 161a]]

19 Oct 1776. Deed with Receipt. Between Elizabeth Pinckard Widow & acting
Executrix of the last Will & Testament of Thomas Pinckard late of
Westmoreland County decd of the one part & James Pinckard junr of the parish
of Christ Church in the county of Lancaster of the other part... Elizabeth
Pinckard in compliance with the last Will and Testament of her said deceased
husband & also for & in consideration of the sum of sixty two pounds ten
shillings lawful money of Virginia to her in hand paid by the said James
Pinckard Junr at & before the sealing & delivery of these presents... for diverse
other good causes and considerations her her thereunto moving hath granted...
unto the said James Pinckard Junr... all that Plantation tract or parcel of land
whereon the said Thomas Pinckard decd formerly lived situate lying & being in
the parish of Christ Church in the county of Lancaster & is bounded as followeth
to wit by the main road leading from Norris's Mill to Davis's Warehouse & the
lands of Thomas Kirk James Gordon & William Edwards containing one
hundred acres... her former husband the said Thomas Pinckard decd was in his
life time & at the time of his death seized in his own right of a good sure perfect
& absolute Estate of Inheritance in Fee Simple of in & all the said Plantation
tract or parcel of land... and also that she the said Elizabeth Pinckard now hath
good right full power & lawful authority as Executrix of the last Will &
Testament of her said deceasd husband Thomas Pinckard to grant bargain sell &
convey all & singular the premises above mentioned with appurtenances unto
the said James Pinckard Junr... [Wit:] James Kirk Junr, William Brown, John
Pinckard, & Thomas Kirk. Received 19 Oct 1776 of the within named James
Pinckard Junr sixty pounds ten shillings lawful money of Virginia being the full
consideration money within mentioned to be paid to me I say received by me
Elizabeth Pinckard. [same witnesses as listed above]. Be it remembered that
this 19 Oct 1776 full quiet & peaceable possession & Seizin was had given &
delivered by the within named Elizabeth Pinckard to the within named James
Pinckard Junr of the within mentioned Plantation tract or parcel of land by the
delivery of Turf & Twig on the premises... [same witnesses as listed above].
Recorded 21 Nov 1776 by Test Thomas B. Griffin, Cl L Cur. [Pages 161a, 162,
162a, & 163]

19 Dec 1776. Power of Attorney. Know all men by these presents that I Daniel
George of the county of Lancaster & commonwealth of Virginia for diverse
good causes & considerations have appointed & do by these presents ordain...
my trusty friend and kindsman Nicholas George my lawfull attorney to ask
demand recover & receive of & from Eppee Timberlake of Faurquier County all

sums that are due me or all negro slaves or other estate that is in the hands of the said Timberlake or any other person that has or may descend to my wife from her father or any other person, & I do grant to the said Nicholas George my sole & full power & authority to take pursue & follow such legal courses for the recovery & receiving of the same as I myself might do were I personally present & I do ratify & confirm all that my said attorney shall lawfully do or cause to be done in or about the execution of the premises by virtue of these presents... [Wit:] Test Thomas B. Griffin. Recorded 19 Dec 1776 by Test Thomas B. Griffin, Cl L Cur. [Pages 163 & 163a]

13 May 1776. Indenture between James Waddel & his wife Mary Waddel of the county of Lancaster of the one part & Elisha Hall of the same county Physician of the other part... James Waddel & his wife Mary Waddel for & in consideration of the sum of seven hundred & fifty pounds current money of Virginia to him by the said Elisha Hall in hand paid before the ensealing & delivery of these presents... [for] all that tract or parcel of land situate lying & being in the county of Lancaster containing three hundred & ninety five acres of land be the same more or less eighty acres part of the said tract or parcel of land was formerly granted to a certain Henry Boatman by a Proprietor's Deed dated 13 Sep 1695, & by the said Henry Boatman by his deed dated 5 Oct 1695 sold & conveyed unto a certain Joseph Tayloe & by the said Joseph Tayloe by his Deed dated 20 Dec 1711, sold & conveyed unto a certain William Olivit/decd/ & by the said William Olivit by his Deed dated 9 Feb 1719 sold & conveyed unto a certain John Bell C L R decd father to the said Charles Bell/Party to these presents/ & three hundred & fifteen acres the other part thereof was purchased by the said John Bell decd of a certain Damerson Pasquet by Deed bearing 9 Feb 1719 which said two tracts of land was by the said John Bell in his last Will & Testament given & bequeathed unto the said Charles Bell & his heirs for ever as by the said Deeds & Will may appear & is bounded on the lands of John Yerby Robert Edmonds and the lands of John Edwards decd... appurtenances whatsoever to the said hereby granted premises. For this Deed see page 160. [Pages 163a & 164]

15 Nov 1776. Deed of Bargain and Sale with Receipt. ...in the first year of the common wealth of Virginia between Thaddeus McCarty of the county of Lancaster Gent & Anne his wife of the one part & John Chinn of the same county Gent of the other part... Thaddeus McCarty & Ann his wife for & in consideration of the sum of eight hundred pounds current money in hand paid to the said Thaddeus McCarty at or before the sealing & delivery of these presents... for ever all that Messuags tract or parcel of land situate in the sd county of Lancaster which formerly belonged to Rawleigh Chinn Gent father of the said Ann & on his death descended unto his two daughters Catharine and the said Ann in copartnership & the said Catharine's part was purchased by the said

Thaddeus McCarty of Francis Humphrey Christian & the said Catharine his wife & is bounded on the lands of the said John Chinn & Rawleigh Downman Gent & Morattico & Ives Creeks containing three hundred & thirty three acres... the Dower therein of Ann Chinn widow of the aforesaid Rawleigh Chinn during her natural life & that they the said Thaddeus McCarty & Ann his wife... shall & will warrant & defend hereafter the sd hereby granted parcel of land & premises... unto the said John Chinn... [Wit:] Richard Mitchell, Henry Tapscot, Robert Chinn, William Hunt, & Thomas Stott. Received the day of the date of the within Indenture of the within named John Chinn the sum of eight hundred pounds current money in full consideration for the within mentioned granted lands & premises. [same witnesses as listed above]. Recorded 19 Nov 1776 by oaths of Henry Tapscot & Robert Chinn and on 16 Jan 1777 was further proved by oath of Richard Mitchell & recorded by Test Thomas B. Griffin, Cl L Cur. [Pages 164, 164a, 165, & 165a]

16 Nov 1776. Commission. In the name of the Commonwealth of Virginia To James Ball Richd Mitchell and John Taylor Gent whereas Thadeus McCarty & Ann McCarty his wife by their certain Indenture of Bargain & Sale bearing date 15 Nov 1776 have sold & conveyed unto John Chinn Gent one tract of land containing three hundred & thirty three acres... with appurtenances lying & being in Lancaster County & whereas the said Ann McCarty cannot conveniently travel to our county court of Lancaster to make acknowledgement of right in the said land therefore we do give unto you or any two or more of you full power to receive the acknowledgement which the said Ann shall be willing to make before you of her right in the land aforesaid contained in the aforesaid Indenture which is hereunto annexed & we do therefore command you that you personally go to the said Ann & receive her acknowledgement of the same & examine her privily & apart from the said Thadeus McCarty her husband whether she does the same freely & voluntarily without the persuasions or threats of her said husband & whether she be willing that the same shall be recorded in our said county court of Lancaster... [Wit:] Thomas B. Griffin Cl L Cur. Recorded 19 Nov 1776 by oaths of Henry Tapscot & Robert Chinn and on 16 Jan 1777 was further proved by oath of Richard Mitchell & recorded by Test Thomas B. Griffin, Cl L Cur. [Pages 164a & 165]

16 Nov 1776. Certificate. By virtue of the within Commission to us directed we the subscribers having examined the within named Ann McCarty privily & apart from her husband the within named Thadeus McCarty do hereby certify that she the said Ann McCarty doth freely & voluntarily without the threats or persuasions of her said husband acknowledge her right to the land and premises contained in a Deed of Bargain of Sale from the said Thadeus McCarty & Ann his wife to John Chinn Gent which is hereunto annexed & that she is willing the same should be recorded in the county court of Lancaster... [Wit:] Richard

Mitchell & John Taylor. Recorded 19 Nov 1776 by oaths of Henry Tapscot & Robert Chinn and on 16 Jan 1777 was further proved by oath of Richard Mitchell & recorded by Test Thomas B. Griffin, Cl L Cur. [Page 165]

29 Oct 1776. Lease. ...in the first year of the United States of America between William Brent of the county of Lancaster & parish of Christ Church of the one part & Thomas Rouand of the same county & parish of the other part... for & in consideration of the rents covenants & agreements herein after reserved & contained he the said William Brent... hath leased demised granted & let to farm to the said Thomas Rouand... all that tract tenement or parcel of land situate lying and being in the county & parish aforesaid & bounded as followeth vizt Beginning at a red oak on the road side called Fleets Bay Road in the line of George Flowers & running along the said line down to the Indian Creek & down the said creek to the line of William Norris thence up the said Norris's line to the said road & up the sd road to the beginning red oak containing by estimation one hundred acres be the same more or less (being a tract or parcel of land leased by the decd George Wale to the said William Brent 21 May 1773)... & all & singular the appurtenances thereunto belonging or in any wise appurtaining together with Liberty for the said Thomas Rouand... to cut down & clear any part of the aforesaid tract of land & plantation also with the further Liberty to cut down & clear twelve thousand Tobo Hills as the said Thomas Rouand thinks most convenient... from & after the first day of January next ensuing the date hereof for and during & unto the end term & expiration of eighteen years beginning at the first day of January next – he the said Thomas Rouand... yielding & paying yearly & every year during this sd term of eighteen years unto the said William Brent... sum of ten pounds current money & the said Thomas Rouand doth for himself... agree with the sd William Brent... to plant or cause to be planted three hundred peach trees and seventy five apple trees on the said tenement or tract of land & lastly the said William Brent for himself... doth... grant to the said Thomas Rouand...(paying yearly the rent aforesaid & performing the covenants aforesaid)... [Wit:] Walker Conway, William Forsyth, & William Norris. 19 Dec 1776 proved in court by oath of William Norris... & ordered to lye for further proof by Test Thomas B. Griffin, Cl L Cur. Recorded 19 Jun 1777 ...Lease from William Brent to Thomas Rouand was acknowledged in court by said Brent & ordered to be recorded. By Test Thomas B. Griffin, Cl L Cur. [Pages 165a & 166]

17 Aug 1776. Deed in Trust with Memorandum. Between Frances Stephens Widow of Richard Stephens late of the county of Lancaster decd of the one part & William Sydnor of the same county Gent of the other part... Frances Stephens for & in consideration of the natural love & affection which she hath for her children William Joseph George Judith & Susanna, & that they pay all debts now due from the said Frances Stephens hath given... unto the said William

124

Sydnor... the following negroes stocks of all kinds household furniture & other
personal estate and land which the said Frances Stephens is possessed of under
the last Will & Testament of her said husband Richard Stephens to wit James
Macns Winny Pleasant Jane Sarah Jacob Sue Hannah Mary Nan Prue Rose Flora
& George, two thirds of the said stocks household furniture & other personal
estate and the tract of land whereon the sd Frances Stephens now dwelleth with
its appurtenances in trust for the use & purpose following that is to say one third
part of the said tract of land for the use of the said Frances Stephens during her
natural life & at her decease to the said William Stephens... & the other two
thirds thereof to the said William Stephens... the said negro Pleasant to & for
the use of the said Frances Stephens during her natural life & at her decease to
be by her disposed off as she shall think proper to or amongst her said children
& if she shall depart this life without disposing of the said Negro & her future
increase as aforesaid then equally divided amongst her said children & all the
remainder of the said negroes stocks of all kinds household furniture & other
personal estate to be equally divided amongst her said children... six months
from the date hereof... The said Frances Stephens is to have her bay riding mare
in her third of the personal estate which she reserves to herself. It is to be
observed it is not the intent of the parties that the growing crop or crop made the
present year be included in this gift but the said Frances reserves the same to
herself. [Wit:] David Currie, Gavin Lowry, & Fortunatus Sydnor. Memdm that
quiet & [blank] possession of the within granted land negroes stock household
furniture & other personal estate was had given by the within named Frances
Stephens unto the within named William Sydnor by delivery of Turf & Twig of
the said Land & delivery of negro Sue in the name of & for the whole use &
purpose within mentioned... [same witnesses as listed above]. 16 Jan 1777
Deed in Trust with Memorandum was proved in court by the oaths of Gavin
Lowry & Fortunatus Sydnor & ordered to lye for further proof. 19 Jun 1777
....further proved by oath of sd David Currie & recorded by Test Thomas B.
Griffin, Cl Lan Cur. [Pages 166a & 167]

22 Nov 1776. Between Lowry Oliver of the county of Lancaster & Ellen his
wife of the one part and William Brumley of the same county of the other part...
Lowry Oliver & Ellen his wife for & in consideration of the sum of one hundred
& ten pounds current money in hand paid by the said William Brumley at or
before the sealing & delivery of these presents... do absolutely grant... for ever
all that tract or parcel of land scituate in the said county of Lancaster bounded on
the east side of the main road that leads from Deep Bottom to Colo James Ball's
Mill on the lands of the said William Brumley Mr Rawleigh Downman & Mr
Henry Tapscot containing by estimation fifty acres... being part of a parcel of
land purchased by the said Lowry Oliver of his brother John Oliver... [Wit:]
Richard Mitchell, John Chinn, James Newby, Henry Tapscot, & John Newby.
Memorandum that on the day of the date of the within Indenture quiet peacable

possession & Livery of Seisin of the within mentioned parcel of land & premises was had & given by the within named Lowry Oliver unto the within named William Brumley by delivery of the handle of the door of the chief mansion house thereon (no other person being therein)... [same witnesses as listed above]. Recorded 16 Jan 1777 by Test Thomas B. Griffin, Cl L Cur [Pages 167, 167a, 168, & 168a]

21 Nov 1776. Commission. In the name of the Commonwealth of Virginia To James Ball Richard Mitchell John Chinn & John Taylor Gent whereas Lowry Oliver & Ellen Oliver his wife by their certain Indenture of Bargain & Sale bearing date 22 Nov 1776 have sold and conveyed unto William Brumley one tract of land containing fifty acres more or less with the appurtenances lying and being in Lancaster County & whereas the said Ellen Oliver can't conveniently travel to our said county court of Lancaster to make acknowledgement of her right in the said land, therefore we do give unto you or any two or more of you full power to receive the acknowledgement which the said Ellen Oliver shall be willing to make before you of her right in the land aforesaid contained in the aforesaid Indenture which is hereto annexed & we do therefore command you that you personally go to the said Ellen Oliver & receive her acknowledgement of the same & examine her privily & apart, from the said Lowry Oliver her husband whether she does the same freely & voluntarily without the persuasions or threats of her sd husband & whether she be willing that the same shall be recorded in our sd county court of Lancaster... in the first year of our said Commonwealth. [Wit:] Thomas B. Griffin,Cl L Cur. Recorded 16 Jan 1777 by Test Thomas B. Griffin, Cl L Cur [Page 168]

23 Nov 1776. Certificate. By virtue of the annexed Commission to us directed & in obedience thereto we the subscribers did personally go to the said Ellen Oliver in the Commission named & examined her privily & apart from her sd husband Lowry Oliver touching & concerning her relinquishment of her right in the land in the annexed Deed mentioned to be sold unto William Brumley & saith that she doth freely & voluntarily of her own accord & without the threats & persuasions of her said husband relinquish all her right & title whatsoever of in & to the said tract or parcel of land... [Wit:] Richard Mitchell & John Chinn. Recorded 16 Jan 1777 by Test Thomas B. Griffin, Cl L Cur. [Pages 168 & 168a]

4 May 1776. Deed. Between George Flowers of the county of Lancaster of the one part & John Flower of the said county of the other part... George Flowers for & in consideration of the natural love & affection which he hath & doth bear to the said John Flowers hath given and granted & by these presents doth give & grant to the said John Flowers... for ever all that peice parcel or tract of land situate lying & being in Fleets Bay Neck in the sd county of Lancaster

126

containing by estimation seventy acres be it more or less bounded as followeth
vizt beginning at an oak tree corner to Richard Hutchings from thence a straight
course to Indian Creek thence along the said creek the several meanders thereof
to Wales line from thence to a markt oak tree & from thence to the beginning...
[Wit:] William Lawson, Thomas Hathaway, & James Pollard. Recorded 16 Jan
1777 by oaths of William Lawson & James Pollard... & ordered to lye for
further proof and on 17 Jul 1777 was proved further in court by oath of Thomas
Hathaway & recorded by Test Thomas B. Griffin, Cl L Cur. [Pages 168a &
169]

18 Mar 1777. Power of Attorney. Know all men by these presents that I Burges
Ball of the county of Lancaster and parish of Christ Church have made
ordained... and appointed... Henry Armistead Thomas B. Griffin & James
Gordon Esqr all of the same county of Lancaster & parish of Christ Church or
either of them jointly & severally my true just & lawful attorney & attornies to
grant bargain sell lease or mortgage in any manner all my real estate or estates
lying & being in the said county of Lancaster & parish of Christ Church
belonging to me Burges Ball by the right of inheritance by the right of purchase
or by virtue of any devices bequests or marriages particularly that plantation
descended to me from my ancestors and known by the name of Foxe's
Plantation containing about fifteen hundred acres also another plantation that I
purchased of James Ewell Esqr containing about four hundred acres and known
by the name of Fair Weathers and also another plantation derived to me by right
of marriage with wife Mary Chichester containing about four hundred acres all
the aforesaid lands lying and being upon the banks of Rappahannock River also
another plantation purchased by me of William Lewis and Rawleigh Carter
containing about two hundred acres and one other plantation that I purchased of
Abraham White the said two plantations adjoining the above mentioned lands &
also all title claim interest & demand whatever of in & unto the said premises
and every part & parcel thereof and also for me & in my name place & stead &
as my proper act & deed to execute sign seal & deliver such conveyances &
assurances of said premises... and according to the Tenor & Design of the
respective agreements whether in Fee Simple for lives or years giving and by
these presents granting unto my said attorney or attornies full power & absolute
authority to do execute & perform any act or acts deed or deeds thing or things
whatsoever that shall be competent & necessary to be done touching or
concerning... the aforesaid premises or the conveying or assuring thereof to the
purchasers lessees or mortgagees in as full & ample a manner to all intents and
purposes as I said Burges Ball might or could do if I was then & there personally
present... [Wit:] John Taylor, John Selden, & Richd Ball. Recorded 20 Mar
1777 by Test Thomas B. Griffin, Cl L Cur. [Pages 169, 169a, & 170]

18 Mar 1777. Power of Attorney. Know all men by these presents that I Burges

Ball of the parish of Christ Church in the county of Lancaster have made
ordained... and appointed Henry Armistead Thomas B. Griffin & James Gordon
Esqr of the said county of Lancaster & parish of Christ Church any one or two of
them jointly or severally my true just & lawful attorney or attornies for me & in
my name and place and to my use absolutely to bargain sell and dispose of the
following negro slaves belonging to me... by Bills of Sale or in whatever other
manner they or either of them shall think most conveniently vizt the following
negro slaves at present being and living in the county of Lancaster aforesaid
Peter Korah Will Ned Bobb Betty Hannah Solomon also Ellerson & her four
children Hannah James Amey & Jonathan, also Lucy & her two children George
& Elijah also Nanny & her two children Tom & Amos also Kate & her child
Sarah also Judith & her two children Betty & Letty also Kitchenor and her three
children Prince Doll & Winny also Sarah & her two children Luckey and Ben,
also the following negro slaves at present being and living upon my plantation in
the county of King George vizt Dinah Letty and also Sillah & her four children
Libb Hagar Charles & Letty & also I do nominate... my above mentioned
attorney or attornies absolutely to bargain sell & dispose of whatever other negro
slaves belonging to me... they my said attorney or attornies shall think proper
together with all my stocks whether cattle sheep hogs & horses or any part
thereof being upon any of my estates or plantations in the aforesaid county of
Lancaster & also all my household furniture & plantation utensils of every sort,
and whatsoever my said attorney or attornies or either of them shall lawfully do
or cause to be done in the above named premises I do hereby ratify confirm and
allow as fully & effectually as if I myself was present and did the same... [Wit:]
John Taylor, John Selden, & Richard Ball. Recorded 20 Mar 1777 by Test
Thomas B. Griffin, Cl L Cur. [Pages 169, 169a, 170, & 170a]

9 Aug 1773. Report. In pursuance of an order of Lancaster County court... we
the subscribers thereby appointed have agreeable to the order layed off and
divided the lands of Thomas Sharp decd betweenBurges Ball of the one part who
purchased one fourth of the said land from Rawleigh Carter & Sarah his wife &
one other fourth of William Lewis & Ann his wife, and William Chowning of
the other part who purchased one fourth of Fortunatus Sydnor & Elizabeth his
wife & holding one other part in right of his wife Thomazin, the said part for
Burges Ball being the upper tract of land seperated from the lower by the land of
Nicholas George's containing two hundred & three acres from the Dower of Mrs
Sarah Bond & bounded on the north by the lands of Henry Towles & Henry
Carter, on the east by Corotomon River on the west by the land of the said
Burges Ball & on the south by the lands of Nicholas George and James Brent the
other part for William Chowning being the lower tract seperated as aforesaid
containing two hundred and sixty five acres subject to the Dower of the said
Sarah Bond & bounded on the north by the lands of James Brent & Nicholas
George on the east by the Corotomon River, on the west by the lands of

Nicholas George & the said Burges Ball & on the south by lands of George
Carter & Gavin Lowry... [Wit:] John Taylor & Jesse Ball. Recorded 20 Mar
1777 by Test Thomas B. Griffin, Cl L Cur. [Pages 170a & 171]

18 Mar 1777. Deed of Gift. To whom all these presents shall concern know ye
that I Burges Ball of the county of Lancaster & parish of Christ Church for & in
consideration of the sum of five shillings current money of Virginia to me in
hand paid by Henry Armistead Esquire of the said county of Lancaster & parish
of Christ Church the receipt whereof I do hereby acknowledge as well as for
diverse other good causes & affectionate brotherly considerations me hereunto
moving have given... unto the said Henry Armistead the following negro slaves
vizt a house wench Rachel with her three children Joe Dennis & Dominy also a
house wench Hetty with her four children Luckey George Moses & Sally, also a
house wench Judy also an out wench Cate with her two children Sarah & Sam
also an out fellow Charles & an out fellow Bob also an out wench Jenny with
her four children Winny Manuel Jenny & Nanny together with Weaver Sarah, to
have & to hold said negro slaves & their increase all being & living at present in
the aforesaid county of Lancaster... [Wit:] John Taylor, John Selden, Richard
Ball, & James Gordon. Recorded 20 Mar 1777 by Test Thomas B. Griffin, Cl L
Cur. [Pages 171 & 171a]

18 Feb 1777. Deed with Receipt. ...between John Pasquet of Lancaster &
colony of Virginia of the one part & Meredith Mahanes of the county & colony
aforesaid of the other part... John Pasquet for the consideration of the full sum
& quantity of fifty five pounds current money of Virginia to him in hand paid by
the said Meredith Mahanes... [for] all that tract parcel or dividend of land
situated lying & being in sd county & containing by estimation fifty acres of
land be the same more or less & bounded as followeth & beginning for the same
at a corner tree by the main branch of Tom Dogget's adjoining the land of
George Edwards & from thence along a line of marked trees to a branch that
leads from Crowther's Pon & from thence bounded by the branch dividing the
said land from John Carter's down to a fork of a swamp & from thence up the
main branch to the beginning & including fifty acres be the same more or less
which said lands &c became the right & property of the said John Pasquet by the
death of his brother William Pasquet decd... [Wit:] Rawleigh Davenport,
George Edwards, & William Allen. Received 20 Feb 1777 Then received of the
within Meredith Mahanes the sum of one hundred & fifty five pounds current
money of Virginia it being the consideration within mentioned recd by me John
Pasquet & Molley Pasquet. Recorded 20 Mar 1777 by Test Thomas B. Griffin,
Cl L Cur. [Pages 171a & 172]

24 Mar 1777. Deed with Receipt. Between Thomas B. Griffin of the county of
Lancaster of the one part & Cyrus Griffin Brother of the said Thomas B. Griffin

of the other part... Thomas B. Griffin for & in the consideration of the sum of five shillings to him in hand paid as well as for the natural affection which he hath for his said brother & for diverse other good causes and considerations him thereunto moving hath given... all that Messuage tenement tract or parcel of land scituate in the said county of Lancaster which the said Thomas B. Griffin purchased of Edward Newby & his mother Mary Newby bounded on the lands of James Tapscot, Lowry Oliver, Samuel Brumley & the said Thomas B. Griffin containing by estimation seventy five acres... [Wit:] James Tapscot, Elias Edmonds, James Newby, John Wormeley, Thomas Edwards, & Joseph Shearman. Received the day of the date of the within Indenture five shillings current money of Virginia being the full satisfaction for the within premises. [Wit:] James Newby & Joseph Shearman. Recorded 17 Apr 1777 by Thomas B. Griffin, Cl L Cur. [Pages 172 & 172a]

15 May 1777. Deed of Feoffment with Memorandum. ...in the first year of the Commonwealth of Virginia Between Jeremiah Doggett of the county of Lancaster & Mary his wife of the one part & & James Ewell of the said county of the other part... Jeremiah Dogget & Mary his wife for & in consideration of the sum of one hundred & twenty pounds current money in hand paid by the said James Ewell at or before the sealing & delivery of these presents... for ever all that tract or parcel of land situate in the said county of Lancaster, binding on the lands of William Stephens & William Arms & Rappahannock River which was devised by Walter Arms unto his daughter Hannah & to her confirmed by a Deed from her brother Walter Arms bearing date 13 Sep 1720 & sold by her Heir at Law Jesse Light unto Mathew Myars & by him sold to the said Jeremiah Dogget containing by estimation eighty eight acres... [Wit:] William Yerby, Thomas Perkins, & John Newby. Memorandum that on the day of the date of the within Indenture quiet & peaceable possession & Livery of Seisin was had & given by the within named Jeremiah Dogget unto the within named James Ewell by delivery of the handle of the door of the chief mansion house thereon... [same witnesses as listed above]. Recorded 15 May 1777 by Test Thomas B. Griffin, Cl Cur. [Pages 173 & 173a]

14 Apr 1777. Deed of Gift. ...I the said Elmor Dogget of the parish of Christ Church & county of Lancaster for & in consideration of the love & good will that I bear to my son John Doggett of the parish & county aforesaid have given & granted & by these presents do freely give... one hundred & sixty acres of land more or less which land was purchased of John Eustace & goes by the name of the Brick House Land... [Wit:] Charles Lee, John Parrott, William Griggs, & Rawh Hazard. At court...held 15 May 1777 Deed of Gift from Elmor Dogget of the one part to John Dogget of the other part was proved... by the oaths of Rawleigh Hazard & William Griggs & ordered to lye for further proof. 19 Jun 1777 further & fully proved by the oaths of Charles Lee & John Parrott &

recorded by Test Thomas B. Griffin,Cl Cur. [Page 174]

4 Jan 1777. Report of Survey. In obedience to the summons of the sheriff of this county by virtue of an order of this county court bearing date 21 Nov 1776. We the subscribers have met on the land adjacent to Dick's Branch where the petitioner William Gibson intends to build a water grist mill & in company with surveyor have seen an acre of land laid off belonging to Richard Hutchings decd which we judge to be of the value of twenty five shillings & upon viewing all the lands &C which join the said run we find that there will be damage to no other person but the said Richard Hutchings decd land which we think will be damaged to the value of thirty shillings to which we sign our hands & seals. [Wit:] Harry Currell, John Moughon, James Currell, William Mason, Anthony Garton, George Flowers, John James, Elmore Doggett, Roger Kelly, William Martin, Benjamin Garton, & William Norris. For Edwin Conway Sheriff by Bailie George SSLC. 19 Jun 1777 Report of Survey & also the view of the jury to establish a mill on the petition of William Gibson, to establish in the possession of the sd acre of land & premises... & ordered to be recorded by Test Thomas B. Griffin Cl L Cur. [Pages 174 & 174a]

15 Jul 1777. Deed of Gift. Between John Rogers of the parish of Christ Church & county of Lancaster of the one part & Betty Rogers of the parish & county aforesaid of the other part... John Rogers for & in consideration of the natural love & affection which he beareth to his sister the above named Betty Rogers & for & towards her future support and maintenance the said John Rogers doth give... to his said sister Betty Rogers one negro girl commonly called & known by the name of Milley with her future increase... which said negro became the property of the said John Rogers as being Heir at Law to his brother Richard Rogers decd... in case the said Betty Rogers shall die without heirs of her body that then the said negro Milley with her future increase shall go & descend unto the said John Rogers & his heirs for ever & whereas there may possibly arise a dispute whether the said John Rogers hath a right to the whole of his said brothers negroes or not, or whether they ought to be divided among the said John Rogers, & Betty Rogers & the children of William Mitchell by his first wife, who was sister to the said decd Richard Rogers should it be in the future determined that a division should take place there the said Betty is to deliver up with the said negro with her future increase to be divided as aforesaid & in consideration of the said negro & her increase shall be satisfied with her portion of a division of the whole of the said decd Richard Rogers negroes. [Wit:] Richard Mitchell, Henry Tapscot, John Chinn, & Thomas Flint. 17 Jul 1777 recorded by Test Thomas B. Griffin, Cl L Cur. [Pages 174a & 175]

15 Jul 1777. Deed of Bargain and Sale with Receipt. ...in the second year of the Commonwealth of Virginia ...between John Chinn & Sarah his wife of the

county of Lancaster of the one part & Henry Tapscot of the county aforesaid of the other part... John Chinn & Sarah his wife for & in consideration of the sum of one hundred & thirty one pounds current money in hand paid at or before the sealing & delivery of these presents... for ever all that tract peice or parcel of land that I bought of John Rogers & part of a peice of land formerly bought by me of Burges Smith situate in the fork of Colo James Ball's Mill Pond in the said county of Lancaster bounded as followeth, beginning at a corner stake that divided this land & Richard Stott's land thence northerly along the said Stott's line to the north branch of Colo Ball's Mill Pond, thence up the said branch to a flax patch in the said branch thence [blank] 6 degrees E to John Rogers line thence up the said line of John Rogers to the beginning containing one hundred & thirty one acres... [Wit:] Richard Mitchell, Thomas Stott, & James Warrick. Recd the day of the date of the within Indenture of the within named Henry Tapscot the sum of one hundred & thirty one pounds current money in full consideration for the within mentioned granted parcel of land & premises. [same witnesses as listed above]. Recorded 17 Jul 1777 by Test Thomas B. Griffin, Cl L Cur. [Pages 175, 175a, & 176]

18 Aug 1777. Deed of Lease and Release. Between Burges Ball of the county of Lancaster & the parish of Christ Church Esquire of the one part & Robert Gilmore of the parish of Wiccomico & county of Northumberland of the other part... Burges Ball for & in consideration of the sum of five shillings current money of Virginia to him in hand paid by the said Robert Gilmour... [for] all that Messuage or Tenement & tract of land called Fox's Plantation & all that Messuage or tenement & tract of land which formerly belonged to John Chichester Esqr of the said county of Lancaster decd & all that other Messuage or tenement & tract of land which the said Burges Ball purchased of James Ewell & Mary his wife of the said county of Lancaster & known by the name of Fairweather's & all that other messuage or tenement & tract of land which he the said Burges Ball purchased of William Lewis & Ann his wife of the county of Northumberland & all that other messuage or tenement & tract of land which he the said Burges Ball purchased of Rawleigh Carter & Sarah his wife of the county of Amelia and all that messuage or tenement & tract of land which he the said Burges Ball purchased of Abraham White & Frankey his wife by whatsoever name or names or howsoever the same or any of them are called or known with their & every of their rights members & appurtenances situate lying & being in the said county of Lancaster & parish of Christ Church which said several messuages or tenements & tracts of land all adjoin the one to the other & contain three thousand acres be it more or less and are bounded as followeth vizt beginning at the mouth of a cove on Rappahannock River & running thence to a marked locust at the head thereof thence N40 E to the main road thence up the road & over the Church Run to Colo Jesse Ball's corner thence along the said Balls line to the head of Pritchard's Swamp thence down the swamp to Davis's

corner, thence along Davis's line to Edward Carter's land thence along the said
Carter's & Henry Towles's lines westerly southerly & easterly to Prices Creek
thence along the said creek including the land purchased of the aforesaid
William Lewis & Rawleigh Carter to Campbell's land thence along the lines of
the said Campbell Nicholas George & William Chowning to George Carter's
land, thence along the lines of the said Carter & Merryman Payne to [blank]
Creek thence down said creek to Rappahannock River thence up the river to the
beginning...unto the said Robert Gilmour... from the first day of this instant for
& during & to the full end & term of one whole year from thence next ensuing
fully to be complete & ended yeilding & paying therefore at the expiration of the
said year one peppercorn... signed by Henry Armistead, Thomas B. Griffin, &
James Gordon, attornies in fact for Burges Ball. [Wit:] James Ball, Cyrus
Griffin, William Chowning, David Galloway, Thomas Rouand, & William
Dunaway. Recorded 21 Aug 1777 by Test Thomas B. Griffin, Cl L Cur. [Pages
176 & 176a]

19 Aug 1777. Deed of Lease and Release. Between Burges Ball of the county
of Lancaster & parish of Christ Church Esqr of the one part & Robert Gilmour
of the parish of Wiccomico & county of Northumberland of the other part...
Burges Ball for & in consideration of the sum of ten thousand pounds current
money of Virginia to him in hand paid by the said Robert Gilmour at or before
the ensealing & delivery hereof... confirm unto the said Robert Gilmour in his
actual possession now being by virtue of a Bargain & Sale to him thereof made
for one whole year by Indenture bearing date the day next before the day of the
date of these presents & by force of the statute for transferring uses into
possession... for ever, all that messuage or tenement & tract of land called Fox's
Plantation and all that other messuages or tenement & tract of land which
formerly belonged to John Chichester Esqr of the county of Lancaster decd and
all that other messuages or tenements & tract of land which the said Burges Ball
purchased of James Ewell & Mary his wife of the said county of Lancaster &
known by the name of Fair Weather's and all that other messuage or tenement &
tract of land which he the said Burges Ball purchased of Wm Lewis & Ann his
wife of the county of Northumberland and all that other messuage or tenement &
tract of land which he the said Burges Ball purchased of Rawleigh Carter &
Sarah his wife of the county of Amelia & all that messuage or tenement & tract
of land which he the said Burges Ball purchased of Abraham White & Frankey
his wife by whatsoever name or names or howsoever the same or any of them
are called or known with their & every rights members and appurtenances
situate lying & being in the said county of Lancaster & parish of Christ Church
which said several messuages or tenements & tracts of land all adjoin one to the
other & contain three thousand acres be it more or less & are bounded as
followeth to wit beginning at the mouth of a cove (on Rappahannock River) &
running thence to a marked locust at the head thereof, thence N40 E to the main

road thence up the road & over the Church Run to Colo James Ball's corner
thence along the said Ball's line to the head of Pritchard's Swamp thence down
the swamp to Davis's corner thence along Davis's line to Edward Carter's land
thence along the said Carters & Henry Towles's line westerly southerly &
easterly to Rice's Creek thence along the said creek including the land purchased
of the aforesaid William Lewis & Rawleigh Carter to Campbell's land thence
along the line of the said Campbell Nicholas George & William Chowning to
George Carter's land, thence along the lines of the said Carter & Merryman
Payne to [blank] creek thence down the creek to Rappahannock River thence up
the river to the beginning... signed by Henry Armistead, Thomas B. Griffin, &
James Gordon attornies in fact for Burges Ball. [Wit:] James Ball, Cyrus
Griffin, Thomas Rouand, David Galloway, & William Chowning. Recorded 21
Aug 1777 by Test Thomas B. Griffin, Cl L Cur. [Pages 177, 177a, 178a, & 179]

19 Aug 1777. Bond. ...I Burges Ball am held and stand bound unto Robert
Gilmour in the sum of twenty thousand pounds currt money of Virginia which
payment well & truly to be made unto the said Robert Gilmour... I bind
myself... by these presents... The condition of the above obligation is such that
whereas Henry Armistead, Thomas B. Griffin, & James Gordon attornies in fact
for the said Burges Ball have executed a Deed of Lease & Release bearing even
date with these presents for conveying certain lands tenements & messuages
therein mentioned if therefore the said Burges Ball... and every of them shall at
all times abide by... all & singular the articles... in the said Deed of Lease &
Release mentioned to be by him his heirs exors & admors performed then the
obligation to be void, otherwise be in full force & power. Signed by Henry
Armistead, Thomas B. Griffin, & James Gordon attornies in fact for Burges
Ball. [Wit:] James Ball, Cyrus Griffin, Thomas Rouand, & William Dunaway.
Recorded 21 Aug 1777 by Test Thomas B. Griffin, Cl L Cur. [Page 179]

20 May 1778. Deed of Bargain and Sale with Receipt. ...in the second year of
the Commonwealth of Virginia... between John Connolly and Mary his wife of
the county of Lancaster and parish of Christ Church of the one part, and Jesse
Harrison of the county of Richmond and parish of Northfarnham of the other
part... John Connolly and Mary his wife for and in consideration of the sum of
one hundred and fifty pounds current money of Virginia in hand paid by the said
Jesse Harrison before the sealing and delivery of these presents... forever a
certain tract or parcel of land containing sixty acres, be the same more or less,
situate lying and being in the aforesaid county of Lancaster on the main branch
of the Corotoman River, beginning at the head of a cove which divides the said
land from Moses Georges land, thence to a hickreenutt tree standing in a valley
which divides the said land from Lazarus Georges land, thence to a marked
white oak, from thence to a corner line that formerly stood between the said
land and Lazarus Georges land, from thence along a straight line of marked

trees, which divides the said land from Lazarus Georges land from thence to the head of a branch and down the branch to the head of a creek called the Old House Creek... [Wit:] Test James Connolly, Sarah Hill, & James Carter. Received the day of the date of the within Indenture of the within named Jesse Harrison the sum of one hundred and fifty pounds current money in full satisfaction for the within mentioned granted parcel of land & premises. [same witnesses as listed above]. Recorded 25 May 1778 by Test Thos Shearman CLC. [Pages 179a & 180]

20 Apr 1778. Deed with Memorandum. Between Rawleigh Carter of the county of Amelia of the one part and Edward Carter of Lancaster County of the other part... for and in consideration of the sum of three hundred and seventy five pounds currt money of Virginia to him in hand paid before the sealing and delivery of these presents by the said Edward Carter... Rawleigh Carter has bargained and sold... unto the said Edward Carter all that parcel of land being devised to Rawleigh Carter by Thomas Carter decd his father by will lying in Lancaster County and is the land where the said Thomas Carter lived containing eighty acres more or less and bounded as followeth joining the lands of James Gordon, John Davis, and William Stephens agreeable to the lines now standing... [Wit:] Nicholas George, John Payne, Wm Chowning, & John Merryman. Memorandum that on the day of the date of the within Indenture peaceable and quiet possession of the within land and premises was made and given unto the within named Edward Carter by the within named Rawleigh Carter agreeable to the form and intent of the within mentioned Deed... [same witnesses as listed above]. Recorded 21 May 1778 by Test Thos Shearman CLC. [Pages 180 & 180a]

11 Nov 1777. ...Between James Blackerby and Ann his wife of the county of Lancaster Planter of the one part and Henry Tapscott of the same county of the other part... James Blackerby and Ann his wife for and in consideration of the sum of twenty pounds currt money in hand paid at or before the sealing and delivery of these presents... for ever all that tract piece or parcel of land situate in the fork of Colo James Ball's Mill Pond in the said county bounded as followeth, beginning at a small white oak on the north side of the south branch of the said Mill Pond, it being a corner tree between John Rogers and Henry Tapscott, thence along the said Rogers's line N22 degrees W 101 3/1 Polls to a dogwood at the head of the branch then along Richd Stotts line to the south branch of Colo James Balls Mill Pond thence up the meanders of the said branch to the beginning containing twenty one and an half acres more or less, being part of a parcel of land descended unto the said Blackerby's wife as coheiress to her father Richd Rogers decd... [Wit:] Jno Galloway, George Scurlock, Leannah Blackerby, Wm Stonum, James Newby, & George Cammell. Recd the day of the date of the within Indenture of the within named Henry Tapscott, the sum of

twenty pounds currt money in full consideration for the within mentioned granted parcel of land and premises. [Wit:] John Galloway, George Scurlock, & Leannah Blackerby. Recorded 21 May 1778 by Test Thos Shearman CLC. [Pages 181 & 181a]

22 Mar 1778. Deed of Trust. Between Richard Hall and Mary his wife of the county of Lancaster of the one part, and Elisha Hall of the county of King William of the other part... Richard Hall and Mary his wife for and in consideration of the settling and assuring, the messuages, lands, tenements, hereditaments, herein after mentioned, to and for the several uses, intents and purposes herein after limited and declared, pursuant to an agreement made by and between the said Richd Hall & the Revd John Leland and Lucy his wife, mother of the said Mary, upon the contract of marriage between the said Richard Hall and the said Mary his wife, they the said Richd Hall and Mary his wife, have granted... unto the said Elisha Hall, all that plantation, tract or parcel of land, situate, lying and being in the county of Lancaster, which descended and came to the said Mary, from her father Thomas Lee, containing by estimation, seven hundred acres, be the same more or less, with the rights members and appurtenances of the same, bounded and adjoining by and to the lands of Charles Lee, Rawleigh Shearman, Wm Griggs, James Currell, George Kelly and George Currell... declared (that is to say) to the use and behoof of the said Richard Hall and his assigns for and during the term of his natural life, without impeachment of waste and from and after the determination of that estate, to the use and behoof of the said Elisha Hall and his heirs for and during the natural life of the said Richard Hall in trust... to permit and suffer the said Richd Hall and his assigns to receive and take the rents, issues and profits thereof to his and their own proper use and benefit during his natural life, and from and after the decease of him the said Richd Hall, to the use and behoof of the said Mary his wife and her assigns, for and during the term of her natural life, and from and after the decease of the survivor of them, the said Richard Hall and Mary his wife, to the use and behoof of the heirs of the body of the said Mary Hall, lawfully begotten, or to be begotten by the said Richard Hall, or in case of his death by another lawful husband, and for want of such heirs or lawful issue as aforesaid of the body of the said Mary, then to the survivors of them... [Wit:] Richard E. Lee, John Fleet, & Thomas Lawson. Recorded 21 May 1778 by Test Thos Shearman CLC. [Pages 181a, 182, & 182a]

20 Mar 1778. Commission. The Commonwealth of Virginia to John Fleet, Thomas Lawson and John Berryman Gent Justices of Lancaster County, Greeting Know ye that we trusting your fidelity and provident circumspection in diligently examining Mary Hall wife of Richard Hall touching and concerning her acknowledgement of the annexed Deed said to be made by her and her said husband do command you or any two or more of you that at such certain days

and places as you shall appoint you assemble yourselves and the said Mary Hall before you or any two or more of you, that you cause to come, and diligently examine her privily and apart from her said husband Richard Hall touching her consent to the said Deed, and whether she doth the same freely and volunatrily without the threats or persuasions of her said husband and is willing that the said Deed with her acknowledgment be recorded... Witness by Test Thomas B. Griffin clerk of [Lancaster County]... Recorded 21 May 1778 by Test Thos Shearman CLC [Page 182a]

22 Mar 1778. Certificate. Lancaster County (to wit) by virtue of the within Commission to us directed, we John Fleet and Thomas Lawson, two of the Justices for the county aforesaid have privately examined Mary Hall wife of Richard Hall, seperately and apart from her said husband, touching her acknowledgment and consent to the annexed Deed from the said Richard Hall and Mary his wife to Elisha Hall, and do find that the same was done freely and voluntarily without the threats or persuasion of her said husband, and that she is willing that the said Deed together with her acknowledgment should be recorded... [Wit:] John Fleet and Thomas Lawson. Recorded 21 May 1778 by Test Thos Shearman CLC [Page 182a]

21 May 1778. Bond. Know all men by these presents that we Edwin Conway, Richard Mitchell & William Brown are held and firmly bound unto the Treasurer of this Commonwealth for the time being in the sum of three thousand pounds current money to be paid to the said Treasurer for the time being, to which payment well and truly to be made in a bind ourselves our heirs exors and admors jointly and severally firmly by these presents... The condition of the above obligation is such, that if the above bound Edwin Conway sheriff of the county of Lancaster during his continuence therein, shall well and truly collect the taxes ordered by an act of the last General Assembly, and duly account for, and pay the same at such times as are presented and limited by the said Act, then the above obligation to be void, else to remain in full force and virtue... signed by Edwin Conway, Richard Mitchell, and William Brown. Recorded 21 May 1778 by Test Thos Shearman CLC. [Page 183]

11 May 1778. Certificate of Election. We James Ball and Richard Mitchell the two senior Justices who attended the election of Commissioners for the said county and Edwin Conway sheriff thereof, do hereby certify that an election was held at the court house of the said county on Tuesday the 10th day of March last Richard Mitchell, James Ball and Henry Towles were elected Commissioners of the taxes for the said county for this present year. Recorded 21 May 1778 by Test Thos Shearman CLC. [Page 183]

18 Mar 1778. Indenture of Feoffment with Memorandum. Between Mary

Neasom of the parish of Christ Church in the county of Lancaster of the one part and Ozwald Newby of the parish and county aforesaid of the other part... Mary Neasom for and in consideration of the sum of forty pounds current money of the Commonwealth of Virginia in hand paid her by the said Ozwald Newby... [for] one certain piece or parcel or tract of land lying and being in the parish and county aforesaid containing by estimation fifty acres of land be the same more or less and bounded by the land of Ozwald Newby, Elizabeth McTire, John McTire, and Samuel Neasom decd... [Wit:] Thomas Flint, John Clutton, William Clutton, & Easter Newby. Memorandum that on the day of the within date quiet and peaceable possession of the within mentioned land and premises was made and given by the within named Mary Neasom to the within named Ozwald Newby by delivery of Turf and Twig... [same witnesses as listed above]. Recorded 19 Mar 1778 by Test Thomas B. Griffin, Cl Cur. [Pages 183a & 184]

4 Jun 1777. Deed with Receipt. ...Between Elisha Hall of the parish of Christ Church and the county of Lancaster of the one part and Edwin Conway Gent of the same parish and county aforesaid of the other part... Elisha Hall for and in consideration of the sum of seven hundred and fifty pounds lawfull money of Virginia to him in hand paid by the said Edwin Conway the receipt whereof the said Elisha Hall doth hereby confess and acknowledge himself therewith sufficiently... paid... and for diverse other good causes and considerations him thereunto moving... release and confirm unto the said Edwin Conway... forever all that plantation tract or parcel of land situate lying and being in the parish of Christ Church and county of Lancaster whereon the Revd James Waddell formerly dwell and now occupied by the said Elisha Hall containing by estimation three hundred and ninety five acres to be the same more or less eighty acres whereof was formerly granted to Henry Boatman by the Proprietor's Deed dated on or about 30 Sep 1695 and by the said Henry Boatman by his Deed dated on or about 5 Oct 1695 sold and conveyed unto Joseph Taylor and by the said Joseph Taylor by his Deed dated 20 Dec 1711 sold and conveyed unto William Olivet and by the said William Olivet by his Deed dated on or about 9 Feb 1719 sold and conveyed unto the Revd John Bell the remaining three hundred and fifteen acres of the said tract was purchased by the said John Bell of Dameron Pasquet by Deed bearing date on or about 9 Feb 1719 which said two tracts of land the said John Bell in and by his last Will and Testament gave and bequeathed his son Charles Ball who by his Deed dated on or about [blank] day of 17[blank] sold and conveyed the same to James Gordon who by his last Will and Testament devised the same to his daughter Mary wife of the said Revd James Waddell who together executed a Deed for the same to the said Elisha Hall bearing date 30 May 1776, as by the said several Deeds Wills and Writings of record among the records of the Secretaries office and of Lancaster County Court... which said plantation tract or parcel of land next adjoins the lands of

John Yerby Elias Edmonds [blank] Edwards and the eastern branch of Corotoman... [Wit:] James Gordon, Cyrus Griffin, Richd Mitchell, & Henry Towles. Received the day and year first within written of the within named Edwin Conway the sum of seven hundred and fifty pounds being the full consideration money within mentioned to be paid to me. I say received by me signed Elisha Hall. Witness James Gordon & Cyrus Griffin. Recorded 20 Nov 1777 by Test Thomas B. Griffin, Cl Cur. [Pages 184, 184a, 185, & 185a]

4 Jun 1777. Bond. Know all men by these presents that we Elisha Hall are held and firmly bound unto Edwin Conway Gent of the county of Lancaster in the just and full sum of two thousand pounds – lawful money of Virginia to be paid to the said Edwin Conway his certain attorney... to which payment well and truly to be made and done we bind ourselves jointly and severally... The condition of the above Obligation is such that if the above bound Elisha Hall... do and shall in all things well and truly perform... all and singular the covenents... whatsoever which on the part and behalf of the said Elisha Hall... are or ought to be observed... in a certain Indenture bearing even date with the above written obligation made or mentioned to be made between the said Elisha Hall of the one part and the said Edwin Conway of the other part... [Wit:] James Gordon, Cyrus Griffin, Richd Mitchell & Henry Towles. Recorded 20 Nov 1777 by Test Thomas B. Griffin, Cl Cur. [Pages 185a & 186]

15 Nov 1777. Deed of Bargain and Sale with Receipt. ...in the second year of the Commonwealth of Virginia... Between Edward Newby and Mary Newby his wife and Mary Newby mother of the said Edward all of the county of Culpepper of the one part and Thomas B. Griffin of the county of Lancaster of the other part... Edward Newby and Mary his wife and Mary Newby for and in consideration of the sum of two hundred and six pounds current money to them in hand paid by the said Thomas B. Griffin at or before the sealing and delivery of these presents... forever all that tract or parcel of land lying in the upper part of the said county of Lancaster which descended to the said Edward Newby from his father Henry Newby, which said Henry inherited the said land from his father Henry who purchased it of one David Smith and bounded by the lands of the said Thomas B. Griffin, Samuel Brumley, the lands of Lowry Oliver now belonging to the said Thomas B. Griffin and James Tapscott, containing by estimation seventy five acres more or less... [Wit:] John Strother, John Slaughter, James Newby, Leroy Newby, Rawleigh Coats, & Ann Newby. Received the day of the date of the within Indenture of the within named Thomas B. Griffin the sum of two hundred and six pounds current money in full consideration for the within granted parcel of land and premises. [Wit:] James Newby, Leroy Newby, Rawleigh Coats, & Ann Newby. Recorded 19 Feb 1778 by [blank]. [Pages 186, 186a, & 187]

15 Nov 1777. Commission. The Commonwealth of Virginia to John Strother and John Slaughter Gent Justices of Culpepper County greeting whereas Edwin Newby and Mary his wife by their certain Indenture of Bargain and Sale bearing date 15 Nov 1777 have sold and conveyed unto Thomas B. Griffin one tract of land containing seventy five acres more or less with the appurtenances lying and being in Lancaster County, and whereas the said cannot conveniently travel to our county court of Lancaster to make acknowledgment of her right in the said lands therefore we do give unto you or any two or more of you full power to receive the acknowledgment of her right in the lands aforesaid certained in the aforesaid Indenture which is hereunto annexed, which the said Mary Newby shall be willing to make before you, and we do therefore command you that you personally go to the said Mary Newby and receive her acknowledgment of the same and examine her privily and apart from the said Edward Newby her husband whether she does the same freely and voluntarily without her said husbands persuasions or threats, and whether she be willing that the same with the annexed Deed should be recorded... Witness Thomas B. Griffin, Clerk of Lancaster County... Recorded 19 Feb 1778 by [blank]. [Pages 186a & 187]

15 Nov 1777. Certificate. Culpepper County Court. By virtue of the within Commission to us directed we the subscribers Justices of the said county did personally go to and examine the within named Mary Newby wife of Edward Newby touching her acknowledgment of the within mentioned Indenture privily and apart from the within named Edward Newby her husband and she relinquishes her right to the land and premises contained in the said Indenture freely and voluntarily without his persuasions or threats and also that she is willing that the said Deed with this Commission executed shall be recorded in the county court of Lancaster... [Wit:] John Strother & John Slaughter. Recorded 19 Feb 1778 by [blank]. [Page 187]

1 Jan 1778. List. A true list of the names of those who have taken the Oath of Allegience and Fidelity before me, the preceding year... **Column 1:** Matthew Myars, Nicholas George, & Charles Rogers-sworn 18 Jul 1777. Rodham Lundsford, Gavin Lowry N5, & John Dye-sworn 21 Jul 1777. William Chowning & John Chowning-sworn 22 Jul 1777. Thomas Carter Junr, James Ewell N10, William Luckham, John Merryman, William Smith, John Wilkerson, William Darby N15, Joseph Carter, John Arms, William Biscoe N2, Henry Carter, William Overstreet N20, Thomas Webb, George Connolly, John Fleming, Thomas Kern, William Stephens N25, Sampson Dimoral, William Hendren[?], Richd Mitchell Junr, George Chitwood, William Chitwood N30, John Hazard, Richard [Steardocte, Sheardocte, Straardock?], & William Dunaway-sworn 23 Jul 1777. **Column 2:** William Wiblin, William Wiblin Junr N35, Henry Davis, Ambrose Pitman, James Fleming, William Chitton Junr, William Newton N40-sworn 23 Jul 1777. Charles Dotson Junr, Thomas Ellit, &

George Carter-sworn 26 Jul 1777. Benjamin George Junr-sworn 29 Jul 1777.
George Conner N45 & James Mercer-sworn 30 Jul 1777. Merryman Payne-
sworn 2 Aug 1777. John Harris, John Lunsford, William Hunt N50, & Richard
Blaid-sworn 3 Aug 1777. Thomas Hunton & Joseph Hubbard-sworn 21 Aug
1777. Jesse Chitton, John Dinovit N55, Vachel Faudree & Jeremiah Doggett-
sworn 23 Aug 1777. Edward Carter, Michael Welch, Thomas Myars N60,
James Kirk, & William Arms-sworn 2 Oct 1777. Sampson Dinovit Junr,
Thomas Bradshaw, & Thomas George-sworn 10 Oct 1777. [Page 187a]

1 Jan 1778. List. A true list of the names of those who have taken the Oath of
Allegience and Fidelity before me, the preceding year...[Continued]   **Column
1:** Robert Chinn, Joseph Shearman, William Newby, George Dale, James
Norris, William Mason, William Carpenter, William Tapscott, Rawleigh Stott,
Robert Clark, William Cornelious, James Warrick, Thomas Crookhorn, Thomas
Stonum, James Pullen, Thomas Mitchell, Thomas Clutton, William Warrick,
Aaron Robinson, George Robinson, Henry Kern, George Cammell, William
Stonum Junr, John Pasquett, Charles Norris, Wiett Riveer, & John Mason-sworn
19 Jul 1777.   **Column 2:** John Clutton, Ozwald Newby, Henry Tapscott Junr,
James Tapscott, & Le Roy Pope-sworn 19 Jul 1777. Thomas Bell-sworn 5 Sep
1777. John Norris, Joseph Norris, Steptimus Norris, Robert Jones, John Riveer
Junr, Andrew Robertson, Robert Belvard, Johnson Riveer, & William Riveer-
sworn 23 Sep 1777. John Riveer & George Hill-sworn 8 Oct 1777. Samuel
Brumley, William Stott, & James Luckham-sworn 11 Oct 1777. George Moore-
sworn 14 Oct 1777. John Carpenter & Martin Tapscott-sworn 18 Oct 1777.
Henry M Horne, William Mitchell, & William Montague-sworn 23 Oct 1777.
All sworn before Henry Tapscott. [Page 188]

27 May 1778. List. A list of persons that have taken the Oath of Allegience and
subscribed the test before Thomas Lawson one of the Magistrates for the
Commonwealth of Lancaster County agreeable to an Act of Assembly for that
purpose. **Column 1:** James Gordon-sworn 17 Jul 1777. Richard E. Lee &
Hugh Brent-sworn 19 Jul 1777. Thomas Perkins, Thomas Lee, & Richard Blaid
Junr-sworn 26 Jul 1777. James Kelly, Thomas Hathaway, Samuel Hunt, Epa
Lawson Junr, John Pearson, Thomas Ingram, James Currell Junr, Isaac Currell,
Aaron Dameron, James Davis, Isham Miller, Joshua Spillman, James Pollard,
John Clayton, Lawson Hathaway, John Airs, John Reeves, Hugh Kelly Junr,
Nathaniel Wilder, Jeremiah Ashburn, John Carter, Morris Wheeler, John
Flowers, David Garland, Michael Wilder, James Harris, Peter Williams, George
Currell Senr, William Hinton, Vincet Brent, & Thomas Shearman-sworn 25 Jul
1777.   **Column 2:** William Currell, Bushrod Riveer, & William Biscoe-sworn
25 Jul 1777. Thomas Carter, Richard Hinton, Isaac Dogge, Jonathan Wilder,
Rawleigh Shearman, & Peter Garton-sworn 2 Aug 1777. Harry Currell-sworn
29 Sep 1777. George Forde-sworn 16 Oct 1777. Epaphroditus Lawson,

Nicholas Currell, & William Steptoe-sworn 1 Nov 1777. Newton Brent, Charles Williams, & George Robinson-sworn 9 Nov 1777. John Nichols-sworn 15 Feb 1778. Roger Kelly & William Martin-sworn 1 May 1778. Henry Hinton, John Edwards, William Riley, Thomas Hill, Thomas Cottrell, Aaron Williams, Thomas Bridgford, Benjamin Garton Junr, Luke Millet Ashburn, Rawleigh James, Martin George, & Stephen Miller-sworn 2 May 1778. Taken by Thomas Lawson. Recorded by Test Thos Shearman CLC. [Pages 188 & 188a]

31 Dec 1777. List. A list of inhabitants of Lancaster County who have taken and subscribed the oath directed by an Act of Assembly (entitled an Act to oblige the free male inhabitants of this state above a certain age to give assurances of allegience to the same, and for other purposes) before me one of the Justices of the peace for the said county appointed by order of the court for that purpose. **Column 1:** Newton Brent-sworn 18 Jul 1777. Henry Lawson-sworn 19 Jul 1777. William Gibson, William Griggs, Job Carter, John James, William Mason, William Kelly, & John Merrideth-sworn 21 Jul 1777. Revd David Currie & Bailie George-sworn 28 Jul 1777. William Merrideth & Elmore Dogget-sworn 31 Jul 1777. John Parrot-sworn 5 Aug 1777. James Brent-sworn 7 Aug 1777. Thomas Pinckard, William Shelton, John Yerby, William Kirk, John Hill, John Merrideth, James Fendla, Tapscott Oliver, William Norris, Minitree [Minitras?] Jones, & William West-sworn 9 Aug 1777. **Column 2:** John Riveer, Christopher Miller, Henry George, William Hayden, Thomas Cox, John Dogget, William Dogget, William Brent, & William Dogget, William Schofield, Thomas Rouand, Daniel Kent, Nicholas Lawson George, William Kent, Jesse Kelly, Merrideth Mahanes, & John Longwith-sworn 9 Aug 1777. William Brent-sworn 13 Aug 1777. Edney Tapscott & Charles Lee-sworn 21 Aug 1777. Isaac Weaver-sworn 6 Oct 1777. Aaron Weaver-sworn 14 Oct 1777. Benjamin George-sworn 16 Oct 1777. John Allen & William Allen-sworn 29 Dec 1777. By John Berryman & recorded by Test Thos Shearman CLC. [Page 189]

21 Mar 1778. Report. Pursuant to an order of Lancaster County court bearing date March 1778. We the subscribers having met, viewed the road petitioned for by Coleman Dogget, and find the intended road to be about four hundred and eighty yards farther than where the road now is, that it will run a small distance upon Spencer George's land, which we think will be of very little disadvantage to him, it will then cross a swamp, which may be made passable, by having two small bridges, and we think will not be much inferior to the old road, as the hills are not steep on either side the swamp, then it will run about one hundred yards on Moses Georges land which we think cannot injure him much, as it's nigh the line, and we imagine it cannot be of much advantage to him to inclose that part of his land, and then it run upon Coleman Doggets land, till it gets to Patrick Connollys, where it will join the old road. The road at present runs about seven

hundred yards upon Coleman Doggets land and cuts off near fifty acres as near we can guess which is the land he wants to inclose, and join his fences if the road is turned and so prevent his having a lane. Recorded 18 Jun 1778 by Test Thos Shearman CLC. [Page 189a]

16 Apr 1778. Report. In obedience to an order of Lancaster court... we the subscribers did go to the clerks office of the said county lately kept by Colo Thomas B. Griffin where we found all the papers and books in good order, and that the records were completed as far up as the first November 1777, and that the said papers and books we in our presence delivered by Colo Thomas B. Griffin's Exors to Mr Thomas Shearman the present clerk... 16 Jul 1778. [Wit:] Richard Mitchell & John Chinn. Recorded 16 Jul 1778 by Test Thos Shearman CLC. [Page 189a]

28 May 1778. Commission. The Commonwealth of Virginia to James Ball, Richard Mitchell and James Ball Junr Gent Whereas John Chinn and Sarah his wife by their certain Indenture of Bargain and Sale bearing date 15 Jul 1777 have sold and conveyed unto Henry Tapscott one tract of land containing one hundred and thirty one acres more or less with the appurtenances lying and being in Lancaster County and whereas the said Sarah cannot conveniently travel to our county court of Lancaster to make acknowledgment of her right in the said land therefore we do give unto you or any two or more of you full power to receive the acknowledgment which the said Sarah shall be willing to make before you of her right in the land aforesaid contained in the aforesaid Indenture which is hereunto annexed and we do therefore command you that you personally go to the said Sarah and receive her acknowledgment of the same and examine her privily and apart from the said John Chinn her husband whether she does the same freely and voluntarily without the persuasions or threats of her said husband, and whether she be willing that the same should be recorded... signed Test Thos Shearman CLC. [Page 190]

16 Jul 1778. Certificate. We the subscribers two of the Commissioners within named do hereby certify that we did personally go to the within named Sarah the wife of the within named John Chinn and examine her touching the within mentioned land and premises whose answer was she freely and voluntarily acknowledged her Right of Dower in and to the land mentioned in the Deed hereto annexed and without the persuasions or threats of her husband and that she is willing the same should be recorded in the county court of Lancaster... [Wit:] James Ball & Richd Mitchell. Recorded 16 Jul 1778 by Test Thos Shearman CLC. [Page 190]

1 Jan 1778. Deed of Feoffment and Receipt. ...in the second year of the Common Wealth between Enoch George and Mary his wife of the county of

Dinwiddie of the one part and Charles Williams of the county of Lancaster of the other part... Enoch George and Mary his wife for and in consideration of the sum of eighty five pounds current money of Virginia to the said Enoch George by the said Charles Williams in hand well and truly paid at or before the sealing and delivery of these presents... [for] all that plantation tract or parcel of land situate lying and being in the parish of Christ Church in the county of Lancaster sometimes formerly known by the name of Mr Enoch George's or Mr Enoch George's Forrest Quarter and adjoins the lands of James Simmonds the orphans of William Waugh decd Charles Hammonds decd and Charles Carter Esq of Shirely containing by estimation fifty acres... [Wit:] William Brown, Charles Hammonds, James Simmons, & Nicholas Lawson George. Received this first day of January 1778 of the within named Charles Williams eighty five pounds current money of Virginia being the full consideration money within mentioned to be paid to me I say received by me-Enoch George. [same witnesses as listed above]. Be it remembered that on the day of the date of this Indenture peaceable and quiet possession and seisin of the plantation and premises in the Deed mentioned and contained was taken and had by the within named Enoch George and by him in like manner given and delivered unto the within named Charles Williams by the delivery of Turf and Twig upon the premises... [same witnesses as listed above]. Recorded 16 Jul 1778 by Test Thos Shearman CLC. [Pages 190, 190a, 191, & 191a]

2 Jan 1778. Commission. The Commonwealth of Virginia to Robert Walker and James Greenway Gent Justices of the county of Dinwiddie know ye that trusting to patriotism integrity and fidelity you are hereby required diligently at such time and place as you shall appoint to examine privily and apart from her husband Mary George wife of Enoch George touching and concerning her acknowledgment of a certain Deed of Indenture hereunto annexed made between the said Enoch the said Mary and Charles Williams of Lancaster County, and whether she doth the same freely and voluntarily without the threats or persuasions of her said husband and her examination having so taken that you immediately return to the Clerk of Lancaster County a distinct and true account of the same... signed Thomas B. Griffin clerk of Lancaster County... Recorded 16 Jul 1778 by Test Thos Shearman CLC. [Page 191a]

11 Jun 1778. Certificate. Dinwiddie Court. By virtue of the within dedimus we have examined the within name Mary George separate and apart from her husband touching her relinquishment of Dower of and to the land mentioned in the Deed hereunto annexed and do find that she is willing to relinquish the same and is willing the said Deed should be recorded in the county court of Lancaster... [Wit:] Robt Walker & James Greenway. Recorded 16 Jul 1778 by Test Thos Shearman CLC. [Page 191a]

1 Jan 1778. Bond. Know all men by these presents that we Enoch George of the county of Dinwiddie and Benjamin George and Merideth Mahanes of the county of Lancaster, are held and firmly bound unto Charles Williams of the county of Lancaster in the just sum of five hundred pounds current money of Virginia to be paid to the said Charles Williams... To which payment well and truly to be made and done we bind ourselves jointly and severally... firmly by these presents... The condition of the above Obligation is such that if the above bound Enoch George... shall in all things well and truly observe... all the covenants... whatsoever which on the part & behalf of the said Enoch George and Mary his wife... ought to be observed... in a certain Indented Deed bearing even date with the above written obligation made between the said Enoch George and Mary his wife of the one part and the said Charles Williams of the other part... [Wit:] William Brown, Charles Hammonds, James Simmons, & Nicholas Lawson George. Recorded 16 Jul 1778 by Test Thos Shearman CLC. [Page 192]

30 Jul 1778. Report. In obedience to an order of Lancaster County Court bearing date July court 1778. We subscribers have met and being sworn by the sheriff of this county have moved an acre of land the property of Mr John Schon which Mr Elias Edmonds craves in order to build a water grist mill, and find the value thereof to be forty shillings cash, also a swamp belonging (in part) to the said Schon, we think will be laid under water to the value of ten pounds cash damages to the said Schon, which we think is all the damages that will accrue to any person (except the petitioner Edmonds) in consequence of Mr Elias Edmonds building a mill over Grace's Run as in his petition set forth... [Wit:] Spencer George, Joshua Hubbard, Stephen Chitton, James Carter, Moses George, Joseph Dobbs, Samuel Yopp, Jonathan Pullen, James Fendla, Thomas Hubbard, John Davis, & Coleman Dogget. In presence of Bailie George SS. Recorded 20 Aug 1778 by Test Thos Shearman CLC. [Pages 192 & 192a]

6 Aug 1778. Report. In obedience to an order of Lancaster County court bearing date July 1778, for valuing an acre of land belonging to Robert Angell orphan of Samuel Angell decd where Capt William Montague intends to build a water grist mill, and also to diligently view and examine what damage the building the said mill will be to any person or persons in the said county by laying their lands under water or prejudicing their timber. We the subscribers being first sworn before James Newby substitute sheriff, and having fully viewed the aforesaid acre of land belonging to Robert Angell orphan of Samuel Angell decd and the lands belonging to the several persons adjacent on both sides of the run where the said mill is intended to be built that may be affected or layed under water by building such mill, are of opinion that there be paid to Robert Angell orphan of Samuel Angell decd eighty two pounds current money of Virginia, also to Mary Robinson fifteen pounds of like money, also to Richard

Ball forty pounds of like money... [Wit:] Benja George, John Selden, Nicho
George, John Miller, Coleman Dogget, James Carter, John Bailey, John
Goodridge, Wm Sydnor, John Longwith, Fortunatus Sydnor, & Ozwald Newby.
Recorded 20 Aug 1778 by Test Thos Shearman CLC. [Page 192a]

17 Sep 1778. Deed of Bargain and Sale with Receipt. ...Between Peter
Conway Esqr and Frances his wife of the parish of Christ Church in the county
of Lancaster and Commonwealth of Virginia of the one part and Job Carter
tavern keeper of the said parish and commonwealth of the other part... Peter
Conway and Frances his wife for and in consideration of the sum of twelve
hundred pounds, good and lawful money of Virginia to us in hand paid... [for] a
certain tract or parcel of land lying being and situate in the said parish of Christ
Church and is a part of a tract of land on which the said Conway now lives and
which descended to the said Peter Conway by the death of his father Major Peter
Conway deceased and is that part of the said land whereon the courthouse of the
said county of Lancaster now stands and the said Peter Conway and Frances his
wife by these presents... sell... unto the said Job Carter... the said tract or parcel
of land containing (by survey made the thirteenth of August of the present year)
ninety eight acres two rods and ten perches and bounded as followeth vizt
beginning at a marked oak standing in the line of this and Boatmans land from
thence running south fifty degrees east fifteen chains to a corner stake, thence
north twenty degrees east twenty three chains thirty links to a marked corner
chesnut, thence north twenty two degrees west twenty six chains thirty links to
Selden's Mill Pond thence by the said pond to a marked tree on Selden's line
and from thence south fifty five degrees west to the corner in the branch where it
strikes the beginning line... [Wit:] John Taylor, William Heale, & James
Gordon. Received 17 Sep 1778 from Mr Job Carter the sum of twelve hundred
pounds in full for the within mentioned tract of land. [same witnesses as listed
above]. Recorded 17 Sep 1778 by Test Thos Shearman CLC. [Pages 193 &
193a]

17 Sep 1778. Commission. The Commonwealth of Virginia to John Taylor,
James Gordon, and Henry Tapscott Gent Justices of Lancaster County greeting
Whereas Peter Conway and Frances his wife by their certain Indenture of
Bargain and Sale bearing date 17 Sep 1778 have sold and conveyed unto Job
Carter one tract of land containing ninety eight acres two rods and ten perches
with the appurtenances lying and being in the said county of Lancaster, and
whereas the said Frances Conway cannot conveniently travel to our county court
of Lancaster to make acknowledgment of her right in the said land therefore we
do give unto you or any two or more of you, full power to receive the
acknowledgment of her right in the lands aforesaid contained in the aforesaid
Indenture which is hereunto annexed, which the said Frances Conway shall be
willing to make before you, and we do therefore command you that you

personally go to the said Frances Conway and receive her acknowledgment of
the same and examine her privily and apart from the said Peter Conway her
husband whether she does the same freely and voluntarily without her said
husbands persuasions or threats, and whether she be willing that the same with
the annexed Deed should be recorded... [Wit:] Thomas Shearman [Lancaster
County Clerk]. Recorded 17 Sep 1778 by Test Thos Shearman CLC. [Page
193a]

17 Sep 1778. Certificate. Agreable to the within writ to us directed, we
personally went to the within mentioned Frances Conway, and examined her
privily and apart from her said husband Peter Conway, when she declared she
freely and voluntarily without the persuasions or threats of her said husband,
acknowledged her right to the land mentioned in the Indenture hereunto
annexed, and that she is willing the same be recorded... [Wit:] John Taylor &
James Gordon. Recorded 17 Sep 1778 by Test Thos Shearman CLC. [Page
193a]

17 Sep 1778. Deed of Bargain and Sale with Receipt. Between Job Carter and
Judith his wife of the county of Lancaster and Common wealth of Virginia of the
one part and James Gordon of the said county and Commonwealth of the other
part... Job Carter and Judith his wife for and in consideration of the sum of six
pounds lawful money of Virginia, which we acknowledge to have received of
the said James Gordon... [for] a certain small tract or parcel of land lying being
and situate in the said county of Lancaster and joining the lott belonging to the
said Gordon whereon are some houses commonly known by the name of Stone
houses and near the courthouse of the said county and bounded as followeth vizt
Begining at a marked red oak standing in the line of the said Job Carter and
Boatmans land thence runing south fifty degrees east four gunters chain and
eighty six links before the said Gordon's Store door to another marked red oak
upon the hillside below the store in the line of the said Carter and the said
Gordon's above mentioned lott, thence runing at right angles to a stake thence
runing north fifty degrees west four chains and eighty six links to another stake
and from thence to the begining tree including one rod thirty two perches...
These words (four chains and eighty six links) between the sixteenth and
seventeenth lines interlined before signed... [Wit:] Edwin Conway &
Fortunatus Sydnor. Received 17 Sep 1778, the sum of six pounds Virginia
money in full for the within land. [same witnesses as listed above]. Recorded 17
Sep 1778 by Test Thos Shearman CLC. [Page 194]

26 Sep 1778. Deed of Bargain and Sale with Receipt. ...in the third year of the
Commonwealth of Virginia... Between Thomas Rouand of the county of
Lancaster & Mary his wife of the one part and Thaddeus McCarty of the county
of Richmond of the other part... Thomas Rouand and Mary his wife for and in

consideration of the sum of fifteen hundred pounds current money of Virginia in hand paid at or before the sealing and delivery of these presents... forever all that tract or parcel of land whereon the said Thomas Rouand now dwelleth and which the said Thomas Rouand purchased of Richard Edwards late of Lancaster County Gent situate lying and being in Fleets Bay Neck in the said county of Lancaster and is bounded as followeth, Begining at a marked pine tree (said to be the begining ...? upon Hathaway's Creek and runing thence down the meanders of the said creek to the mouth of Ivans [?] Bay thence along and up the meanders of the said bay to a point that makes Keets [?] Bay thence down Fleets Bay to the great bay of Chesapeak thence up the said bay to a point that makes the mouth of Indian Creek thence up the meanders of the said creek to a marked corner pine between the said land and the land of Mr James Brent thence 59 degrees west to the begining containing by estimation two hundred acres... [Wit:] William Yerby, Richd E Lee, Richard Hall, & John Fleet. Received the day of the date of the within Indenture the consideration money of Thaddeus McCarty being fifteen hundred pounds. [Wit:] Test Edwin Conway & Robt Brown. Recorded 15 Oct 1778 by Test Thads McCarty CLC [Pages 194a, 195, & 195a]

25 Sep 1778. Commission. The Commonwealth to John Fleet William Yerby and Thomas Lawson Gent Greeting whereas Thomas Rouand and Mary his wife by their certain Indenture of Bargain and Sale bearing date 26 Sep 1778 have sold and conveyed unto Thaddeus McCarty on tract of land containing two hundred acres more or less with the appurtenances lying and being in the county of Lancaster and whereas the said Mary Rouand wife of the said Thomas Rouand cannot conveniently travel to our county court of Lancaster to make adknowledgment and relinquishment of her right in the said land therefore we do give unto you or any two or more of you full power to receive the acknowledgment which the said Mary shall be willing to make before you of her right in the land aforesaid contained in the aforesaid Indenture which is hereunto annexed and we do therefore command you that you personally go to the said Mary and receive her acknowledgment and relinquishment of the same and examine her privily and apart from the said Thomas Rouand her husband whether she does the same freely and voluntarily without his persuasions or threats and whether she be willing that the same should be recorded in our county court of Lancaster... witness Thomas Shearman clerk of our said court... Recorded 15 Oct 1778 by Test Thads McCarty CLC [Pages 195 & 195a]

26 Sep 1778. Certificate. By virtue of the written Commission to us directed we this day examined Mrs Mary Rouand wife of the above mentioned Thomas Rouand and she the said Mary Rouand did freely and voluntarily acknowledge the said Indenture hereunto annexed to Thaddeus McCarty and declared she did the same without the persuasions or threats of her said husband and that she be

willing the same should be recorded... [Wit:] John Fleet & William Yerby.
Recorded 15 Oct 1778 by Test Thads McCarty CLC [Page 195a]

15 Oct 1778. Deed of Bargain and Sale with Receipt. Between William
Schofield Senior and Betty his wife of the parish of Christ Church in the county
of Lancaster and the Commonwealth of Virginia of the one part and William
Schofield Junior of the same parish, county and commonwealth of the other
part... William Schofield Senior and Betty his wife for and in consideration of
the sum of two hundred pounds good and lawful money of Virginia which we
acknowledge to have received of the said William Schofield Junior and
ourselves to be fully satisfied and paid hath given... unto the said William
Schofield Junior... a certain tract or parcel of land lying being and situate on the
eastern side of Corotomon River and in the said county of Lancaster and is part
of a tract of land which descended to the said William Schofield Senior by the
death of his father and the said land is bounded as followeth viz Begining at a
marked sassafrass standing near a cove called Yerby's Cove in the line between
this land and the land of John Yerby deceased thence along the said line to a
marked corner pine tree standing in the main road thence making a new line and
runing (between this land now sold and a part of afore mentioned tract which the
said William Schofield Senior reserves and still keeps) to a marked wild cherry
tree thence to a marked pine thence down a valley to a marked red oak upon
Taffs Creek thence runing down the said creek to James Fendla's line thence
along the said Fendla's line to the main creek called the Eastern Branch thence
along the main shore to the cove first mentioned and so to the begining tree
containing by estimation one hundred acres be the same more or less saving and
reserving to the said William Schofield Senior a half acre of land where the
grave yard is... [Wit:] James Gordon, Bailie George, & Thos Shearman.
Received 15 Oct 1778 from William Schofield Junior the sum of two hundred
pounds Virginia money in full for the within-[Wit:] Thos Shearman & Bailie
George. Recorded 15 Oct 1778 by Test Thads McCarty CLC. [Pages 195a,
196, & 196a]

1 Apr 1778. Bill of Sale. Know all men by these presents that I Thomas Cottrel
of the county of Lancaster and parish of Christ Church have bargained sold and
delivered unto Michael Wilder of the said county and parish one bay horse one
saddle and bridle & for the valuable consideration of twenty one pounds
nineteen shillings current money to me in hand paid the receipt I do hereby
acknowledge and my self to be fully satisfied and paid for aforesaid... [Wit:]
Test Bailie George. Recorded 15 Oct 1778 by Test Thads McCarty CLC. [Page
196a]

2 Nov 1778. Deed of Bargain and Sale with Receipt. ...between Richard Locke
and Winnifred his wife of the parish of Wicomico and county of Lancaster of the

one part and Stephen Locke of the said parish and county of Northumberland of the other part... Richard Locke and Winnifred his wife for and in consideration of the sum of three hundred pounds current money of Virginia to him the said Richard Locke in hand paid or secured to be paid by the said Stephen Locke... [for] one hundred acres of land situate lying and being in the parish of Wicomico in the county of Lancaster part of the tract of land William Sanders now lives on and bounded as followeth (vizt) Begining at a stake inclosed with four small[?] saplings marked in the line of Mr Tapscotts and runing along the said line south five degrees west 136 ½ poles to the line of Edward Sanders thence along the said line north seventy four degrees west 140 poles thence along two other lines of the said Edward Sanders's land north six degrees east 64 poles and north twenty degrees west 33 poles thence north eighty nine degrees east 151 poles dividing this from the aforesaid William Sanders's land to the place it began. Containing one hundred acres of land... [Wit:] J. Eusstace, Edwin Conway, William Brown, John Bean, & Craven Everitt. Memorandum that quiet and peaceable possession and seizen was this day delivered of the within granted land and premises by the within named Richard Locke unto the within named Stephen Locke by the delivery of Turf and Twig... [same witnesses as listed above]. Received 2 Nov 1778 of the within named Stephen Locke three hundred pounds being the full consideration money within mentioned to be paid to me I say received by me Richard Locke. [same witnesses as listed above]. Recorded 19 Nov 1778 by Test Thads McCarty CLC. [Pages 196a, 197, & 197a]

17 Dec 1778. Deed of Bargain and Sale with Receipt. ...in the third year of the Commonwealth Elmore Doggett of Lancaster County and Christ Church Parish of the one part and Rawleigh Hazard of the same parish and county of the other part... Elmore Doggett for and in consideration of the sum of thirty pounds current money of Virginia to him in hand paid by the said Rawleigh Hazard... [for] a certain piece or parcel of land situate lying and being in the parish and county aforesaid containing three acres more or less bounded as follows, Begining at a chestnut tree that divides the said land from Mr Thos Pollards lott at Kilmarnock and runing down the county road to a small dogwood tree and from thence straight across to a small pissimmon that stands on the side of the Church Road and up the said road to the line that divides the said land from the said Hazards at Kilmarnock that he purchased of Mr Thos Pollard & thence straight across to the begining... [Wit:] Test Michael Wilder, David Garland, & John Sebree. 17 Dec 1778 Delivery and Seisen was this day made and acknowledged by the within named Elmore Doggett to the within named Rawleigh Hazard for the within mentioned tract of land and premises by the delivery of Turf and Twig... [same witnesses as listed above]. 17 Dec 1778 Received of the within mentioned Rawleigh Hazard the sum of thirty pounds current money it being the sum mentioned in this Indenture I say received by me-Elmore Doggett. Recorded 17 Dec 1778 by Test Thads McCarty CLC.

150

[Pages 198 & 198a]

17 Dec 1778. Report. In obedience to an order of Lancaster Court... we the
subscribers did go to the Clerk's office of the said county lately kept by Mr
Thomas Shearman where we found all the papers and books in good order and
that the records were completed as far up as October court 1778 and that the said
papers and books were in our presence delivered by Mrs. Shearman Widow of
Mr Thomas Shearman to Col Thaddeus McCarty the present clerk given under
our hands 7 Jan 1779. [Wit:] John Berryman & William Yerby. Recorded 10
Feb 1779 by Test Thads McCarty CLC. [Page 198a]

13 Jan 1779. Deed of Bargain and Sale with Receipt. In the third year of the
Commonwealth... between Richard Hall and Mary his wife of the parish of
Wiccomico in the county of Northumberland of the one part and Peter Conway
of the parish of Christ Church of the county of Lancaster of the other part...
Richard Hall and Mary his wife for and in consideration of the sum of ten
thousand pounds current money of Virginia to him... in hand paid by the said
Peter Conway at and before the sealing and delivery of these presents... forever
all that plantation tract or parcel of land situate lying and being in the parish of
Christ Church and county of Lancaster whereon the said Richard Hall lately
lived being that plantation whereon Thomas Lee father of the said Mary
formerly lived adjoining the lands of Epaphroditus Lawson, George Currell,
James Currell, William Griggs, Rawleigh Shearman, and George Shelly
containing by estimation seven hundred acres be the same more or less including
the whole of the lands that were given or descended or came to the said Mary
from her said father Thomas Lee and her brother George Lee deceased... and
lastly the said Richard Hall and Mary his wife have made... and by these
presents do make ordain... Richard Evers Lee their true and lawful attorney for
them and in their name... [Wit:] James Gordon, Henry Tapscott, Edwin
Conway, James Tapscott, & Elizabeth Tapscott. Received 13 Jan 1779 of the
within named Peter Conway ten thousand pounds lawfull money of Virginia
being the full consideration money within mentioned to be paid to me I say
received by me Richard Hall. [Wit:] James Gordon, Henry Tapscott, Edwin
Conway, & James Tapscott. Recorded 18 Feb 1779 by Test Thads McCarty
CLC. [Pages 199, 199a, 200, 200a, & 201]

21 Jan 1779. Commission. The Commonwealth of Virginia to Richard
Mitchell, Henry Tapscott, and James Gordon Gent Justices greeting whereas
Richard Hall and Mary his wife by this Indenture Deed hereunto annexed have
bargained and sold unto Peter Conway a certain tract or parcel of land in this
county of Lancaster containing seven hundred acres be the same more or less
now have ye that we are trusting to your fidelity and circumspection in
examining the said Mary as we are informed that she cannot conveniently travel

to our county court of Lancaster we command you or any two or more of you that you personally go to the said Mary and her privily and apart from her said husband examine and inquire whether she doth acknowledge the said Deed freely and voluntarily without the threats or persuasions of her said husband... such acknowledgment in the premises as she shall be willing to make... witness Thad McCarty Clerk of our said county... Recorded 18 Feb 1779 by Test Thads McCarty CLC. [Pages 200 & 200a]

28 Jan 1779. Certificate. Agreeable to the within writ to us we this day went personally to Mrs Mary Hall and examined her privily and apart from her husband the within mentioned Richard Hall where she declared she was willing the Indenture hereto annexed should be recorded in the county court of Lancaster and that she consented to the same without the threats or persuasions of her said husband... [Wit:] Henry Tapscott and James Gordon. Recorded 18 Feb 1779 by Test Thads McCarty CLC. [Page 200a]

13 Jan 1779. Bond. Know all men by these presents that I Richard Hall am held and firmly bound unto Peter Conway in the just and full sum of twenty thousand pounds lawfull money of Virginia to be paid to the said Peter Conway... To which payment well and truly to be made and done... The condition of the above obligation is such that if the above bound Richard Hall and Mary his wife... shall in all things well and truly observe preform fulfill and keep all and singular the covenants... whatsoever on the part and behalf of the said Richard Hall and Mary his wife... are or ought to be observed... in a certain Deed of Indenture bearing even date with the above written obligation... [Wit:] Edwin Conway and James Tapscott. Recorded 18 Feb 1779 by Test Thads McCarty CLC. [Pages 200a & 201]

20 May 1777. Commission. The Commonwealth of Virginia To John Chinn and James Ball Junr Gent. Whereas James Blackerby and Ann his wife by their certain Indenture of Bargain and Sale bearing date 11 Nov 1777 have sold and conveyed to Henry Tapscott one tract of land containing twenty one and a half acres more or less with the appurtenances lying and being in Lancaster County and whereas the said Ann cannot conveniently travel to county court of Lancaster to make her acknowledgment of her right in the said land therefore we do give unto you or any two or more of you full power to receive the acknowledgment which the said Ann shall be willing to make before you of her right in the land aforesaid contained in the aforesaid Indenture which is hereunto annexed and we do therefore command you that you personally go to the said Ann and receive her acknowledgment of the same and examine her privily and apart from James Blackerby her said husband whether she does the same freely and voluntarily without the persuasions or threats of her said husband and whether she be willing the same should be recorded in our county court of

152

Lancaster... [Wit:] Thos Shearman. [Page 201]

14 Oct 1778. Certificate. By virtue of the written Commission to us directed, we the subscribers having examined the within named Ann Blackerby privately and apart from her husband the within named James Blackerby do hereby certify that the said Ann Blackerby doth freely and voluntarily without the threats or persuasions of her said husband acknowledge her right to the land and premises contained in a Deed of Bargain and Sale from the said James Blackerby & Ann his wife to Henry Tapscott Gent which is hereunto annexed and that she is willing the same should be recorded in the county court of Lancaster... [Wit:] James Chinn & James Ball Junr. Recorded 18 Feb 1779 by Test Thads McCarty CLC. [Pages 201 & 201a]

21 Jan 1779. Deed of Feoffment with Receipt. Between Thomas Dunaway and Susannah his wife of the parish of Christ Church and county of Lancaster and Edwin Gaskins and Sarah his wife of the parish of Wiccomoco in the county of Northumberland of the one part and William Doggett of the parish of Christ Church in the county of Lancaster of the other part... Thomas Dunaway and Susannah his wife and the said Edwin Gaskins and Sarah his wife for and in consideration of the sum of three hundred pounds current money of Virginia... in hand well and truly paid by the said William Doggett before the sealing and delivery of these presents the receipt whereof is hereby confessed by the said Thomas Dunaway and Edwin Gaskins and for divers other good causes and considerations them thereunto moving... have given... unto the said William Doggett... all that plantation tract or parcel of land situate lying and being in the parish of Christ Church and county of Lancaster which Gabriel Thatcher by his Deed bearing date on or about 14 Feb 1704 sold and conveyed unto James Kirk and was afterwards to writ on or about 11 Apr 1738 sold and conveyed by James Kirk son of the aforementioned James Kirk to John Fendley from whom the said land descended and came to his son John Fendley deceased from whom the said land descended and came to his two daughters the aforesaid Susannah and Sarah parties to these presents bounded as followeth begining at a chestnutt standing at the mouth of a small branch of Hutchings's Creek thence runing up to the head of a valley to a marked red oak thence across the neck to a red oak standing at the head of a branch runing out of Thatchers's Mill Pond and down that branch to a marked white oak standing at the said branch from thence to the said Hutchings's Creek and afterwards down the said creek to the begining containing by estimation eighty acres... [Wit:] William Kirk, William Brent, & Jonathan Pullen. Received 21 Jan 1779 of the within named William Doggett the sum of three hundred pounds current money of Virginia being the full consideration money within mentioned to be paid to us I say received by us Thomas Dunaway and Edwin Gaskins. [same witnesses as listed above]. Be it remembered that this 21 Jan 1779 full quiet and peaceable possession and seisin

of the plantation and premises in this Deed mentioned and contained was taken
and had by the within named Thomas Dunaway and Edwin Gaskins and by them
in like manner given and delivered unto the within named William Doggett by
the delivery of Turf and Twig... [same witnesses as listed above]. Recorded 18
Feb 1779 by Test Thads McCarty CLC. [Pages 201a, 202, 202a, 203, & 203a]

21 Jan 1779. Bond. Know all men by these presents that Thomas Dunaway of
the county of Lancaster am held and firmly bound unto William Doggett of the
same county in the just and full sum of four hundred pounds lawfull money of
Virginia to be paid to the said William Doggett... The condition of the above
obligation is such that if the above bound Thomas Dunaway... shall in all things
well and truly observe... all and singular the covenants... whatsoever which on
the part and behalf of the said Thomas Dunaway and Susannah his wife... are or
ought to be observed... in a certain Indenture of Feofment bearing even date
with the above obligation... [Wit:] William Kirk, Willam Brent, & Jonathan
Pullen. Recorded 18 Feb 1779 by Test Thads McCarty CLC. [Page 203]

21 Jan 1779. Bond. Know all men by these presents that I Edward Gaskins of
the county of Northumberland am held and firmly bound unto William Doggett
of Lancaster County in the just and full sum of four hundred pounds lawfull
money of Virginia to be paid to the said William Doggett... To which payment
well and truly to be made and done I bind myself... firmly by these presents...
The condition of the above obligation is such that if the above bound Edward
Gaskins... shall in all things well and truly observe... all and singular the
covenants... whatsoever which on the part and behalf of the said Edward
Gaskins and Sarah his wife... are or ought to be observed... in a certain
Indenture of Feoffment bearing even date with the above obligation... [Wit:]
William Kirk, William Brent, & Jonathan Pullen. Recorded 18 Feb 1779 by Test
Thads McCarty CLC. [Page 203a]

18 Feb 1779. Deed of Gift. ...third year of the Commonwealth of Virginia
between Ann Shearman of Christ Church Parish and county of Lancaster of the
one part and Joseph Shearman of the parish and county aforesaid of the other
part... Ann Shearman for and in consideration of the natural love and affection
which she hath her son the above named Joseph Shearman and for and towards
his future support doth give and grant unto her said son Joseph Shearman... all
that tract or parcel of land lying and being in the parish and county aforesaid
whereon the said Ann now lives containing by estimation two hundred acres...
being bounded by the lands of CL James Ball Henry Tapscott Thomas Stott
Richard Mitchell and William Stott... [Wit:] Richard Mitchell, Thomas Stott, &
Elizabeth Shearman. Recorded 18 Feb 1779 proved by oaths of Richard
Mitchell and Thomas Stott... and ordered to lie for further proof by Test Thads
McCarty CLC. [Pages 203a & 204]

24 Feb 1779. Report. In obedience to an order of Lancaster county court in November last we the subscribers freeholders in the said county having been summoned by James Newby Deputy Sheriff... on and at the place where Fortunatus Sydnor proposes to build his water grist mill, did accordingly meet on the place showed to us by the said Sydnor on his land and have viewed & valued one acre of land on the other side of Thomas Schofield decd and value the same twenty shillings, We also value the damages that the low ground or swamp of the said Schofield will sustain by the water of the said Mill Pond to twelve pounds. We also value the low ground or swamp of the orphans of William King decd that will be suffered by the pond of the said millto thirty pounds, and we also value the low ground and swamp of William Brown that will be injured and overflowed to one hundred and fifty pounds lawfull money of Virginia... [Wit:] Thomas Garner, Henry M. Horne, Job Carter, William Schofield, John Miller, James Carter, Benjamin George, Edney Tapscott, John Bean, Joseph Sullivan, Joshua Hubbard, & Samuel Yop. Recorded 18 Mar 1779 by Test Thads McCarty CLC. [Pages 204 & 204a]

3 Mar 1779. Report. In obedience to an order of Lancaster County court bearing date February court 1779. We the subscribers being summoned by James Newby to meet on the land whereon John Clayton proposes to build a water grist mill did accordingly meet on the same this 3 Mar 1779, and being first sworn before the sheriff did diligently examine the lands adjacent thereto on both sides of the run that we think will be affected or laid under water by the said Clayton building the said mill and do find that Edney Tapscott will thereby sustain damages to the amount of one hundred and twenty five pounds for his land and timber that the pond of the sd proposed mill will overflow... [Wit:] John Yerby, Joshua Hubbard, Elias Edmonds, William Doggett, James Carter, Thos Garner, Benjamin George, Samuel Yop, John Bean, Fortunatus Sydnor, Joseph Sullivan, & John Miller. Recorded 18 Mar 1779. [Page 204a]

17 Mar 1779. Report. In obedience to an order of the worshipfull court of Lancaster. We the subscribs have viewed the road altered by Andw Robertson and find it sufficient and the difference in distance sixty five yards... [Wit:] John McTyer, Johnson Riveer, Thomas Flint, & Ozwald Newby. Recorded 18 Mar 1779 by Test Thads McCarty CLC. [Page 205]

8 Feb 1779. Deed of Bargain and Sale with Receipt. Between Edwin Conway and Sarah Conway his wife of the parish of Christ Church in the county of Lancaster of the one part and Charles Bell of the same parish and county aforesaid of the other part... Edwin Conway and Sarah Conway his wife for and in consideration of the sum of seven hundred and fifty pounds current money of Virginia to the said Edwin Conway in hand well and truly paid by the said Charles Bell at and before the sealing and delivery of these presents... [for] all

that plantation tract or parcel of land situate lying and being in the parish of Christ Church and county of Lancaster whereon the said Charles Bell now lives and which was sold and conveyed unto the said Edwin Conway by Elisha Hall by his Deed bearing date on or about 14 Jun 1777. Containing by estimation three hundred and ninety five acres... [Wit:] Martha McAdam, Walker Conway, & William Brown. Received 8 Feb 1779 of the within named Charles Bell seven hundred and fifty pounds being the full consideration money within mentioned to be paid to me I say received by me Edwin Conway. [same witnesses as listed above]. Recorded 18 Mar 1779 by Test Thads McCarty. [Pages 205, 205a, & 206]

15 Mar 1779. Deed with Receipt. Between Edwin Conway Gent and Sarah Conway his wife of the parish of Christ Church and the county of Lancaster of the one part and John Cundiff of the parish of Wiccomicco in the county aforesaid of the other part... Edwin Conway and Sarah Conway his wife for and in consideration of the sum of two hundred and twelve pounds sixteen shillings and three pence current money of Virginia to the said Edwin Conway in hand well and truly paid by the said John Cundiff at and before the sealing and delivery of these presents... [for] all that plantation tract or parcel of land whereon the said John Cundiff now liveth situate lying and being in the county of Lancaster bounded as follows begining at a bunch of marked chestnutts a corner to this land that of Hannah Owens William Yop and the lands of the sd Edwin Conway thence runing S10 W210 Po. By marked trees up to the road leading from Carters Mill to Lancaster Court House thence along the sd road N60 W 60 Po. To a stake standing in a bottom by the road side, thence down the said bottom and runing to a point in the swamp where two runs meet, thence N65 E10 Po. To a marked tree between this of Wm Schofields land, thence N55 E by marked trees to the main road thence down the sd road to a corner of Wm Hubbards, thence N272 E 145 Po. To a corner red oak on ...? branch side, thence up the said branch to the begining containing two hundred and fifty acres... Received 15 Mar AD 1779 of the within named John Cundiff two hundred and twelve pounds sixteen shillings and three pence current money of Virginia being the full consideration money within mentioned to be paid to me I say received by me Edwin Conway. [Wit:] William Brown, John Bean, & William Yop. Recorded 18 Mar 1779 by Test Thads McCarty CLC. [Pages 206, 206a, 207]

9 Mar 1779. Certificate of Election of Commissioners. We John Taylor sheriff of the said county [Lancaster] & James Ball & James Gordon two senior Justices present at an election of commissioners of the tax for the said county this day held at the court house... do hereby certify that James Ball, James Gordon, & Edwin Conway serve then and there duely elected to that office [Wit:] John Taylor, James Ball, & James Gordon. Recorded 15 Apr 1779 by Test Thads

McCarty CLC. [Page 207]

Mar 1779. Report. In obedience to an order of Lancaster court... we the
subscribers have met, and viewed the road petitioned for, and find that there may
be full as good a road maid and the distance not more than sixty yards diference
in turning the said road and will save the said Bushrod Riveer about two or three
thousand rails... [Wit:] Henry Lawson, Thos. Carter, & Wm. Hathaway.
Recorded 15 Apr 1779 by Test Thads McCarty CLC. [Pages 207 & 207a]

16 Mar 1779. Deed of Gift. Robert Chinn of the parish of Christ Church and
county of Lancaster for and in consideration of the natural love and affection
which he hath and beareth unto his five daughters, Sarah Chinn, Elizabeth
Chinn, Susannah Chinn, Mary Chinn of Ann Mitchell Chinn and his son Robert
Chinn and for and towards their future support and maintenance and in order to
encourage the friends and relations of my above mentioned five daughters and
my son aforesaid to aid and assist me in bringing up my aforesaid children, have
given and granted unto my aforesaid daughters... and aforesaid son... the
following negroes with their future increase vizt my negro woman Delilah my
negro boy Dick, my negro boy Allen, my negro girl Mary, my negro girl Nell
my negro girl Nanny, and my negro girl Sarah with their future increase to my
above mentioned children and their heirs to be equally divided among them... as
they arrive to age twenty one or marries or at my death as the case may happen,
reserving to myself the use off in and to the above mentioned negroes and their
future increase for and during my natural life and no longer... [Wit:] William
Brumley, Griffin Fauntleroy, & Ricd Mitchell. Recorded 15 Apr 1779 by Test
Thads McCarty CLC. [Pages 207a & 208]

2 Apr 1779. Deed of Gift. ... I William Chilton of the parish of Christ Church
and county of Lancaster do send greeting... for and in consideration of the love
good will & effection which I have and do bear to my grandson William Chilton
late of the county of Culpepper, but now of the county of Lancaster and parish
aforesaid have given... my negro girl Rachel, who (before signing of these
presents) I have delivered to my said grandson William Chilton... [Wit:] Matt
Myars & Gavin Lowry. Recorded 18 Apr 1779 by Test Thads McCarty CLC.
[Page 208]

15 May 1779. Deed of Gift. ...between Richard Ball of the county of Lancaster
Gent of the one part and James Wallace Ball son of heir at law of the said
Richard Ball of the other part, Whereas there is a marriage shortly intended to be
solemnized between the said James Wallace Ball and Anne the daughter James
Ball Gent...Richard Ball for and in consideration of the natural love and
affection which he hath for his said son & for his and the said Anne's future
support and maintenance and for divers other good causes and considerations,

hath given... all that tract or parcel of land whereon the said Richard Ball now dwelleth containing by estimation four hundred acres be it more or less, also all that tract or parcel of land whereon Mrs Margaret Ball, mother of said Richard Ball now dwelleth, containing by estimation two hundred and seventy acres... also the following negro slaves, to wit, Pluto, Peter, Syphase[?], Joe, Daniel, Arguile, Tom, Cupid, Corinna, Zilpha, Sukey, Milly, Nelly & Peg, and their future increase of the said females, also one moity of all the stocks of all kinds of moveables now the property of the said Richard Ball... in manner following, that is to say, one moiety of the said tract of land & premises of four hundred acres from the date of these presents & the other moiety thereof at the death of the said Richard Ball, and the other tract of land & premises whereon the said Margaret Ball now dwelleth at the death of the said Margaret, and the said slaves, stocks of moveables from the date of these presents provided nonetheless, it is hereby agreed... that if the said Richard shall survive the said Margaret, he shall or may then possess occupy & enjoy the said tract of land & premises whereon the said Margaret now dwelleth during his natural life, in lieu of his moiety of the tract whereon he now dwelleth, and that if the said Anne shall survive the said James Wallace Ball in the lifetime of the said Richard & Margaret, or either of them, that she shall or may possess occupy & enjoy her dower of both the sd tracts or parcels of land & premises with their appurtenances during her natural life... [Wit:] John Smither, John Boyd, & Richard Cundiff. Memorandum that quiet and peaceable possession of Livery of Seisen was had & given by the within named Richard Ball unto the within named James Wallace Ball, by delivery of Turf & Twig of the tract of four hundred acres of land within mentioned & delivery of Syphase one of the within mentioned negros in name of the whole within mentioned lands & slaves & moveables... [same witnesses as listed above]. Recorded 15 Jul 1779 by Test Thads McCarty. [Pages 208, 208a, & 209]

19 Nov 1778. Deed of Bargain and Sale. Between John Hathaway (one of the sons of William Hathaway of the parish of Christ Church and county of Lancaster) and Sarah his wife of the parish of Leeds and the county of Fauquier, James Hathaway another of the sons of the above said William Hathaway and Ivanna his wife of the parish and county last mentioned, Thomas Hathaway another of th sons of the said William Hathaway deceased and Elizabeth his wife Zachariah Linton and Mary his wife one of the daughters of the aforesaid William Hathaway & Isaac Currell and Dolly his wife another of the daughters of the aforesaid William Hathaway of the one part and Lawson Hathaway of the parish of Christ Church and county of Lancaster aforesaid of the other part. Whereas the aforesaid William Hathaway by his last Will in writing duly made and published by him in his lifetime gave & bequeathed to his son the aforesaid Lawson Hathaway his plantation and tract of land the said William Hathaway bought of Andrew Donaldson called by the name of Andrews and the aforesaid

William Hathaway by his said Will declared his Will and device to be... that the remainder of his estate should be equally divided between his sons and daughters the aforesaid John Hathaway, James Hathaway, Thomas Hathaway Mary Hathaway Lawson Hathaway and Dolly Hathaway... the said Lawson Hathaway is and standeth seized for the term of his natural life of and in the aforesd plantation and tract of land... John Hathaway and Sarah his wife, James Hathaway and Ivanna his wife, Thomas Hathaway and Elizabeth his wife Zachariah Linton and Mary his wife Isaac Currell and Dolly his wife for and in consideration of the sum of six shillings lawful money of Virginia to them in hand paid by the said Lawson Hathaway at or before the ensealing and delivery... forever all that remainder and reversion of five six parts of all that plantation and tract of land which the aforesaid William Hathaway bought of Andrew Donaldson called by the name of Andrews with the rights members and appurtenances thereof situate lying and being in the parish of Christ Church and county of Lancaster aforesaid... [Wit:] William Kirk, Thos Hathaway, Eppa Fielding, William Lawson, & James Currell. Recorded 19 Aug 1779 by Test Thads McCarty CLC. [Pages 209, 209a, & 210]

19 Aug 1779. Deed of Bargain and Sale with Receipt. ... in the fourth year of the Commonwealth between John Payne of the county of Lancaster and Ellen his wife of the one part and Moses Lunsford of the county of Northumberland of the other part... John Payne and Ellen his wife for and in consideration of the sum of seven hundred & eighteen pounds current money of Virginia in hand paid at or before the sealing and delivery of these presents... for ever all that tract or parcel of land situate in the said county of Lancater which was devised unto the said John Payne by his father George Payne Gent deceased binding on the lands of Richard Housing Payne, Joseph Samsson, John Clutton, William Raines, and Andrew Robertson containing by estimation two hundred & thirty acres... [Wit:] John Smither, John Gibbons, & Rodham Lunsford. Received the day of the date of the within Indenture the sum of seven hundred & eighteen pounds current money in full consideration for the within granted parcel of land and premises. [same witnesses as listed above]. Recorded 19 Aug 1779 by Test Thads McCarty CLC. [Pages 210a & 211]

3 Sep 1779. Inquisition to Estate. Lancaster County to wit. Inquisition indented taken at the parish of Christ Church and county aforesaid... in the fourth year of the Commonwealth of Virginia... by the oath of Thomas Hunton Nicholas Currell William Griggs Charles Lee Rawleigh Shearman James Currell John James William Mason, William Martin, Harry Currell Fortunatus Sydnor and Thomas Lawson good and lawfull men of the county aforesaid before John Taylor Esquire sheriff of the said county by virtue of an Act of the General Assembly... that Robert Bristow Esquire of the kingdom of Great Britain if now in life and if the said Robert Bristow in dead those who claim under him by

devise... on 19 Apr 1775 an inhabitant of the kingdom of Great Britain and a
subject of the aforesaid king from the 19 Apr 1775 to the time of taking this
inquisition and also that the said Robert Bristow if alive was on 19 Apr 1775 and
if dead the person or persons who claim under the said Robert Bristow by devise
descent or purchase was seized in his or her domyne as of fee and now at the
time of taking this inquisition is so seized of and in a tract of land with
appurtenances containing by estimation one thousand acres... commonly called
Bristows Plantation and situate lying and being in the parish and county
aforesaid and also possessed of the following negroe slaves and personal estate,
vizt, Doll a woman, Nell a woman, Esther a girl, Dick a boy, George a man,
Kate a woman, George a boy, Robin a child, Stephen a man, Gabriel a man,
Nany a woman, Stephen a child, Ned a child, Jenny a child, Nan a woman, Will
a boy, Patt a child, Moses a child, Manuel a child, a negro child a boy just born
not christened, Mary a woman, James a boy, Isaac a boy, Peter a boy, Sarah a
woman, Tom a man, Milly a woman, Jack a child, Armistead a boy, Anthony a
man, Esther a woman, Patt a girl, Kitt a boy, Mary a girl, Tamar a girl, Anthony
a small boy, Ben a child, Letty a child, Esther a woman, David a man, Charles a
child, David a man, Moll a woman, Sillah a girl, Sam a child, David a child,
Doll a woman, Solomon a man and Ann Betty, ninety one head of black cattle,
eighty sheep, thirty five grown hogs, three bay mares and one gray mare, one
gray one black and one sorrel geldings, three hogsheads of tobacco in Dymers
warehouse inspected the weight not known the overseer has a right to a ninth
part of the said tobacco as his share, five narrow acres, seven broad hoes, five
narrow hoes, three grubing hoes, six ploughs fixed, an old whipsaw, an old
chest, a hand mill, and the crop of corn and tobacco now growing on the
aforesaid tract of land also two ox chains, four ox yokes furnished, two ox carts
and two pair of cart wheels... [Wit:] John Taylor, Sheriff. Recorded 16 Sep
1779 by Test Thads McCarty CLC. [Pages 211 & 211a]

21 Oct 1779. Deed of Gift. Between Elmore Doggett of the county of Lancaster
of the one part & William Dogget son of the said Elmore Dogget of the other
part... Elmore Dogget for and in consideration of the natural love and affection
which he hath for his sd son William and for other good causes and
considerations hereunto moving hath given... all that tract or parcel of land
which the said Elmore Doggett purchased of Eusstace Gent of the county of
Northumberland lying and being in the county of Lancaster, adjoining the land
whereon the said Elmore Doggett now dwelleth, containing by estimation one
hundred and forty seven acres... [Wit:] William Gibson & Rawh Hazard.
Recorded 21 Oct 1779 by Test Thads McCarty CLC. [Pages 211a & 212]

18 Aug 1779. Deed of Bargain and Sale with Receipt. Between John Eusstace
and Alice Corbin his wife of Northumberland County of the one part and Elmore
Doggett of the county of Lancaster of the other part... John Eustace and Alice

Corbin his wife for and in consideration of the sum of three hundred pounds current money to them in hand paid by the said Elmore Doggett... [for] a certain tract or parcel of land situate lying and being in the parish of Christ Church and county of Lancaster, containing one hundred forty seven and a quarter acres of land purchased by the said John Eusstace of Colo Charles Carter of the county of King George and known by the name of the brick house tract, begining by a survey of plot made by Griffin Garland dated 17 Mar 1769 begins at ...? Dicks branch thence up a small branch to a white oak corner with Richard Huthchings thence N76 E56 poles to far the road thence up the road to K [?] thence S87 W poles to a large red oak thence S66.30 W103 poles to M a large red oak thence S19.30 E106 pole to N in Dicks Branch & down the same to the begining which includes one hundred and forty seven and a quarter acres... [Wit:] Rawh Hazard, John Doggett, & William Doggett. Received 18 Aug 1779 of Elmore Doggett the sum of three hundred pounds current money it being the sum mentioned in this Indenture. [Wit:] Test Rawh Hazard & Jno Doggett. Recorded 21 Oct 1779 by Test Thads McCarty CLC. [Pages 212, 212a, & 213]

20 Oct 1779. Commission. To Thomas Lawson William Yerby & Henry Lawson Gent... Whereas John Eustace and Alice Corbin Eustace his wife by their certain Indenture of Bargain and Sale bearing date 20 Oct 1779 have sold and conveyed unto Elmore Doggett one tract or parcel of land containing 147 ¼ acres more or less with the appurtenances lying and being in the county of Lancaster and whereas Alice Corbin Eustace wife of the said John Eustace cannot conveniently travel to our said county court of Lancaster to make acknowledgment & relinquishment of her right in the said land therefore we do give unto you or any two or more of you full power to receive the acknowledgment to which the sd Alice Corbin Eustace shall be willing to make before you of her right in the land aforesaid contained in the aforementioned Indenture which is hereunto annexed & we do therefore command you that you personally go to the Alice Corbin Eustace and receive her acknowledgment of relinquishment of the same and examine her privily and apart from the said John Eustace her husband whether she does the same freely and voluntarily without the persuasions or threats of her said husband and whether she be willing the same should be recorded... [Wit:] Thads McCarty. Recorded 21 Oct 1779 by Test Thads McCarty CLC. [Pages 212a & 213]

20 Oct 1779. Certificate. By virtue of the within Commission to us directed we have examined the within named Alice Corbin Eustace apart from her husband & she doth voluntarily of her own free will acknowledge all her right title & interest of Dower to the said land & premises mentioned in the Deed hereto annexed & without the persuasion or threats of her sd husband & is willing the same shall be entered upon record... [Wit:] William Yerby & Henry Lawson. Recorded 21 Oct 1779 by Test Thads McCarty CLC. [Page 213]

21 Oct 1779. Deed of Bargain and Sale with Receipt. Between Mary Schofield of the county of Lancaster and the parish of Christ Church and colony of Virginia Planter of the one part & John Hutcherson of the county aforesaid and parish of Wiccomico Blacksmith of the other part... Mary Schofield for and in consideration of the sum of one hundred pounds current money of Virginia to her in hand paid by the said John Hutcherson before the ensealing and delivery of these presents... for ever sixty acres of land situate & lying in the aforesaid parish of Christ Church and county of Lancaster being a parcel of land containing in a Pattant from the Proprietors office bearing date 20 Oct 1696 and is all that plantation which Sarah Cotes now dwells which the aforesaid Mary Schofield in the aforesaid Pattent claims a title to and is bounded by the land of Mr John Clayton Mr William Brown & Mr Natis Sydnor... [Wit:] Henry Towles, Elijah Perciful, & William Schofield Junr. Memorandum that this day to wit 20 Oct 1779 peaceable & quiet possession & seizen of the lands and premises in the within mentioned Deed was given and delivered unto the within named John Hutcherson by the within named Mary Schofield by the delivery of Turf & Twig... [Wit:] Elijah Perciful & William Schofield Junr. Received the day of the date of the within Indenture of the within mentioned John Hutcherson the sum of one hundred pounds current money... [Wit:] Test Henry Towles, Elijah Percifull & Wm Schofield Junr. Recorded 21 Oct 1779 by Test Thads McCarty CLC. [Pages 213, 213a, & 214]

23 Sep 1779. Deed of Bargain and Sale with Receipt. Between John Berryman and Sarah his wife of the parish of Christ Church and the county of Lancaster Gent of the one part and Henry George of the aforesaid parish and county Planter of the other part... John Berryman and Sarah his wife for and in consideration of the sum of three thousand pounds to them in hand paid by the said Henry George at or before the sealing and delivery of these presents... for ever all that tract or parcel of land which the said John Berryman purchased of Thomas Rouand Gent of the county of Lancaster situate lying and being in the said county of Lancaster binding on the lands of John Meredith, John Eustace, William [Moson, Moron, Moren?] Issac George, & John Moughon in the county aforesaid containing by estimation three hundred acres... [Wit:] Thomas Lawson, Henry Lawson, & William Gibson. Received the day of the date of the within named Henry George the sum of three thousand pounds current money of Virginia in full consideration for the within granted part of land & premises. [same witnesses as listed above]. Recorded 21 Oct 1779 by Test Thads McCarty CLC. [Pages 214, 214a, 215, & 215a]

23 Sep 1779. Commission. To John Fleet Thomas Lawson & Henry Lawson Gent greeting whereas John Berryman and Sarah his wife by their certain Indenture of Bargain and Sale bearing date 23 Sep have sold and conveyed unto Henry George one tract or parcel of land contain three hundred acres more or

less with the appurtenances lying and being in the county of Lancaster &
whereas Sarah the wife of the said John Berryman cannot conveniently travel to
our county court of Lancaster to make acknowledgement and relinquishment of
her right in the said land therefore we do give you or any two or more of you full
power to receive the acknowledgment which the said Sarah shall be willing to
make before you of her right in the land aforesaid contained in the aforesaid
Indenture which is hereunto annexed and we do therefore command you or any
two or more of you that you personally go to the said Sarah & receive her
acknowledgment and relinquishment of the same & examine her privily and
apart from the said John Berryman her husband whether she does the same
freely & voluntarily without the persuations or threats of her said husband and
whether she be willing the same should be recorded... Thads McCarty.
Recorded 21 Oct 1779 by Test Thads McCarty CLC. [Page 215]

23 Sep 1779. Certificate. By virtue of the within Commission to us directed We
have examined the within named Sarah Berryman apart from her husband and
she doth voluntarily of her own free will acknowledge all her right title interest
of dower to the said land & premises mentioned in the Deed hereunto annexed
without the persuation or threats of her sd husband & is willing the same should
be entered upon record... [Wit:] Thos Lawson & Henry Lawson. Recorded 21
Oct 1779 by Test Thads McCarty CLC. [Page 215]

30 Sep 1779. Deed of Bargain and Sale with Receipt. Between George Heale
of the county of Fauquier & Commonwealth of Virginia Gent & Sarah his wife
of the one part and William Warren of the same county and Commonwealth
Gent of the other part... George Heale and Sarah his wife for and in
consideration of the sum of four thousand six hundred pounds current money of
Virginia To them in hand paid by the said William Warren at and before the
sealing and delivery of these presents... for ever four certain tracts or parcels of
land containing by estimation seven hundred & fifty acres be the same more or
less situate lying and being in the parish of St Marys Wt [*White*] Chapel in
Lancaster County, one of which said tracts or parcels of land was purchased by
Ellen Heale late of Lancaster County from a certain Thomas Taylor and wife as
appears by their Deed dated 21 Jan 1706 which said Deed is recorded among the
records of said Lancaster County relation... and is bounded as followeth
Beginning at a corner stake of Capt Richard Ball standing on a point in Theriotts
head line thence S degree V 50 pol to a branch of Foxes Mill Swamp thence
down the said branch the several courses thereof to a corner ash standing near
the mouth of the said branch by the turn being also in Therriots line, thence
down the said branch and Foxes Mill Swamp S degree NV 90 poles thence W
W 32 p thence S degree S degree W 70 p thence S degree W 37 p to a corner
white oak standing by to the side of the main swamp, Thence N degree 44 W
334 pole to a corner chestnut thence N E by N 180 pole to the first begining

stake containing five hundred acres, a second tract or parcel of land containing thirty five acres adjoining the above described five hundred acres tract was purchasesd by Geo Heale party to these presents from a Captain Thomas Lee of Lancaster County as appears by Deed recorded among the records of said county... a third tract or parcel of land was also purchased by George Heale Gent party of these presents from a certain Lyndsy Opie and Sarah his wife as appears by their Deed dated 13 Aug 1742 which Deed is recorded among the records of Lancaster County... and is bounded as followeth Beginning at a corner tree standing on the south side of the main road at Capt Jesse Ball's Mill Dam thence down the said road N degree 54 ½ E 164 pole to the land of John Kennedy and thence along the said Kennedy's land N degree 39 ½ W to a swamp that parts the land from Joseph Ball Esqr thence along the said swamp to coves & meanders to the place where it first begun containing one hundred & nine acres also a fourth tract or parcel of land was purchased by the said George Heale Gent party to these presents from a certain John Kennedy as appears by Deed dated 13 Aug 1742 which Deed is recorded among the records of Lancaster County... and is bounded as followeth Beginning at the upper corner of the land of Lyndsey Opie on the south side of the main road and runing thence along the said road N 50 E to the lower most corner of the land of Wm Davenport & Moore Fauntleroy thence N degree 53 ¾ W a long the land of the said Davenport and Fauntleroy to a swamp that parts his land from the land of Joseph Ball Esqr. Thence along to said swamp its several courses to the land of the said Lyndsy Opie & from thence along the said Opie's line to the place where it first began, containing one hundred & fourteen acres... [Wit:] Chas Chilton, Thos Carter, & A Churchill. Received 13 Sep 1779 from William Warren four thousand six hundred pounds Virginia currency being the consideration in full expressed in the within Deed... [Wit:] Test A Churchill & Thos Carter. Recorded 21 Oct 1779 by Test Thads McCarty CLC. [Pages 215a, 216, 216a, 217, & 217a]

7 Oct 1779. Commission. The Commonwealth of Virginia to A Churchill Chas Chilton & Thos Degges Gent Justices of Fauquier County greeting whereas George Heale & Sarah Heale by their certain Indenture of Bargain & Sale bearing date 30 Sep 1779 have sold and conveyed unto William Warren one tract or parcel of land containing seven hundred & fifty eight acres of land with appurtenances lying and being in the said county of Lancaster and whereas the said Sarah Heale cannot conveniently travel to our county court of Lancaster to make acknowledgment of her right in the said lands there fore we do give unto you or any two or more of you full power to receive the acknowledgment of her right in the lands aforesaid contained in the aforesaid Indenture which whereunto annexed which the said Sarah Heale shall be willing to make before you... therefore command you that you personally go to the sd Sarah Heale & receive her acknowledgment of the same & examine her privily & apart from the said

164

George Heale her husband whether she does the same freely & voluntarily
without her said husbands persuations or threats & whether she be willing that
the same with the annexed Deed should be recorded... Thads McCarty.
Recorded 21 Oct 1779 by Test Thads McCarty CLC. [Pages 217 & 217a]

7 Oct 1779. Certificate. In obedience to the within order we have examined
Mrs Sarah Heale apart from the said George Heale and find her very willing to
relinquish her right of dower in the said lands... [Wit:] A Churchill & Charles
Chilton. [Page 217a]

9 Oct 1779. Between Spencer Hinton of the county of Lancaster of the one part
and Thomas Lawson of the same county of the other part... Spencer Hinton for
and in consideration of the sum of one hundred pounds current money of
Virginia in hand paid at or before the sealing & delivery of these presents...
grant bargain... unto said Thomas Lawson... forever all that tract or parcel of
land situate lying and being on Musqueto Creek in the county of Lancaster &
bounded as followeth beginning at a pine tree on the side of the said creek
adjoining the land of William Boatman & runing along the said Boatmans line to
a corner that divides this land from the land of Thomas Hunton thence runing
along the said Huntons line to a corner stone thence from the said stone to the
north head branch of Musquito Creek in a straight line & so down the meanders
of the said creek containing one hundred acres... [Wit:] John Parrott, Rawl
Hazard, & Henry Fleet. Received the day of the date of the within Indenture of
the within named Thomas Lawson one hundred & seventy pounds current
money of Virginia in full consideration for the within mentioned granted parcel
of land and premises... [same witnesses as listed above]. Recorded 21 Oct 1779
by Test Thads McCarty CLC. [Pages 217a, 218, & 218a]

18 Oct 1779. Deed of Bargain and Sale with Receipt. Between Thomas Lawson
& Lettice his wife of the county of Lancaster of the one part and William
Lawson of the same county of the other part... Thomas Lawson & Lettice his
wife for and in consideration of the sum of one hundred & eighty pounds current
money of Virginia in hand paid at or before the sealing & delivery of these
presents... unto the said William Lawson... for ever all that tract or parcel of
land situate lying and being on Mosquito Creek in the county of Lancaster and is
bounded as followeth Beginning at a pine tree on the side of the said creek
adjoining the land of William Boatman and runing along the said Boatmans line
to a corner that divides this land from the land of Thomas Hunton thence runing
along the said Huntons line to a corner stone thence from the said stone to the
north head branch of Mosquito Creek in a straight line and so down the
meanders of the said creek containing one hundred acres... [Wit:] John
Berryman, Henry Lawson, & Nicholas Currell Junr. Received the day of the
date of the within Indenture of the within named William Lawson the sum of

one hundred & eighty pounds current money of Virginia in full consideration for the within mentioned granted parcel of land and premises. [same witnesses as listed above]. Recorded 21 Oct 1779 by Test Thads McCarty CLC. [Pages 218a, 219, 219a, 220, & 220a]

17 Oct 1779. Commission. The Common Wealth of Virginia to John Berryman William Yerby Henry Lawson & John Fleet Gent Justices, whereas Thomas Lawson & Lettice his wife by their certain Indenture of Bargain and Sale bearing date 18 Oct sold and conveyed unto William Lawson one tract or parcel of land containing 100 acres more or less with the appurtenances lying and being in the county of Lancaster and whereas Lettice wife of the aforesaid Thomas Lawson cannot conveniently travel to our said court to make her acknowledgment & relinquishment of her right in the land aforesaid therefore we do give unto you or any two or more of you full power to receive the acknowledgment which they said Lettice shall be willing to make before you of the land aforesaid contained in the aforesaid Indenture which is hereunto annexed and we do therefore command you that you personally go to the said Lettice and receive her acknowledgment and relinquishment of the same and examine her privily and apart from the said Thomas her husband whether she doth the same freely and voluntarily without the persuations or threats of her said husband and whether she be willing the same should be recorded... witness Thads McCarty. Recorded 21 Oct 1779 by Test Thads McCarty CLC. [Page 220]

18 Oct 1779. Certificate. By virtue of the within Commission to us directed we have examined the within named Lettice Lawson apart from her husband and she doth voluntarily of her own free will acknowlege all her right title & interest of dower to the said land and premises mentioned in the Deed hereunto annexed without the persuations or threats of her said husband and is willing the same should be entered upon record... [Wit:] John Berryman & Henry Lawson. Recorded 21 Oct 1779 by Test Thads McCarty CLC. [Page 220]

22 Oct 1779. Between James Tapscott of the county of Lancaster Merchant and Elizabeth his wife of the one part & William Sydnor of the same county Gent of the other part... James Tapscott and Elizabeth his wife for and in consideration of the sum of two thousand two hundred pounds current money in hand paid at or before the sealing & delivery of these presents... unto the said William Sydnor... all that tract or parcel of land situate in the county of Lancaster which John Stott grandfather of the said James Tapscott purchased of William Sammon and Catharine his wife and devised the same to his said grandson and is bounded as followeth beginning at the bogs at the head line of Colo Corbin Griffin's land and runing along the said line to Colo James Ball's land thence from sd land by William Stotts & said Sydnors line to the beginning containing one hundred & six acres... [no witnesses listed]. Received the day of the date of the within

166

Indenture of the within named William Sydnor the sum of two thousand two
hundred pounds current money in full consideration for the within mentioned
parcel of land and premises. [no witnesses listed]. Recorded 21 Oct 1779 by
Test Thads McCarty CLC. [Pages 220a & 221]

19 May 1779. Deed of Bargain and Sale with Receipt. Between William
Montague and Lucy his wife of Lancaster County of the one part and Revd John
Leland of Northumberland County of the other part... for and in consideration of
the sum of eleven hundred & sixty six pounds thirteen shillings and four pence
current money of Virginia to him the said William Montague in hand paid by the
said John Leland a certain parcel or piece of land situate lying and being in the
aforesaid county of Lancaster which said parcel or piece of land is part of a tract
of land which the said William Montague purchas'd of William Graham of
Northumberland County which said tract of land formerly belonged to Mrs Anne
Taite and by her sold to Newton Keine, containing three hundred and fifty acres
to be the same more or less and is bounded by as followeth vizt Beginning at a
water fence the reputed boundary between this tract and Capt John Seldens land
formerly Capt Richard Ball's decd thence N30 degree W along a line of marked
trees to a large black oak standing by the road side that leads from Capt John
Seldens Mill to Northumberland [?] thence up the said road to a small black oak
standing by the side of Capt William Montagues ditch thence S87 degrees E
eight poles sixteen links to an old hickory stump, a former corner between Anne
Taite Elizabeth Lee & Capt Richard Ball decd thence S47 degrees E along a line
of marked trees the ancient boundary between this tract & Elizabeth Lee's land
to a corner white oak standing upon a point a little above the mouth of a branch
that runs into Capt Seldens Mill Pond thence down the said mill pond the several
courses thereof to the beginning... [no witnesses listed]. Received on the day of
the date of the within written Indenture of the within named John Leland eleven
hundred and sixty six pounds thirteen shillings and four pence current money of
Virginia in full consideration for the within mentioned granted parcel of land and
premises. Recorded 21 Oct 1779 by Test Thads McCarty CLC. [Pages 221,
221a, & 222]

17 Jan 1780. Deed of Feoffment with Receipt. Between John Selden Gent and
Ann his wife of the parish of Christ Church in the county of Lancaster of the one
part and Peter Conway of the same parish and county aforesaid of the other
part... John Selden and Ann his wife for and in consideration of the sum of
twenty thousand pounds current money of Virginia... in hand well and truly paid
by the said Peter Conway at and before the sealing and delivery of these
presents... John Selden doth hereby confess and acknowledge therewith
sufficiently... paid and for divers other good causes and considerations them
thereunto moving, they the said John Selden and Ann his wife have granted...
unto the said Peter Conway... forever all that plantation tract or parcel of land

situate lying and being in the parish of Christ Church within the county of Lancaster whereon the said John Selden now liveth and dwelleth which adjoins the lands of William Montague John Taylor John Leland Job Carter and Margaret Boatman and by estimation contains four hundred and fifty acres to be the same more or less and also one water grist mill situate on the tract of land commonly known by the name of Seldens Mill with two pair of mill stones one of which is known by the name of French Burr... [Wit:] Charles Bell, Edwin Conway, Walker Conway & Ann Selden. Received 17 Jan 1780 of the within named Peter Conway the sum of twenty thousand pounds current money of Virginia being the full consideration money within mentioned to be paid to me I say received by me John Selden. [Wit:] Charles Bell, Edwin Conway, & Walker Conway. Be it remembered that on the day of the date of the within Indenture full quiet and peaceable possession and seisen was had and taken of the within mentioned land and premises by the within named John Selden party to these presents and by him delivered over unto Peter Conway the other party to this Indenture by the delivery of Turf and Twig... [Wit:] Charles Bell, Edwin Conway, & Walker Conway. Recorded 17 Feb 1780 by Test Thads McCarty CLC. [Pages 222, 222a, 223, 223a, & 224]

17 Jan 1780. Commission. The Commonwealth of Virginia To Edwin Conway James Gordon and Chas Bell Gent greeting whereas John Selden and Ann his wife by their certain Indenture of Bargain and Sale bearing date 17 Jan 1780 have sold and conveyed unto Peter Conway one tract or parcel of land with the appurtenances containing 450 acres more or less with a water grist mill adjoining lying and being in the county of Lancaster and whereas Ann Selden wife of the said John cannot conveniently travel to our said court to make acknowledgment and relinquishment of her right in the aforesaid land therefore we do give unto you or any two or more of you full power to receive the acknowledgment which the said Ann shall be willing to make before you of the land aforesaid contained in the aforesaid Indenture which is hereunto annexed and we do therefore command you that you personally go to the said Ann and receive her acknowledgment and relinquishment of the same and examine her privily and apart from her said husband whether she does the same freely and voluntarily without the persuasions or threats of the said John her husband & whether she be willing the same shall be recorded... Recorded 17 Feb 1780 by Test Thads McCarty CLC. [Pages 223a & 224]

17 Jan 1780. Certificate. By virtue of the Commission hereunto annexed we the subscribers did... go to the within nam'd Ann Selden and having examined her privately and apart from John Selden her husband, do certify that she declared that it was without the persuasions or threats of her said husband, she voluntarily and freely acknowledged the conveyance contained in the Indenture hereunto annexed that she was willing that the same should be recorded... [Wit:] Edwin

Conway & Charles Bell. Recorded 17 Feb 1780 by Test Thads McCarty CLC. [Page 224]

30 Nov 1779. Report. (Returned to the Secretary's Office by T Mc) Pursuant to an order of Lancaster County Court... we the subscribers having met did view the road petitioned for by Edward Carter leading to Davis's Warehouse and find the new road which he means to establish to be little farther than the present road and are think full as good, except that the hill is some what steeper than the hill over which the road now runs, So that we think it will be no disadvantage to the publick and a considerable advantage to Mr. Carter... [Wit:] James Gordon, James Carter, & William Stephens. Recorded 20 Jan 1780 by Test Thads McCarty CLC. [Page 224]

Jan 1780. Division of Land. In obedience to an order of Lancaster Court... we the subscribers being approved have met and divided the land of Henry Mayes decd as followeth vizt Beginning at a stake that stands on the line of Jesse Robinson from thence south east along a line of marked trees to a white oak standing by the side of a branch which divides Sinah Mayes's William Mason and Sarah Mayes's land begining at a stake on the line of Sinah Mayes south west along a line of marked trees to a small willow near the main branch thence up the main branch to the mouth of a small branch thence up the said branch to the dividing white oak including William Masons part, thence from the willow down the main branch to a persimmon tree on the line of Jesse Robinson, thence up the said line to the stake at the beginning including Sarah Mayes's part... [Wit:] Richd Goodridge, Jesse Robinson Junr, & Peter Riveer. Recorded 17 Feb 1780 by Test Thads McCarty CLC. [Page 224a]

25 Oct 1779. Deed of Bargain and Sale with Receipt. Between George Heale of the county of Fauquier of the one part and John McTyre, Richard Cundiff, and Richard Mitchell Junr of the county of Lancaster of the other part... George Heale and Sarah his wife for and in consideration of the sum of seven thousand six hundred and fifty one pounds & fifteen shillings current money of Virginia in hand paid at or before the sealing and delivery of these presents... [to] John McTyre, Richard Cundiff, and Richard Mitchell Junr... for ever all that tract or parcel of land situate in the said county of Lancaster and bounded as followeth Beginning at the crossroads thence down the road to Mrs Margaret Balls Mill thence down the meanders of the run to the creek thence the meanders of the creek to the line of John Williams Junr thence along the said line to the line of the aforesaid Richard Mitchell Junr thence along the said line to the line of James Webb decd thence along the said line to the line of William Sydnor thence along the road bounds to the said Sydnor to the begining containing six hundred and thirty five acres... [Wit:] John Chinn, Mungo Harvey, William Mitchell, John Pasquett, & Derby Dunaway. Received the day of the date of the

within Indenture of the within named John McTyre the sum of two thousand four hundred and ten pounds current money of Virginia and also the further sum of two thousand four hundred and ten pounds current money of the within named Richard Cundiff and also the further sum of two thousand eight hundred and thirty one pounds fifteen shillings current money of the within named Richard Mitchell being in whole the sum of seven thousand six hundred and fifty one pounds & fifteen shillings current money in full consideration for the whole within mentioned granted tract of land & premises. [same witnesses as listed above]. Recorded 20 Apr 1780 by Test Thads McCarty CLC. [Pages 224a, 225 & 225a]

13 Aug 1779. Deed of Bargain and Sale. Between John Arms of the county of Lancaster and Judith his wife of the one part and James Ewell of the same county of the other part... John Arms and Judith his wife for and in consideration of the sum of twenty five pounds current money in hand paid at or before the sealing and delivery of these presents... for ever all that piece parcel or tract of land situate in the said county of Lancaster being all that part of a tract of land whereon the said John Arms ow dwelleth which lyeth on the east side of the main road that leads from Chiltons Ferry to the church and is bounded by the said road & the lands of the said James Ewell and William Arms containing by estimation twenty five acres... [Wit:] Henry Towles, John Selden, & Richard Selden. Received the day of the date of the within Indenture of the within named James Ewell the sum of twenty five pounds current money in full consideration for the written mentioned granted parcel of land and premises... [same witnesses as listed above]. Court held 17 Feb 1779 Indenture of Bargain and Sale... was proved in court by the oaths of John and Richard Selden... and asked to lie for further proof and on 20 Apr next following was further proved in court by the oath of Henry Towles Gent...by Test Thads McCarty CLC. [Pages 225a, 226, & 226a]

13 Aug 1779. Commission. The Commonwealth of Virginia to Henry Towles and John Selden Gent greeting Whereas John Arms & Judith his wife by their certain Indenture of Bargain & Sale bearing date 13 Aug 1779 have sold and conveyed unto James Ewell one tract of land containing twenty five acres more or less with the appurtenances lying and being in the county of Lancaster and whereas Judith the wife of John Arms cannot conveniently travel to our county court of Lancaster to make acknowledgment & relinquishment of her rights in the said land, therefore we do give unto you or any two or more of you full power to receive the acknowledgment which the said Judith shall be willing to make before you of her right in land aforesaid contained in the aforesaid Indenture which is hereunto annexed, and we do therefore command you that you personally go to the said Judith and receive her acknowledgment & relinquishment of the same & examine her privily & apart from the said John

Arms her husband whether she does the same freely & voluntarily without the persuasions or threats and whether she be willing that the same should be recorded... Thads McCarty. Court held 17 Feb 1779 Indenture of Bargain and Sale... was proved in court by the oaths of John and Richard Selden... and asked to lie for further proof and on 20 Apr next following was further proved in court by the oath of Henry Towles Gent...by Test Thads McCarty CLC. [Pages 226 & 226a]

13 Aug 1779. Certificate. In obedience to the within Commission we have this day examined Judith the wife of the within mentioned John Arms and have received her acknowledgment & relinquishment of her right in the said land mentioned in the Deed hereunto annexed that she does the same freely and voluntarily without the threats or persuasions of her said husband John Arms and that she is willing the said Deed shall be recorded.. [Wit:] Henry Towles & John Selden. Court held 17 Feb 1779 Indenture of Bargain and Sale... was proved in court by the oaths of John and Richard Selden... and asked to lie for further proof and on 20 Apr next following was further proved in court by the oath of Henry Towles Gent...by Test Thads McCarty CLC. [Page 226a]

7 Sep 1779. Report with the Plat. Lancaster Court. Pursuant to an order of said county court dated Aug 1779. We the subscribers being first sworn having viewed the acre of land petitioned for by John McTire to build a mill and the lands that will be laid under water by means of said mill, are of opinion that the said acre belonging to Ozwald Newby is of the value of five pounds current money and that said Newby will be damaged forty pounds current by flowing of the water of said mill, and that Mrs Elizabeth McTire will be likewise damaged forty shillings by flowing of said water... [Wit:] Elias Edmonds, Elijah Percifull, Joseph Norris, Johnson Riveer, Coleman Doggett, Jas Carter, Thomas Dunaway, Job Carter, Thos Bell, Richard Cundiff, William Yopp, & Eleazer Robinson. Surveyed the above figure or piece of land per order Lancaster court for Mr John McTyre for the use of a mill begining at letter A at the side of the swamp near a small sassafrass marked as a side line runing N2 W 6 poles to a small stake thence N80 E22 poles to a branch that divides the said McTyre's land and Mr Ozwald Newby's thence down the sd branch S8 E7 poles to the main swamp thence up the meanders of the sd swamp S70 & W&S 30 W to the begining including 154 poles or ¾ of an acre & 34 poles. Surveyed by Henry Tapscott. Recorded 20 Apr 1780 by Test Thads McCarty CLC. [Pages 227 & 227a]

29 Feb 1780. Report. We the subscribers being summoned by James Newby sub sheriff of Lancaster County and being first sworn upon the Holy Evangelist of Almighty God did... in obedience to an order of the court of said county for laying off an acre of land petitioned for by Edwin Conway Gent for the building

of a water grist mill, attended Henry Tapscott Get who was mutually chosen by the parties to lay off the said acre, and are of opinion that the heirs of Thomas Edwards decd be paid the sum of twenty pounds for the said acre of land, also that William Yopp be paid the sum of fifty pounds for the damage he will sustain by the flowing of the water of the said mill pond... [Wit:] Richard Ball, John Carter, Job Carter, Benjamin George, James Brent, Fortunatus Sydnor, Thads McCarty, William Doggett, Joseph Dobbs, Colm Doggett, Elijah Percifull, & John Cundiff. Recorded 20 Apr 1780 by Thads McCarty CLC. [Page 227a]

17 Apr 1780. Report with Plat. Agreeable to an order of Lancaster County Court, the subscribers surveyed and laid off one acre of land formerly the property of [blank] Schofield & now possessed by John Hutchinson opposite to the land Fortunatus Sydnor is building a water grist mill, and for the use of the said mill whereof is an annex'd plat, begining at the north east end of the mill dam at "A" thence runing S 34 ½ E10 poles to a marked oak at "B" thence north 55 ½ # 10 poles to a stake "C", thence N34 ½ W20 poles by marked trees to "D" on the edge of a branch marking out of the main swamp, including one acre of land. [Wit:] William Brown. Recorded 20 Apr 1780 by Test Thads McCarty CLC. [Page 227a]

26 Apr 1780. Deed of Bargain and Sale. Between Peter Conway and Frances his wife of the county of Lancaster and parish of Christ Church of the one part and James Tapscott of the said parish and county aforesaid of the other part... Peter Conway and Frances his wife for and in consideration of the sum of six thousand three hundred pounds current money of Virginia in hand paid at or before the sealing and delivery of these presents... grant... unto the said James Tapscott... forever a parcel or tract of land lying and situate in the county and parish aforesaid. Bounded as followeth Begining at a small hickory upon the north side of a valley that divides the said land and the land of Thomas Edwards deceased runing a straight course through the old field to a marked white oak in the head of a branch that divides the said land and the land by the name of Drews from thence down the said branch to Conways Mill Pond thence down the said pond to Job Carters line thence along the said line to the land of Col James Gordon along the said line a cross the main road from Davis's Warehouse down to a branch which divides the said land and the lands of Mary Pinckard & James Pinckard down to the main branch of Norris's Mill Pond thence up the said branch to a branch which divides aforesaid land and the land of Col Edwin Conway up the said branch to the straight line that makes the white stone that divides the said land and the land of Thomas Edwards decd from the white stone to the small hickory at the aforesaid begining containing eight hundred and seventy nine acres... [Wit:] Richard Mitchell, John Selden, William Sydnor, & Robert Chinn. Received the day of the date of the within Indenture of the within

172

named James Tapscott the sum of six thousand three hundred pounds current money of Virginia in full consideration for the within mentioned granted parcel or tract of land and premises. [same witnesses as listed above]. Recorded 10 May 1780 by Test Thads McCarty CLC. [Pages 228, 228a, 229, & 229a]

26 Apr 1780. Commission. The Commonwealth of Virginia To Richard Mitchell James Gordon & John Selden Gent whereas Peter Conway and Frances his wife by their certain Indenture of Bargain and Sale bearing date 26 Apr 1780 have sold and conveyed unto James Tapscott one tract of land containing eight hundred and seventy nine acres more or less with the appurtenances lying and being in Lancaster County and whereas the said Frances cannot conveniently travel to our county court of Lancaster to make acknowledgmt of her right in the said land therefore we do give unto you or any two or more of you full power to receive the acknowledgment which the said Frances shall be willing to make before you... we do therefore command you that you personally go to the said Frances and receive her acknowledgment of the same and examine her privily and apart from the said Peter Conway her husband whether she does the same freely and voluntarily without the persuasions or threats of her said husband and whether she be willing the same should be recorded... Thads McCarty. Recorded 10 May 1780 by Test Thads McCarty CLC. [Page 229]

27 Apr 1780. Certificate. We the subscribers did personally go to the within named Frances Conway and examined her privily and apart from her husband touching the annexed Indenture who answered that she consented the same freely and voluntarily of her own consent without any persuasions or threats of her husband and she be willing the same should be recorded... Recorded 10 May 1780 by Test Thads McCarty CLC. [Page 229]

///4098115_00241

1 Oct 1779. Deed of Bargain and Sale with Receipt. Between John Hathaway and Sarah his wife James Hathaway and Ivannah his wife Zachariah Linton & Mary his wife of the county of Fauquier Lawson Hathaway and Judith his wife Isaac Currell & Dolly his wife of the county of Lancaster of the one part and Thomas Hathaway of the county of Lancaster of the other part... John Hathaway & Sarah his wife James and Ivannah his wife Zachariah Linton & Mary his wife Lawson Hathaway and Judith his wife and Isaac Currell and Dolly his wife for and in consideration of the sum of three hundred pounds current money of Virginia to them in hand well and truly paid by the said Thomas Hathaway at and before the sealing and delivery of these presents... and also for divers other good causes and considerations them thereunto moving they... have granted... unto the said Thomas Hathaway... forever all that tract or parcel of land situate lying and being in the parish of Christ Church and county of Lancaster formerly

the property of William Hathaway decd purchased of Ezekiel Gilbert containing by estimation two hundred and forty acres... and lastly that they the said John Hathaway and Sarah his wife James Hathaway and Ivannah his wife Zachariah Linton and Mary his wife Lawson Hathaway and Judith his wife and Isaac Currell and Dolly his wife or someone or more of them in the name of the whole will within one month after the date hereof into the aforesaid tract or parcel of land or some part thereof in the name of the whole premises above mentioned to be herein & hereby granted... [Wit:] Thomas Carter, John Cook, Charles Bell, William Mullikin, John Fleet, & Thomas Lawson. October 14, 1779-Received of Thomas Hathaway the consideration of three hundred pounds being the sum within mentioned... [Wit:] Test Thomas Carter & John Cook. At a court held 10 Nov 1779 this Indenture of Bargain and Sale... was proved by the oath of John Cooke... and ordered to lie for further proof... and recorded 18 May 1780 by Test Thads McCarty CLC. [Pages 229a, 230, 230a, 231 & 231a]

25 Oct 1779. Commission. The Commonwealth of Virginia to William Edmonds William Pickett Francis Triplett, John Fleet Thomas Lawson and Henry Lawson Gent whereas by their Indenture of Bargain and Sale have sold and conveyed unto Thomas Hathaway one tract or parcel of land containing two hundred and forty acres be the same more or less with the appurtenances lying and being in the county of Lancaster and whereas Sarah, Ivannah & Judith Hathaway, Mary Linton and Dolly Currell wives of the said John, James & Lawson Hathaway & Zachariah Linton & Isaac Currell cannot conveniently travel to our county court to make acknowledgment and relinquishment of their right in the land aforesaid therefore we do give unto you or any two or more of you full power to receive the acknowledgment which the said Sarah Ivannah & Judith Hathaway, Mary Linton & Dolly Currell shall be willing to make before you of their rights in the land aforesaid contained in the aforesaid Indenture which is hereunto annexed and we do therefore command you that you personally go to the sd Sarah, Ivannah & Judith Hathaway, Mary Linton and Dolly Currell and receive their and each of their relinquishment & acknowledgment of the same and examine them privily and apart from John, James & Lawson Hathaway, Zachariah Linton and Isaac Currell their husbands whether they do the same freely and voluntarily without the threats or persuasions of their said husbands and whether they be willing the same should be recorded... [Wit:] Thads McCarty. At a court held 10 Nov 1779 this Indenture of Bargain and Sale... was proved by the oath of John Cooke... and ordered to lie for further proof... and recorded 18 May 1780 by Test Thads McCarty CLC. [Page 231]

17 May 1780. Certificate. Lancaster County. By virtue of the within Dedimus to us directed we have examined the within named Judith Hathaway and Dolly Currell apart from their husbands and they doth voluntarily of their own free

174

wills acknowledge all their rights titles and interest of dower to the said land premises mentioned in the Deed hereto annexed without the persuasions or threats of their sd husbands and are willing the same shall be entered upon record... {Wit:] John Fleet & Thomas Lawson. At a court held 10 Nov 1779 this Indenture of Bargain and Sale... was proved by the oath of John Cooke... and ordered to lie for further proof... and recorded 18 May 1780 by Test Thads McCarty CLC. [Page 231a]

25 Oct 1779. Certificate. Fauqr County. Pursuant to the within Dedimus, we the subscribers have examined sd Sarah and Ivannah Hathaway the wives of John and James Hathaway and Mary Linton wife of Zachariah Linton separate and apart from their said husbands and they freely and voluntarily acknowledge & relinquish their Right of Dower in the lands within mentioned... [Wit:] W. Edmonds & William Pickett. At a court held 10 Nov 1779 this Indenture of Bargain and Sale... was proved by the oath of John Cooke... and ordered to lie for further proof... and recorded 18 May 1780 by Test Thads McCarty CLC. [Page 231a]

18 Nov 1779. Deed of Bargain and Sale with Receipt. Between Thomas Edwards and Betty his wife of the parish of Wiccomoco and county of Northumberland of the one part and John Sullivant of the parish and county aforesaid of the other part... Thomas and Betty Edwards are lawfully possessed of and in a tract of land situate lying and being part in Northumberland and part in Lancaster county containing by estimation one hundred acres... Thomas and Betty Edwards for and in consideration of the sum of three hundred and fifty pounds lawful money of Virginia to them in hand paid by the aforesd John Sullivant before the sealing and delivery of these presents... forever all the before mentioned tract or parcel of land situate as aforesaid containing one hundred acres... [Wit:] Jas Waddey, Geo Phillips, & Ben. Waddey Junr. Memorandum that this 18 Nov 1779 quiet and peaceable possession and seizen of the within parcel of land was given and delivered unto the within named John Sullivant by the within named Thomas Edwards by the delivery of Turf and Twig... [Wit:] James Waddey, Geo Phillips, & Ben. Waddey Junr. Received the day of the date of the within Indenture of and from the within named John Sullivant the sum of three hundred and fifty pounds lawful money of Virginia being the consideration within mentioned to be paid. [same witnesses as listed above]. Recorded 18 May 1780 by Test Thads McCarty CLC. [Pages 231a, 232, & 232a]

11 Dec 1779. Commission. The Commonwealth of Virginia to Thomas Gaskins Charles Lee and William Nutt Gent greeting whereas Thomas Edwards and Betty his wife by their certain Indenture of Bargain and Sale bearing date 18 Nov 1779 have sold and conveyed unto John Sullivant one tract or parcel of land

with the appurtanences containing one hundred acres more or less lying and being in the county of Lancaster and whereas Betty Edwards wife of the said Thomas Edwards cannot conveniently travel to our county court of Lancaster to make acknowledgment and relinquishment of her right in the land aforesaid therefore we do give unto or any two or more of you full power to receive the acknowledgment which the said Betty Edwards shall be willing to make before you of the land was contained in the aforesaid Indenture which is hereunto annexed, and we do therefore command you to personally go to the said Betty Edwards and receive her acknowledgment and relinquishment of the same and examine her privily and apart from her said husband whether she does the same freely and voluntarily without the persuasions or threats of the sd Thomas Edwards her husband and whether she be willing the same should be recorded in our said court of Lancaster...[by] Thads McCarty. Recorded 18 May 1780 by Test Thads McCarty CLC. [Page 232a]

4 May 1780. Certificate. Northumberld Crt. In obedience to the within Commission we the subscribers did go to the house of Thomas Edwards and have examined Betty his wife apart from her husband concerning the land within mentioned sold by her husband Thomas Edwards to John Sullivant, and she says she was no ways compelled by her husband but doth it of her own free will and inclination and desirus that the sd Deed within mentioned may be recorded... [Wit:] Charles Lee & William Nutt. Recorded 18 May 1780 by Test Thads McCarty CLC. [Page 232a]

13 Jan 1779. Deed of Bargain and Sale with Receipt. Between Richard Hall & Mary his wife of the parish of Christ Church and county of Lancaster of the one part and John Selden of the same parish and county of the other part... Richard Hall and Mary his wife for and in consideration of the sum of sixty pounds lawful money of Virginia to them in hand paid by the said John Selden at or before the ensealing and delivery of these presents... [for] all that messuage tenement and tract of land of which Thomas Lee of the parish and county aforesaid father of the said Mary party to these presents died seized and possessed of at the time of his death and which after his death descended unto the said Mary as his only surviving child and heir at law containing one hundred and twenty acres be the same more or less situate lying and being in the parish and county aforesaid in the upper part thereof and bounded on Seldens and Everitts Mill Ponds and on the lands of William Montague and Richard Ball being the evidence of a larger tract of land which the aforesaid Thomas Lee was seized possessed in his lifetime the other part of which he sold and conveyed unto William Griggs of the parish and county aforesaid... and to and with every of them by these presents in manner and form following (that is to say) that the said Richard Hall and Mary his wife now are the true and lawful owners of all and singular the said messuages tenement and tract of land... [Wit:] Thos

Gaskins, Chas Lee, & Sally Gaskins. Received the day of the date of the within written Indenture of the within named John Selden the sum of sixty pounds lawful money of Virginia being the consideration money within mentioned. I say received by me-Richard Hall. Recorded 18 May 1780 by Test Thads McCarty CLC. [Pages 233, 233a, 234, & 234a]

10 Jan 1779. Commission. The Commonwealth of Virginia to Thomas Gaskins Charles Lee & Thos Edwards Gent greeting whereas Richard Hall and Mary his wife by their certain Indenture of Bargain and Sale bearing date 13 Jan 1779 have sold and conveyed unto John Selden one tract of land containing one hundred and twenty acres more or less with the appurtanences lying and being in the county of Lancaster and whereas Mary Hall wife of the said Richard Hall cannot conveniently travel to our county court of Lancaster to make acknowledgment and relinquishment of her right in the said land therefore we do give unto you or any two or more of you full power to receive the acknowledgment which the said Mary shall be willing to make before you of her right in the land aforesaid contained in the aforesaid Indenture which is hereunto annexed and we do therefore command you that you personally go to the sd Mary and receive her acknowledgment and relinquishment of the same and examine her privily and apart from the said Richard Hall her husband whether she does the same freely and voluntarily without the persuasions or threats and whether she be willing that the same should be recorded... Thads McCarty. Recorded 18 May 1780 by Test Thads McCarty CLC. [Pages 234 & 234a]

9 Mar 1780. Certificate. Northumberland County crt. Pursuant to the within Commission to us directed we the subscribers have privately and apart from her husband Richard Hall examined Mary the wife of said Richard Hall whether she was willing to the sale of the land specified in the Deed annexed and have taken her acknowledgment thereof which is that she agrees to the sale of the land of her own free voluntary will without the persuasions or threats of her husband Richd Hall and that she is willing the same shall be recorded... [Wit:] Thomas Gaskins & Chas Lee. Recorded 18 May 1780 by Test Thads McCarty CLC. [Page 234a]

20 Apr 1780. Deed of Bargain and Sale with Livery and Seisen and Receipt. Between Richard Cundiff Junr and Susannah his wife of Lancaster County of the one part and Bartholomew Dammeron of Northumberland County of the other part... Richard Cundiff and Susannah his wife for and in consideration of the sum of four thousand pounds current money of Virginia to him in hand paid by the said Bartholomew Dammeron... [for] a certain parcel or piece of land containing two hundred and six acres lying and being in the county of Lancaster and is part of a tract of land which formerly belonged to Col George Heale and by him sold to Richard Mitchell Junr John McTyre and him the sd Richard

Cundiff Junr as by Indenture of Bargain and Sale bearing date 25 Oct 1779... bounded as followeth begining at a marked oak tree standing in Mrs Margaret Balls Mill Swamp South 85 West to a cedar stake standing by the road side that divides this land and William Sydnors land thence along the road and a line of marked trees that divides this land and Mary Webbs land to a marked white oak N 71 degrees East to above mentioned Mill Swamp so up the said Mill Run the several courses thereof to the begining... [Wit:] David Ball, Josia Gaskins, & George Ball. Received on the day of the date of the within written Indenture of the within named Bartholomew Dammeron the sum of four thousand pounds current money of Virginia being the consideration for the within mentioned land and premises signed Richard Cundiff. Memorandum that on the day of the date of the within written Indenture full and peaceable possession of Livery and Seizen of the within mentioned premises was by me had and taken and delivered unto the said Bartholomew Dammeron... [same witnesses as listed above]. Recorded 18 May 1780 by Test Thads McCarty CLC. [Pages 234a, 235 & 235a]

20 Apr 1780. Deed of Bargain and Sale with Livery and Seisen and Receipt. Between Bartholomew Dammerson and Mary his wife of Northumberland County of the one part and Richard Cundiff Junr of Lancaster County of the other part... Bartholomew Dammerson for and in consideration of the sum of four thousand pounds current money of Virginia to him in hand paid by the said Richard Cundiff... [for] all that messuage plantation and tract of land which he the said Bartholomew Dammeron is now possessed lying and being in the county of Lancaster known by the name of hickory neck and bounded by the land of William Warren John Taylor Isaac Baisey and the above mentioned Richard Cundiff containing by estimation two hundred acres... [Wit:] David Ball, Josia Gaskins, & George Ball. Received on the day of the date of the within written Indenture of the within named Richard Cundiff the sum of four thousand pounds current money of Virginia being the consideration for the within mentioned land and premises. [same witnesses as listed above]. Memorandum that on the day of the date of the within written Indenture full & peaceable possession & Livery of Seizen of the within named premises was by me had and taken & delivered unto the within named Richard Cundiff... [same witnesses as listed above]. Recorded 18 May 1780 by Test Thads McCarty CLC. [Pages 235a, 236, & 236a]

17 May 1780. Deed. Between Richard Mitchell Junr of Lancaster County of the one part and Bartholomew Dameron of Northumberland County of the other part... Richard Mitchell Junr for and in consideration of the sum of two thousand pounds current money of Virginia to him in hand paid by him the said Bartholomew Dameron... [for] a certain parcel or piece of marsh formerly belonged to by Col. George Heale and sold by him to the said Mitchell supposed

to be ten acres be the same more or less begining at the oak landing and so along the creek and land side up to the spring including the same... [Wit:] James Simmonds, Isaac Bayse, & Craven Everitt. Received on the day of the date of the within written Indenture of the within named Bartholomew Dameron the sum of two thousand pounds current money of Virginia being the consideration for the within mentioned land & premises. [same witnesses as listed above]. Memorandum that on the day of the date of the written Indenture full and peaceable possession of Livery and Seizen of the within mentioned premises was by me had and taken and delivered to the within named Bartholomew Dameron... [same witnessses as listed above]. Recorded 18 May 1780 by Test Thads McCarty CLC. [Pages 236a & 237]

18 Feb 1777. Bill of Sale. Know all men by these presents that I John Wormley of Lancaster County for and in consideration of the sum of sixty pounds current money to me in hand paid by John McTyre of the county aforesaid... [for] one negro boy named Abraham... [Wit:] John Miller & Peter Conway. Recorded 19 May 1780 by Test Thads McCarty CLC. [Page 237a]

7 Apr 1778. Bill of Sale. Know all men by these presents that I James Connolly of Richmond County for & in consideration of the sum of two hundred pounds current money to him in hand paid by Maurice Wheeler of the county of Lancaster... [for] one negro man named Ned... [Wit:] John Booth, Rodham Hudson, & Lucy Codman. Recorded 18 May 1780 by Test Thads McCarty CLC. [Page 237a]

2 May 1780. Report. In obedience to an order of Lancaster County court dated April 1780. We the subscribers being summoned by James Newby T. Sheriff to attend as jurymen at the place where Charles Carter Esqr proposes to build a water grist mill did accordingly meet on the land... and being first sworn on the Holy Evangelist of Almighty God before the said James Newby have valued the acre of land petitioned for by the said Charles Carter the property of John Hutchings, the same being laid off and surveyed before us by William Brown by consent of the said Carter and Hutchings to thirty pounds current money which acres is bounded as followeth Begining at a stake on the side of the pond thence runing N6 E3 chains 33 1/3 links to a stake thence S8 E3 chains 33 1/3 links thence S6 W3 ch 33 1/3 links by marked trees to a marked pine thence to the begining and we assess the damage that the said John Hutchings will sustain by the building the said mill to three hundred and twenty pounds currency and that no other persons lands will be affected thereby... [Wit:] John James, Elmore Doggett, George Currell, John Parrott, John Sullivant, Edney Tapscott, Isaac Degge, James Pollard, Jesse George, William Doggett, Fortunatus Sydnor, & William Mason. Recorded 18 May 1780 by Test Thads McCarty CLC. [Page 238]

14 Mar 1780. Certificate. This is to certify that at a meeting of the freeholders
and housekeepers of Lancaster County that on Tuesday the fourteenth of March
1780 for the purpose of electing commisioners of the tax for the said county that
James Ball Edwin Conway and Richard Mitchell Esqur were duly elected for
that purpose... [Wit:] John Taylor, Sheriff. I do hereby certify that James Ball
Richard Mitchell and Edwin Conway Gent have taken the oath of
Commissioners as the law directs... [Wit:] Henry Tapscott. Recorded 18 May
1780 by Test Thads McCarty CLC. [Pages 238 & 238a]

5 Mar 1780. Deed of Bargain and Sale. Between George Kelly of Bourough of
Norfolk of the one part and John Parrott of the county of Lancaster of the other
part... George Kelly for and in consideration of the sum of two thousand pounds
current money to him in hand paid... [for] a certain tract or parcel of land in the
county of Lancaster and parish of Christ Church containing by estimation sixty
acres more or less and bounded by the lands of Epaphroditus Lawson, George
Currell, John Hall & James Currell... [Wit:] Jesse George, Lawson Hathaway,
& Thos Ashburn. Received 17 Apr 1780 from John Parrott the within
mentioned sum of two thousand pounds on acct of George Kelly in full for the
within mentioned land and premises. [Wit:] Richd E. Lee. At a court held for
Lancaster County 20 Apr 1780... was proved by the oaths of Jesse George &
Lawson Hathaway & ordered to lye for further proof... 15 Jun 1780... further
proved by Thomas Ashburn and ordered to be recorded by Test Thads McCarty
CLC. [Pages 238a & 239]

13 Jun 1780. Deed of Bargain and Sale with Receipt. Between Bailie George &
Judith his wife of the county of Lancaster of the one part and Jesse George of the
same county of the other part... Bailie George and Judith his wife for and in
consideration of the sum of five hundred pounds current money of Virginia to
them in hand well and truly paid by the said Jesse George at or before the
sealing and delivery of these presents... forever a certain tract parcel or piece of
land situate in the said county of Lancaster whereon Nicholas Lawson formerly
lived and which after his death descended to his surviving daughters Katharine
and Sarah which was equally divided between them and the aforesaid Jesse
George who intermarried with Sarah aforesaid did by this Indenture bearing date
the [blank] day of [blank] (recourse being thereunto had will more clearly
appear) sell and convey unto the said Bailie George the aforesaid Sarah's part
thereof being on the north side of the said plantation and which is now by these
presents granted... by the said Bailie George and Judith his wife unto the said
Jesse George... containing fifty acres be the same more or less and whereon the
said Jesse George now liveth... [Wit:] Thomas Lawson & Henry Lawson.
Received the day of the date of the within Indenture of the within named Jesse
George the sum of five hundred pounds current money being the consideration
within mentioned for the aforesaid land and premises. [same witnesses as listed

above]. Recorded 15 Jun 1780 by Test Thads McCarty CLC. [Pages 239a & 240]

13 Jun 1780. Commission. The Commonwealth of Virginia to Thomas Lawson John Berryman and Henry Lawson Gent greeting whereas Bailie George and Judith his wife by their Indenture of Bargain and Sale bearing date 13 June 1780 have sold and conveyed unto Jesse George one tract or parcel of land with the appurtenances containing fifty acres more or less lying and being in the county of Lancaster and whereas Judith wife of the said Bailie cannot conveniently travel to our said court to make acknowledgment of her right in the aforesaid land therefore we do give you or any two or more of you full power to receive the acknowledgment which the said Judith shall be willing to make before you of the land contained in the said Indenture which is hereunto annexed and we do therefore command you that you personally go to the said Judith and examine her privily and apart from Bailie her said husband whether she does the same freely and voluntarily without his persuasions or threats and whether she is willing that the same shall be recorded in our county court of Lancaster... Thads McCarty. Recorded 15 Jun 1780 by Test Thads McCarty CLC. [Page 240]

13 Jun 1780. Certificate. By virtue of the within Commission to us directed we have examined the within named Judith George apart from her husband and she doth voluntarily and of her own free will acknowledge all her right title & interest of dower to the said land and premises mentioned in the Deed hereto annexed without the persuasions or threats of her said husband and is willing the same shall be entered upon record... [Wit:] Thomas Lawson & Henry Lawson. Recorded 15 Jun 1780 by Test Thads McCarty CLC. [Page 240]

27 Jul 1779. Deed of Mortgage with Receipt. Between John Hall a native of Maryland of the one part and Thomas Pinckard of Lancaster County Virginia of the other part... John Hall in the consideration of the sum of seventeen thousand three hundred and thirty three pounds six shillings & eight pence current money of Virginia to the said John Hall in hand well and truly paid by the said Thomas Pinckard at and before the sealing and delivery of these presents... [for] all that capital messuage plantation tract or parcel of land situate lying and being in the parish of Christ Church within the county of Lancaster containing by estimation seven hundred acres adjoining the lands of George Currell William Griggs, James Currell Rawleigh Shearman and George Kelly... whatsoever to the said plantation tract or parcel of land or any part or parcel thereof belonging or in anywise appurtaining in a large and ample a manner as the said John Hall purchased the same of a certain Peter Conway and his wife Frances... appurtenances unto the said Thomas Pinckard... for and during the full term of ten thousand years next immediately ensuing and following fully to be compleat and ended yielding and paying therefore during the said term one ear of Indian

corn on Christmas Day only (if demanded) and also the following negro slaves
Phill, Poll, Daniel, with their future increase... unto the said Thomas Pinckard...
for and during the full term of ten thousand years next ensuing and following
full to be compleated and ended yielding and pay therefore yearly during the
said term one ear of Indian corn on Christmas Day only (if demanded) provided
always and upon condition that of the said John Hall... do or shall well and truly
pay or cause to be paid unto Cuthbert Bullett Esqr of Dumfries of the county of
Prince William the full and just sum of seven thousand one hundred and one
pounds two shillings & two pence on or before the first day of December next
ensuing after the date of these presents and also the following sum of seven
thousand one hundred twenty one pounds two shillings & two pence one or
before the first day of June which shall be in the year 1780 and also the sum of
three thousand one hundred and eleven pounds two shillings & two pence one or
before the first day of December which shall be in the year 1780 without any
deduction or abatement whatsoever... and lastly it is covenented... that untill
default shall be made in performance... herein contained he the said John Hall...
shall and may hold and enjoy all and singular the said premises above mentioned
and receive and take the rents... thereof to his and their own proper use and
benefit... [Wit:] William Lee, Peter Conway, & Christopher Miller. Received
the twenty seventh day of July of the within named Thomas Pinckard seventeen
thousand three hundred and thirty three pounds six shillings & eight pence
current money of Virginia being the full consideration money within mentioned
to be paid to me I say paid by me John Hall. [same witnesses as listed above].
Recorded 17 Feb 1780 proved by the oaths of Peter Conway and Christopher
Miller... and ordered to lie for further proof, but upon the request of Mr Thos
Pinckard is recorded by Test Thads McCarty CLC. [Pages 240a, 241, & 241a]

18 May 1780. Settlement. In obedience to an order of Lancaster County court
dated Feb 1780. We the subscribers did meet and settle the bounds of the land
in dispute between Capt William Montague and Mr Richard Ball as followeth
vizt Begining at a red oak in the fork of the main branch which divides the said
Montague and Balls land from thence to a thorn bush standing near Mr Richard
Balls cornfield fence and from thence to the old road which leads to Cundiffs...
[Wit:] Richard Mitchell & Edwin Conway. Recorded 15 Jun 1780 by Test
Thads McCarty CLC. [Page 241a]

5 Jun 1780. Deed of Bargain and Sale with Receipt. Between James Gordon
Gent and Ann his wife of the parish of Christ Church in the county of Lancaster
of the one part and George Norris of the same parish and county aforesaid of the
other part... James Gordon and Ann his wife for and in consideration of the sum
or quantity of one hundred and twenty five barrels of sound merchantable Indian
corn to him the said James Gordon in hand well and truly paid and delivered by
the said George Norris at and before the sealing and delivery of these presents...

forever all the right title interest and property, the said James Gordon had and claims under and agreeable to the last Will and Testament of his father James Gordon Gent deceased dated 6 Jan 1767 one full moiety of a water grist mill situate in the county of Lancaster adjoining the lands of James Kirk Junr decd and James Pinckard Junr commonly called Norris's Mill... which said mill James Gordon Gent decd purchased of John Norris decd father to the said George Norris by articles of agreement made concluded and agreed upon 20 Feb 1761, and the said John Norris decd bought the above mentioned mill of Thomas Edward decd agreeable to a Deed bearing date 15 Aug 1760, related to the above mentioned instruments of writing... [Wit:] Edwin Conway, Chas Bell, & Philip Payne. Received 5 Jun 1780 of the within George Norris one hundred and twenty five barrels of sound merchantable Indian corn being the full consideration within mentioned to be paid to me. [Wit:] Edwin Conway & Chas Bell. Recorded 20 July 1780 by Test Thads McCarty CLC. [Pages 242, 242a, & 243]

6 Jun 1780. Commission. The Commonwealth of Virginia to Edwin Conway William Yerby and Charles Bell Gent greeting whereas James Gordon Gent and Ann his wife by their certain Indenture of Bargain and Sale bearing date 5 Jun 1780 have sold and conveyed unto George Norris a parcel of land with the appurtenances containing about one acre more or less lying & being in the county of Lancaster & whereas Ann Gordon wife of the said James Gordon cannot conveniently travel to our said court to make acknowledgment and relinquishment of her right in the land and mill aforesaid therefore we do give you or any two or more of you full power to receive the acknowledgment which the said Ann Gordon shall be willing to make before you of the land and mill aforesaid contained in the aforesaid Indenture which is hereunto annexed and we do therefore command you that you personally go to the said Ann and receive her acknowledgment and relinquishment of the same and examine her privily and apart from her said husband whether she does the same freely and voluntarily without the persuasions or threats of the sd James Gordon her husband and whether she be willing the same shall be recorded... Thads McCarty. Recorded 20 July 1780 by Test Thads McCarty CLC. [Pages 242a & 243]

6 Jun 1780. Certificate. ...we the subscribers did go personally to the within named Ann wife to the said James Gordon and examined her privily and apart from her said husband ... the Deed within mentioned when she declared that she freely and voluntarily relinquished the right to the said mill and appurtenances and signed the said Deed without the persuasions or threats of her said husband... [Wit:] Edwin Conway & Chas Bell. Recorded 20 July 1780 by Test Thads McCarty CLC. [Page 243]

... Jul 1780. Bill of Sale. Know all men by these presents that I James Brent of the parish of Christ Church and county of Lancaster as well for and in consideration of the love and affection which I have and bear unto my brother George Brent as for and in consideration of one hundred pounds current money to me in hand paid by the said George Brent have given... unto the said George Brent... one negro boy named Isaac... [Wit:] Newton Brent, John Parrott, & Epps Lawson. Recorded 20 Jul 1780 by Thads McCarty CLC. [Pages 243 & 243a]

13 Jun 1780. Deed of Bargain and Sale with Receipt. Between Henry George & Judith his wife of the county of Lancaster of the one part and Jesse George of the aforesaid county of the other part... Henry George and Judith his wife for and in consideration of the sum of eleven hundred and sixty pounds current money of Virginia to them in hand well and truly paid by him the said Jesse George at or before the sealing and delivery of these presents... [for] a certain tract or parcel of land lying and being in the county of Lancaster and a part of the tract of land the said Henry George purchased of John Berryman Gent of the aforesaid county and is bounded as followeth Begining at a willow tree standing on the side of the swamp that divides the land of the said Jesse George and John Mahone runing up the said swamp to a corner oak between the said Mahone and Jesse George thence along the said Georges line to a pine tree at the lower end of a place called Angels Base(?) Ground that divides William Mason James Pollard and the said Jesse George thence along the said Masons line to a pine tree at a place called and known by the name of Sandy Vally that divides the aforesaid Henry George and Jesse George thence W79 W to the begining containing one hundred acres... [Wit:] Thomas Lawson, Henry Lawson & Bailie George. Received the day of the date of the within written Indenture of the within Jesse George the sum of eleven hundred and sixty pounds current money of Virginia being the consideration for the within mentioned land and premises. [same witnesses as listed above]. Recorded 20 Jul 1780 by Test Thads McCarty CLC. [Pages 243a, 244, & 244a]

13 Jun 1780. Bond. Know all men by these presents that I Henry George of the county of Lancaster & parish of Christ Church am held and firmly bound unto Jesse George of the same county & parish in the just sum of five thousand pounds current money of Virginia for the same valuable consideration recd of him to which payments well and truly to be made to said Jesse George.... Dated [blank] day of [blank] 1780. The condition of this obligation is such that whereas the above bound Henry George has bargained... unto and possessed the above said Jesse George with a certain tract of land by estimation one hundred acres be the same more or less (it being part of a tract or parcel of land that the said Henry George purchased of Capt John Berryman) for which he the said Henry received of the said Jesse the sum of one thousand one hundred and sixty

184

pounds current money of Virginia (in full) as will appear by one certain Deed of
Indenture bearing date 13 Jun 1780. Executed and delivered by the said Henry
to the said Jesse but Judith the wife of the said Henry George refuses to sign the
sd Deed of Indenture or to relinquish her right of dower. Now it is that if the
said Henry George... in full peaceable and quiet possession of the said land and
premises against the claim or claims of the sd Judith wife of the said Henry...
[Wit:] John Thrall & Ellen Thrall. Recorded 20 Jul 1780 by Test Thads
McCarty CLC. [Page 244a]

1 Aug 1780. Deed of Bargain and Sale with Receipt. Between James Tapscott
& Elizabeth Tapscott his wife of the parish of Christ Church in the county of
Lancaster of the one part and Charles Bell of the same parish and county
aforesaid of the other part... James Tapscott and Elizabeth his wife for and in
consideration of the sum of two thousand eight hundred and fifty nine lawful
money of Virginia to him in hand paid by the said Charles Bell... forever a
certain tract or parcel of land situate lying and being in the parish of Christ
Church and county of Lancaster being part of a certain tract of land whereon
Peter Conway Gent lately lived on and conveyed unto the said James Tapscott
so by Deed bearing date 26 Apr will more fully show containing by survey made
thereon 17 Jul 1779. Three hundred and ninety four and three quarters acres be
the same more or less which said plantation tract or parcel of land adjoins the
land of Col James Gordon Begining at the head of the said Gordon Mill Pond
N268 ½ W62 p up the swamp to a small ash at the side of the run at the letter B
thence N 26 ½ W21 p N32 W29 ½ p along Pinckard's line to a corner hiccory at
the letter C. thence S64 W102 p near a large white oak at Col Gordons line at the
letter D. thence along the said Gordons line N37 W57 p to a walnut tree at the
letter E thence along the said line N50 W126 p to the road at the letter F now
upon the several meanders of the road N30 E50 p to the head of a swamp at the
road heading from Col. Conways to Davis's Warehouse at the letter H thence
down the several meanders of the said swamp N85 E18 ¾ p S83 E38 p N79 E20
p S72 E25 p S47 E31 p S28 E12 ¼ p S17 ½ E19 ½ p S36 E25 p S50 E14 p S15
E12 ½ p S26 E131 p S11 ½ E39 p and S[blank] 79 p to the begining at the letter
A... [Wit:] James Gordon, Henry Tapscott Junr, & Peter Conway. Received the
day and year first written of the within named Charles Bell the sum of two
thousand eight hundred and fifty nine pounds being the full consideration money
within mentioned to be paid to me. [same witnesses as listed above]. Be it
remembered that 1 Aug 1780 full quiet and peaceable possession and Seizen of
the plantation tract or parcel of land and other the premises with the
appurtenances in this Deed mentioned and contained was given and delivered by
the within named James Tapscott and Elizabeth his wife to the within named
Charles Bell by the delivery of Turf and Twig upon the premises... Recorded 17
Aug 1780 by Test Thads McCarty CLC. [Pages 245, 245a, 246, 246a & 247]

2 Aug 1780. Commission. The Commonwealth of Virginia to James Gordon
and Henry Towles Gent greeting whereas James Tapscott and Elizabeth Tapscott
his wife by their certain Indenture of Bargain and Sale bearing date 1 Aug 1780
have sold and conveyed unto Charles Bell one tract or parcel of land with the
appurtenances containing three hundred and ninety five acres more or less lying
and being in the county of Lancaster and whereas Elizabeth Tapscott wife of the
said James Tapscott cannot conveniently travel to our said county court to make
acknowledgment of her right in the land aforesd therefore we do give you or any
two or more of you full power to receive the acknowledgment which the said
Elizabeth Tapscott shall be willing to make before you of the land aforesaid
contained in the aforesaid Indenture which is hereunto annexed and we do
therefore command you that you personally go to the same and examine her
privily and apart from her said husband whether she does the same freely and
voluntarily without the persuasions or threats of the said James Tapscott her
husband and whether she be willing the same shall be recorded... in the fifth
year of our Commonwealth... Thads McCarty Recorded 17 Aug 1780 by Test
Thads McCarty CLC. [Page 246a]

17 Apr 1780. Certificate. By virtue of the within Commission we the
subscribers did personally apply to the within named Elizabeth Tapscott &
examined her privily and apart from her husband touching the annexed Indenture
who answered that she consented the same freely and voluntarily without any
persuasions or threats from her husband and that she is willing the same should
be recorded...[Wit:] James Gordon and Henry Towles. Recorded 17 Aug 1780
by Test Thads McCarty CLC. [Page 247]

17 Aug 1780. Deed of Bargain and Sale with Receipt. Between Richard
Mitchell and Mary his wife of the county of Lancaster of the one part and
William Mitchell of the same county of the other part... Richard Mitchell and
Mary his wife for and in consideration of the sum of one thousand nine hundred
pounds current money in hand paid at or before the sealing and delivery of these
presents... forever all that tract or parcel of land devised by William Mitchell
(grandfather of the said Richard) unto his son William (unkle of the said
Richard) from whom it descended unto his son Thomas who sold the same unto
John Mitchell (father of the said Richard) who devised the same to the said
Richard situate in the said county of Lancaster bounded on the main western
branch of Corotomon River, the lands of the said William Mitchell, Thomas
Williams and Mungo Harvey and the land the said Richard purchased of George
Heale Gent containing one hundred and thirty acres... [Wit:] Richard Ball,
Ozwald Newby, & Colm Doggett. Received the day of the date of the within
Indenture of the within named William Mitchell the sum of one thousand nine
hundred pounds current money in full consideration for the within mentioned

parcel of land and premises. [same witnesses as listed above]. Recoreded 17 Aug 1780 by Test Thads McCarty CLC. [Pages 247, 247a & 248]

26 Jun 1780. Deed of Bargain and Sale with Receipt. Between Joseph McAdam of the parish of St Stephen and county of Northumberland Gent and Sarah his wife of the one part and John Clayton of Wiccomoco and county of Lancaster of the other part... Joseph McAdam and Sarah his wife for and in consideration of the sum of five hundred pounds current money to them in hand paid by the said John Clayton at or before the ensealing and delivery... forever all that tract of land and plantation where John Pinckard Gent deceased lived & died and whereon the said Joseph McAdam after the said John Pinckard did also for some time live containing two hundred and ninety three acres and bounded as followeth vizt begining at a dead corner red oak of Col Carter thence north five deg thirty minutes east two hundred and thirty three poles to the corner red oak of Henry Tapscott on the side of the main swamp of Col. Carters Mill thence south seventy four degrees east one hundred and sixty five poles to a corner red oak of Simmons thence south six degrees west two hundred and thirty three poles to a corner hiccory in Clement Lattimores line thence north seventy four degrees west one hundred & sixty two poles to the begining with the rights members and appurtenances thereof situate lying & being in the parish of Great Wiccomoco and county of Lancaster aforesaid... [Wit:] Edwin Conway, Thos Pollard, William Brown, & Janeta Brown. Received the day of the date of the within written Indenture of the within named John Clayton the sum of five hundred pounds current money of Virginia being the consideration money within mentioned. I say received by me Joseph McAdam. [same witnesses as listed above]. Recorded 17 Aug 1780 by Test Thads McCarty CLC. [Pages 248, 248a & 249]

21 Sep 1780. Deed of Bargain and Sale with Receipt. Between Thomas Pollard of the county of Lancaster & Mary his wife of the one part & Rawleigh Hazard of the same county of the other part... Thos Pollard and Mary his wife for and in consideration of the sum of three hundred pounds current money in hand paid at or before the sealing and delivery of these presents... [for] part of that tract or parcel of land that he the said Pollard purchased of Wm Steptoe as far as the Church and Ferry Roads which the said Hazard now lives on situate in the said county of Lancaster binding in the lands of John Eustace Thos Pinckard Elmore Doggett & the sd Pollard containing by estimation two acres more or less... [no witnesses listed]. Recorded 21 Sep 1780 by Thads McCarty CLC. [Pages249 & 249a]

21 Dec 1780. Deed of Bargain and Sale with Receipt. ...Between Moses George and Wilmoth his wife of the parish of Christ Church in the county of Lancaster and Common wealth of Virginia of the one part and William Chilton

the younger by trade a carpenter of the same parish county and Common wealth of the other part... Moses George and Wilmoth his wife for and in consideration of the sum of six hundred pounds current money of Virginia... forever a certain tract or parcel of land situate lying and being in the said county of Lancaster between the branches of the Corotoman River adjoining the western branch of the said river and bounded as followeth begining at the head of a small creek which receives the waters of Porringes (?) branch and up the said branch to the head thereof and along a strait line to the main road that leads to the following point, thence along the said road to a white oak between Lazarus Georges and this said tract of land thence along Lazarus Georges line to the corner between this land Lazarus Georges and Jesse Harrisons, thence along Jesse Harrisons line down to a place called the great marsh at the head of a creek and up the said creek to the begining at the head thereof... [Wit:] Jesse Harrison, John Miller, & Richard Ball. December 20 1780 received of Mr William Chilton of Christ Church Parish six hundred pounds current money of Virginia in full for the within mentioned thirty acres of land be the same more or less. [same witnesses as listed above]. Recorded 21 Dec 1780 by Test Thads McCarty CLC. [Pages 250 & 250a]

16 Jan 1781. Deed of Bargain and Sale with Receipt. Between John Hall of the county of Newkent of the one part & Peter Conway of the county of Northumberland of the other part... John Hall for and in consideration of the sum of two hundred and fifty thousand pounds of Rappahannock Crop Tobacco to him the said John Hall in hand well and truly paid by the said Peter Conway at and before the sealing and delivery of these presents... forever all that plantation tract or parcel of land situate lying and being in the parish of Christ Church & county of Lancaster adjoining the lands of George Currell, John Parrott, William Griggs, Rawleigh Shearman, Charles Lee and James Currell containing by estimation seven hundred acres more or less... [Wit:] James Tapscott, William Tapscott, & Robt Clt(?) Jacob. Received the day of the date of this Indenture of the within named Peter Conway two hundred and fifty thousand pounds of Rappahannock Crop Tobacco being the full consideration within mentioned to be paid to me. [same witnesses as listed above]. Recorded 16 Jan 1781 by Test Thads McCarty CLC. [Pages 250a, 251, & 251a]

13 Mar 1777. Deed of Bargain and Sale. Between Richard Payne and Ailce his wife of the county of Lancaster and parish of [blank] of the one part and Joseph Sampson of the county of Northumberland and parish of Wiccomoco of the other part... Richard Payne and Ailse his wife for and in consideration of ninety pounds of good & lawful money of this Commonwealth of Virginia to him in hand paid by the said Joseph Sampson... forever a certain tract or parcel of land situate lying and being in the county aforesaid and parish of Wiccomoco contain one hundred and forty acres which sd land is bounded as follows begining at a

mark standing on the path commonly called the Machodoch Path and starting from the corner of Jesse Cluttons cornfield fence runs south easterly first to markd black oak standing in the old field thence forward to mark'd trees as may or shall be found on that corner or answerable to the first two to mention to a branch dividing William Bean from the sd land thence down the said branch to a branch and run falling into Mrs Balls Mill and is the main branch thereof which two aforesaid branches falls into one and forms a fork thence up the said main branch dividing the aforesaid land from the land of George Payne to a marked tree standing in the fork of the sd main branch and one making out of it into the sd land runing east northerly thence up the said main branch through the middle of the same dividing the aforesd land from the land of John Payne or from that tract of land in the parish of St Marys White Chappel called Islington as will more fully appear by a Deed made to George Payne by his brother William Payne bearing date 1708 and so along up the middle of the sd main branch to another fork the fork still making up the said land east northerly thence along up a branch commonly called and known by the name of Millers Grave Branch to the dividing line between the sd land and John Clutton and along the said Cluttons line or land easterly to a sandy bottom to the other corner of the above mentioned Jesse Cluttons cornfield and the said Jesse having trespassed on sd land and set his fence thereon the sd line from the aforesaid sandy bottom runs through the sd Jesse's inclosure along an old road (the sign of which is now plain and is answerable to the above Machodoch Path) to the mark from whence begun the sd bounds including the quantity or number of acres aforesaid with all the profits priviledges and advantages thereunto belonging excepting the wheat now growing on the premises unto the said Joseph Sampson... forever... [Wit:] Thomas Davis, Dennis Sulevan, & John Davis. At a court dated [blank] day of [blank] this Indenture of Bargain and Sale... was proved by Thomas and John Davis & Dennis Sullivan... and ordered to lie for further proof and at a court held for the sd county 18 Feb 1781 was further proved by John Davis... [Wit:] Test Thads McCarty CLC. [Pages 251a, 252, &252a]

27 Nov 1780. Deed of Lease and Release. Between Peter Conway and Frances his wife of the county of Lancaster of the one part and Robert Clark Jacob of the county of Northumberland of the other part... Peter Conway and Frances his wife for and in consideration of the sum of two thousand pounds in gold & silver lawful money of Virginia to the said Peter Conway in hand well and truly paid by the said Robert C. Jacob at and before the sealing and delivery of these presents... unto the said Robert Clark Jacob (In his actual possession now being by virtue of a Bargain and Sale to him thereof made for one whole year by Indenture bearing date twenty fifth day of this present November last past and by force of the statute for transferring uses into possession)... all that plantation tract or parcel of land situate lying & being in the parish of Christ Church and county of Lancaster whereon the sd Peter Conway now lives and which the said

Peter Conway purchased of John Selden by Deed bearing date on or about the seventeenth of January last past containing by estimation four hundred and fifty acres more or less adjoining the lands of William Montague John Taylor John Leland Job Carter and Margaret Boatman and also one water grist mill adjoining the said plantation with the houses dam pond stones standing and runing gear and all and every appurtenances to the same mill... [no witnesses listed]. [Pages 252a, 253, 253a, & 254]

28 Nov 1780. Commission. The Commonwealth of Virginia to John Taylor James Gordon and Edwin Conway Gent Greeting whereas Peter Conway and Frances his wife by their certain Indenture of Lease and Release bearing date 27 Nov 1780 hath bargained and sold unto Robert Clark Jacob one tract or parcel of land and water grist mill adjoining thereunto containing 450 acres more or less lying and being in the county of Lancaster and whereas Frances wife of the said Peter Conway cannot conveniently travel to our said court of Lancaster to make her acknowledgment and relinquishment of her right contained in the aforesaid Deed therefore we do give unto you or any two or more of you full power to receive the acknowledgment and relinquishment which the said Frances Conway shall be willing to make before you or any two or more of you and we do therefore command you that you personally go to the said Frances and examine her privily and apart from Peter Conway her husband whether she does the same freely and voluntarily without his persuasions or threats and whether she is willing the same shall be recorded... Thads McCarty. [Page 254]

24 Jan 1781. Certificate. ...We the subscribers did go personally to the said Frances Conway wife of the said Peter Conway and did examine her privily and apart from her husband respecting the Lease and Release within mentioned and she acknowledged she signed the same freely and voluntarily of her own will and consent and without the threats or persuasions of her said husband and that she is willing the same shall be recorded... [Wit:] James Gordon & Edwin Conway. [Page 254]

25 Nov 1780. Deed of Lease and Release. Between Peter Conway and Frances his wife of the parish of Christ Church in the county of Lancaster of the one part and Robert Clark Jacob of the county of Northumberland of the other part... Peter Conway & Frances his wife for and in consideration of the sum of five shillings lawful money of Virginia to the said Peter Conway in hand well and truly paid by the said Robert C. Jacob at and before the sealing and delivery of these presents... [for] all that plantation tract or parcel of land situate lying and being in the parish of Christ Church and county of Lancaster whereon the said Peter Conway now lives containing by estimation four hundred and fifty acres be the same more or less and also one water grist mill adjoining the said plantation... and after the twenty fifth day of this present month of November in

the year aforesaid yielding and paying one ear of Indian corn yearly if the same shall be lawfully demanded to the intent that by virtue of these presents and of the statute of transferring uses into possession He the said Robert C. Jacob may be in the actual possession of all and singular the said premises above mentioned... [Wit:] John Taylor, Richd E. Lee, John Selden, George Lee, Henry Tapscott, James Tapscott, & William Tapscott. Recorded 15 Feb 1781 by Thads McCarty CLC. [Pages 254 & 254a]

24 Jan 1781. Deed of Lease and Release. Between Peter Conway and Frances his wife of the parish of Wicocomoco in the county of Northumberland of the one part and Robert Clark Jacob of the county of Lancaster of the other part... the said Peter Conway and Frances his wife for and in consideration of the sum of twenty five hundred pounds of gold and silver lawful money of Virginia to the sd Peter Conway in hand well and truly paid by the said Robert Clark Jacob at and before the sealing and delivery of these presents... unto the said Robert Clark Jacob (In his actual possession now being by virtue of a Bargain and Sale to him thereof made for one whole year by Indenture bearing date the day next before the day of the date of these presents and by force of the statute for transferring uses into possession)... all that plantation tract or parcel of land situate lying & being in the parish of Christ Church and county of Lancaster which the said Peter Conway lately purchased of John Hall and adjoins the lands of James Currell John Parrott George Currell Charles Lee William Griggs and Rawleigh Shearman containing by estimation seven hundred acres... [Wit:] Edwin Conway, John Taylor, James Gordon, & James Tapscott. Received 24 Jan 1781 of the within named Robert Clark Jacob twenty five hundred pounds gold and silver lawful money of Virginia being the full consideration money within mentioned to be paid to me-Peter Conway. [Wit:] James Tapscott & James Gordon. Recorded 15 Feb 1781 by Test Thads McCarty CLC. [Pages 255, 255a, 256 & 256a]

25 Jan 1781. Commission. The Commonwealth of Virginia to John Taylor James Gordon & Edwin Conway Gent greeting whereas Peter Conway and Frances his wife by their certain Indenture of Lease and Release having date the lease the twenty third and the release the twenty fourth of this instant January 1780 and have sold and conveyed unto Robert C. Jacob a tract of land containing seven hundred acres more or less situated and being in Lancaster County with the appurtenances and whereas the said Frances Conway cannot conveniently travel to our county court of Lancaster to make acknowledgment of her right in the said land therefore we do give unto you or any two or more of you full power to receive of her right in the said land contained in the aforesaid Indentures which are hereunto annexed which the said Frances shall be willing to make before you and we therefore command you that you personally go to the said Frances Conway and receive her acknowledgment of the same and examine

her privily and apart from her said husband whether she does the same freely and voluntarily without his threats or persuasions and whether she be willing that the same should be recorded... Thads McCarty. Recorded 15 Feb 1781 by Test Thads McCarty CLC. [Page 256]

24 Jan 1781. Certificate. ...we the subscribers did go personally to Mrs Frances Conway wife of the within mentioned Peter Conway and did examine her privily and apart from her said husband respecting the Lease and Release within mentioned and hereunto annexed where she acknowledged she signed the same freely and voluntarily of her own will and consent and without the threats or persuasions of her said husband and that she is willing the same shall be recorded... [Wit:] James Gordon & Edwin Conway. Recorded 15 Feb 1781 by Test Thads McCarty CLC. [Page 256]

23 Jan 1781. Deed of Lease and Release. Between Peter Conway and Frances his wife of the county of Northumberland of the one part and Robert Clark Jacob of the county of Lancaster of the other part... Peter Conway for and in consideration of the sum of five shillings lawful money of Virginia to him in hand paid by the said Robert C. Jacob at and before the sealing and delivery of these presents... [for] all that plantation tract or parcel of land situate lying & being in the parish of Christ Church within the county of Lancaster adjoining the lands of George Currell John Parrott James Currell Charles Lee William Griggs and Rawleigh Shearman containing by estimation seven hundred acres... from the first day of this instant January... unto the full and said term of one whole year from thence next ensuing and fully to be compleat and ended yielding & paying therefore at the expiration of the said year one ear of Indian corn if the same is lawfully demanded to the intent that by virtue of these presents and of the statute for transferring usses into possession He the said Robert Clark Jacob may be in the actual possession of all and singular the said premises above mentioned with the appurtenances and thereby inabled to take and accept grant and release of the reversion and inheritance thereof to him... [Wit:] Edwin Conway, John Taylor, James Gordon, & James Tapscott. Recorded 15 Feb 1781 by Test Thads McCarty CLC. [Page 256a]

26 Jun 1780. Bond. Know all men by these presents that we Joseph McAdam and John McAdam of the parish of Wiccomoco and county of Lancaster in the sum of ten thousand pounds lawful money of Virginia to be paid to the said John Clayton... for which payment well and truly to be made We bind ourselves... The condition of this obligation is such that if the above bound Joseph McAdam... shall in all things well and truly observe... all and singular the covenants... which on the part and behalf of the said Joseph McAdam... are or might be observed... in certain Indentures biparticle bearing even date with the above written obligation made... between the said Joseph McAdam of the first

part and the above named John Clayton of the other part... [Wit:] Edwin Conway & Thos Pollard. Recorded 15 Jan 1781 by Test Thads McCarty CLC. [Page 257]

21 Dec 1780. Deed of Bargain and Sale with Receipt. Between Roger Kelly and Betty his wife of the parish of Christ Church in the county of Lancaster of the one part and Jesse Crowder of the parish of Wiccomoco in the county of Northumberland of the other part... Roger Kelly and Betty his wife for and in consideration of the sum of fifteen thousand pounds of crop tobacco and casks or the value in lawful money of Virginia by the said Jesse Crowder to him the said Roger Kelly in hand well and truly paid at and before the sealing and delivery of these presents... forever all that plantation tract or parcel of land situate lying and being in the parish of Christ Church within the county of Lancaster whereon the said Roger Kelly and Betty his wife now live adjoining the lands of Aaron Williams Lawson Wale William Martin Benjamin Garton Henry Currell Isaac Degge and Walter James by Nantepoison Creek and the marked tree lines and boundaries as the said Roger Kelly now holds... containing by estimation one hundred acres... provided always that the said Roger Kelly and Betty his wife shall have full power... to live upon...and enjoy the houses and buildings now standing and being at the said plantation with full liberty to work and tend at least ten thousand corn hills on the same and to cut and cart as much wood and timber thereon being as shall be... necessary to repair the fences houses and to burn firewood in his the said Roger Kelly's dwelling house kitchen or quarter For and during the lives of them and each of them the said Roger Kelly and Betty his wife and the survivor of them yielding and paying unto the said Jesse Crowder... one ear of Indian corn on Christmas Day annually and every year if lawfully demanded during the term aforesaid... [Wit:] Thos Carter, Isaac Degge, & Wm James. Received 21 Dec 1780 of the within named Jesse Crowder the sum of fifteen thousand pounds of crop tobacco or the value in lawfull money of Virginia being the full consideration money for the within mentioned to be paid to me... [same witnesses as listed above]. Be it remembered that on the day of the date of this Indenture full quiet and peaceable possession and seizen of the within mentioned plantation tract or parcel of land was had and given by the within named Roger Kelly to the within named Jesse Crowder by the delivery of Turf and Twig upon the premises... [same witnesses as listed above]. Recorded 19 Apr 1781 by Test Thads McCarty CLC. [Pages 257, 257a, 258, & 258a]

12 May 1781. Deed of Bargain and Sale with Receipt. Between Nathan Pullen and Elizabeth his wife of Northumberland County of the one part and Jeduthun Moore of Lancaster County of the other part... Nathan Pullen and Elizabeth his wife for and in consideration of the sum of twenty six pounds current money of Virginia to him in hand paid by the said Jeduthun Moore... [for] all that

messuage plantation and tract of land which the said Nathan Pullen is now
possessed with lying and being in the county of Lancaster all that messuage
plantation and tract of land which was given to Elizabeth Pullen by her father
Richard Cundiff and bounded by the land of Richard Ball John Goodridge
Benjamin Cundiff and John Boyd containing by estimation thirty two & one half
acres... [Wit:] Wm Hunt, Ben. Cundiff, & Johnson Riveer. Received on the
day of the date of the within written Indenture of the within named Jeduthun
Moore the sum of twenty six pounds current money of Virginia being the
consideration for the within mentioned land and premises. [same witness as
listed above]. Memdm that on the day of the date of the within written Indenture
full and peaceable possession of Livery and Seizin of the within mentioned
premises was by me had and taken and delivered unto the said Jeduthun Moore.
[same witnesses as listed above]. Recorded 17 May 1781 by Test Thads
McCarty CLC. [Pages 258a, 259 & 259a]

17 May 1781. Deed of Bargain and Sale with Receipt. Between Jesse Robinson
of the county of Lancaster of the one part and James Norris of the same county
of the other part... Jesse Robinson for and in consideration of the sum of fifteen
hundred pounds of lawful tobacco in hand paid at or before the sealing and
delivery of these presents... forever all that tract piece or parcel of land whereon
the said Jesse Robinson now dwelleth and is bounded as followeth Begining at a
stake (by a cedar bush) in the line between the said parties & runing thence to a
marked willow tree in the main branch of Col James Balls Mill Swamp thence to
the corner (in said swamp) between said Jesse Robinson and James Norris
thence along this line to the begining containing by estimation ten acres... [Wit:]
Wm Sydnor, Wm Stonum, & Johnson Riveer. Received the day of the date of of
the within named James Norris the sum of fifteen hundred pounds of lawful
tobacco in full consideration for the within granted parcel of land and premises.
[same witnesses as listed above]. Signed by Jesse Robinson Jnr. Recorded 17
May 1781 by Test Thads McCarty CLC. [Pages260 & 260a]

31 Oct 1780. Deed of Bargain and Sale with Receipt. ...in the fifth year of the
Commonwealth Between Richard Chilton of the county of Culpeper & Judith his
wife of the one part and William Chilton Junr of the county of Lancaster of the
other part... Richard Chilton and Judith his wife for and in consideration of the
sum of three thousand pounds current money in hand paid at or before the
sealing and delivery of these presents... forever all that tract or parcel of land
situate within said county of Lancaster which the said Richard Chilton purchased
of Thomas Lee by two several Deeds of Conveyances and is bounded by the
lands of William Chilton Junr & John Harris the creeks and branches thereof
anciently known by the names of Berrys and [blank] Creeks as by the said two
Deeds of Conveyances... containing by estimation one hundred acres... [Wit:]
Thads McCarty, Vachal Faundrie, & Eppa. Lawson. Received the day of the

date of the within Indenture of the within named William Chilton Junr the sum of three thousand pounds current money in full consideration for the within granted tract or parcel of land and premises. [same witnesses as listed above]. At a court held for Lancaster County 19 Apr 1781 This Indenture of Bargain and Sale... was proved by the oaths of Thads McCarty and Vachal Faundrie... & ordered to lie for further proof and... 17 May following was further proved by Eppas Lawson & recorded by Test Thads McCarty CLC. [Pages 260a, 261, & 261a]

21 Jun 1781. Deed of Bargain and Sale with Receipt. Between James Gordon and Ann his wife of the parish of Christ Church in the county of Lancaster and Common Wealth of Virginia of the one part and Thaddeus McCarty of the same parish county and commonwealth of the other part... James Gordon and Ann his wife for and in the consideration of the sum of thirty thousand pounds of crop tobacco to them in hand paid by the said Thaddeus McCarty... [for] two certain tracts or parcels of land situate lying and being in the said parish of Christ Church and county of Lancaster, one of which containing two hundred and fifty acres according to estimation be the same more or less and is bounded by the lands of John Wormeley John Miller, Thomas Robb, Thomas Hubbard another tract belonging to the said James Gordon and the land of James Hill deceased, also one other tract of land containing by estimation three hundred and twelve acres be the same more or less and is bounded by the lands of James Tapscott, Charles Bell deceased, James Pinckard, Thomas Robb, John Miller and John Wormeley part of which last mentioned tract being two hundred and twelve acres was devised to the said James Gordon by the last Will and Testament of his father the late James Gordon deceased and which the said James Gordon deceased purchased of Col. Edwin Conway deceased, the other part being one hundred acres the said James Gordon purchased of James Pinckard late of this county and which one hundred acres Mrs. Mary Pinckard, widow now lives upon and has the use of during her natural life and which the said James Gordon hereby saves and reserves for the use of the said Mrs. Mary Pinckard during her natural life agreeable to the Tenor of a Bond the said James Gordon executed to the said Mrs Mary Pinckard for that purpose at the time he purchased the said one hundred acres of land of the said James Pinckard... the said first mentioned tract of two hundred and fifty acres was also devised to the said James Gordon by the last Will and Testament of his father the said James Gordon deceased and which the said James Gordon deceased bought of John Bell... forever the said two tracts of land above mentioned containing in the whole five hundred and sixty two acres... [no witnesses listed]. Received the 21 Jun 1781 from Col. Thaddeus McCarty thirty thousand pounds of crop tobacco in full for the within. Recorded 21 Jun 1781 by Test Thads McCarty CLC. [Pages 261a, 262, & 262a]

2 Feb 1781. Deed of Bargain and Sale with Receipt. Between Thads McCarty and Mary his wife of the county of Lancaster of the one part and James Gordon Gent of the said county of Lancaster of the other part... Thads McCarty and Mary his wife for and in consideration of the sum of thirty thousand pounds lawful money of Virginia to them in hand paid by the said James Gordon at or before the sealing and delivery of these presents... forever all that tract or parcel of land whereon the said Thads McCarty lately lived being the land and plantation the said Thads McCarty purchased of Thomas Rouand and which the said Rouand purchased of Richard Edwards Gent late of the said county of Lancaster situate lying and being in Fleets Bay Neck in the aforesaid county of Lancaster and is bounded as followeth begining at a marked pine tree (said to be the begining corner) upon Hathaways Creek and runing thence down the meanders of the said creek to the mouth of Swans Bay, thence along and up the meanders of the said bay to a point that makes Fleets Bay thence down Fleets Bay to the great bay of Chesapeak thence up the said bay to a point that makes the mouth of Indian Creek thence up the meanders of the said creek to a marked corner pine between sd land and the land of Mr James Brent thence 57 degrees W to the begining containing by estimation two hundred acres... [no witnesses listed]. Received the day of the within Indenture of the within named James Gordon the sum of thirty thousand pounds current money of Virginia being the full consideration within mentioned [by] Thads McCarty. Recorded 21 Jun 1781 by Test Thads McCarty. [Pages 262a, 263, 263a & 264]

3 Feb 1781. Commission. ... To James Ball, Richard Mitchell and James Ball Junr Gent greeting whereas Thads McCarty and Mary his wife by their certain Indenture of Bargain and Sale bearing date 2 Feb 1781 hath sold and conveyed unto James Gordon Gent of the county of Lancaster one certain tract or parcel of land and appurtenances lying and being in the aforesaid county of Lancaster containing two hundred acres more or less and whereas Mary the wife of the said Thads McCarty cannot conveniently travel to our said court to make her acknowledgment and relinquishment of her right in the land aforesaid therefore we do give you or any two or more of you full power to receive the acknowledgment and relinquishment that the said Mary shall be willing to make... we do therefore command you that you go personally to the said Mary and examine her privily & apart from the said Thads McCarty her husband whether she does the same freely and voluntarily without his persuasions or threats... Thads McCarty. Recorded 21 Jun 1781 by Test Thads McCarty. [Page 263a]

3 Feb 1781. Certificate. By virtue of the within Commission we the subscribers having examined the within named Mary privately and apart from the within named Thads McCarty her husband, do hereby certify that she doth freely and voluntarily without the persuasions or threats of her said husband acknowledge

her right to the land mentioned and contained in the within mentioned Deed which is hereunto annexed & that she is willing the said Deed should be recorded... [Wit:] Jas Ball & James Ball Junr. Recorded 21 Jun 1781 by Test Thads McCarty. [Page 264]

16 Mar 1767. Bond. Know all men by these presents that we Jesse Robinson and James Robinson of Lancaster County are held and firmly bound and indebted unto William Lattimore of Wiccomoco Parish in the county of Northumberland in the full and just sum of one thousand pounds current money of Virginia to which payment well and truly to be made to the said William Lattimore... The condition of this obligation is such that whereas the above bounden Jesse Robinson and James Robinson hath this day covenated... unto the above named William Lattimore... forever, all their the said Jesse Robinson and James Robinson's claim... to the negroes and other personal estate of Jesse Robinson late of Wiccomoco Parish in the county of Northumberland decd for the consideration of six pounds current money of Virginia to them the said Jesse & James Robinson well and truly paid by the said William Lattimore Now if the said Jesse Robinson and James Robinson... shall at any time hereafter share thereunto required by the said Wm Lattimore... do and consents at the cost and charges of the said Wm Lattimore a proper Bill of Sale or any other instrument of writing and the same acknowledged in the county court to convey and absolute right in all the negroes and personal estate of Jesse Robinson decd... [Wit:] Wm Angell, John Mahanes, & Alexr Hinton. Recorded 19 Jul 1781 by Test Thads McCarty CLC. [Pages 264 & 264a]

15 Aug 1781. Deed of Bargain and Sale with Receipt. Between John Heath Senior of the parish Wiccomoco & county Northumberland of the one part and John Heath Junior of the parish & county aforesaid of the other part... for and in consideration of the sum of two hundred pounds lawful money in hand paid by the sd John Heath Junior to the sd John Heath Senior at or before the sealing and delivery of these presents... forever all that tract or parcel of land lying situate & being in the county of Lancaster containing by estimation three hundred & five acres more or less as also another tract or parcel of land adjoining the same containing by estimation one hundred acres both which tracts or parcels of lands the sd Heath purchased of Conway & Cundiff the latter of who is at present subject to the incumberance & inconvenience of William Galloways life & sd tract or parcel of land was conveyed to a certain Dr Nicholas Flood in his lifetime by a Deed exacted under duress & imprisonment of the sd Heath the livery of seizen & possession were never delivered the said Flood & are bounded as follows the former of wh[ich] begins at a black stump running NW to a large hiccory binding on the two orphan Webbs & the same direct course to forked dogwood thence runing this a small old field to a large old red oak border'd on Lizenbys land & thence from the corner of the sd Lizenbys fence over the head

of a branch to an old hiccory stump & thence a direct course to a great swamp & down the sd swamp a S W course to Everitts & S E to a large white oak & thence over a branch across the old Lancaster Road to a large chestnutt bind'd on George Webbs orphan & from thence over the swamp to the latter tract or parcel of land before mentioned wh[ich] is binding on Carter on the one side & Pearcifull on the other... [Wit:] Thos Yerby, Chas Coppedge, & Isaac Peed. Be it remembered that on the same day & year within written that the sd John Heath Senr did surrender and deliver unto the sd John Heath Junr quiet and lawful possession of the within premises of Livery of Seizen of Twig & Turf before the within named witnesses on the premises & doth likewise acknowledge the receipt of two hundred pounds lawful money from the sd John Heath Junr... [same witnesses as listed above]. Recorded 16 Aug 1781 by Test Thads McCarty CLC. [Pages 264a, 265 & 265a]

19 Apr 1781. Deed of Bargain and Sale with Receipt. Between Mungo Harvey of the county of Lancaster and Priscilla his wife of the one part and John Selden of the same county of the other part... Mungo Harvey and Prissilla his wife for and in consideration of the sum of one hundred thousand pounds of crop tobacco and casks by the said John Selden in hand paid at or before the sealing and delivery of these presents... forever the two following tracts or parcels of land situate in the county of Lancaster, to wit, all that tract or parcel of land whereon the said Mungo Harvey now dwelleth on the west side of the westward branch of Corotomon River and by him purchased of George Heale Gent and Sarah his wife containing by estimation two hundred acres be it more or less and all that tract or parcel of land purchased by said George Heale Gent of James Webb at two different times containing by estimation eighty four acres be it more or less and are bounded as mentioned in the Deed from the said George Heale to the said Mungo Harvey as by the said Deed... from and after the first day of January next forever... the said John Selden... quietly peaceably have... granted parcel of land & premises... [Wit:] Jas Ball, James Gordon, & Henry Towles. Received the day of the date of the within Indenture of the within named John Selden the sum of one hundred thousand pounds of crop tobo and casks in full consideration of the within mentioned two parcels of land and premises. [same witnesses as listed above]. Recorded 16 Aug 1781 by Test Thads McCarty. [Pages 265a, 266, & 266a]

20 Apr 1781. Commission. The Commonwealth of Virginia To James Ball James Gordon and Henry Towles Gent greeting Whereas Mungo Harvey and Prissilla his wife by their certain Indenture of Bargain and Sale bearing date 13 Apr 1781 have sold and conveyed unto John Selden two tracts of land with the appurtenances containing 284 acres more or less lying and being in the county of Lancaster and whereas Prissilla wife of the said Mungo Harvey cannot conveniently travel to our said county court of Lancaster to make

acknowledgment of her right in the land aforesd therefore we do give unto you or any two or more of you full power to receive the acknowledgment which the said Prissilla shall be willing to make before you of the land aforesaid contained in the aforesaid Indenture which is hereunto annexed and we do therefore command you that you personally go to the sd Prissilla and receive her acknowledgment and relinquishment and examine her privily and apart from her said husband whether she does the same freely and voluntarily without his persuasions or threats and whether she is willing the same shall be recorded... Thads McCarty. Recorded 16 Aug 1781 by Test Thads McCarty. [Pages 266 & 266a]

20 Apr 1781. Certificate. By virtue of the within Commission We the subscribers have examined the within named Prissilla Harvey privately and apart from her husband the within named Mungo Harvey & do certify the said Prissilla doth freely & voluntarily without the threats or persuasions of her said husband acknowledge the dower to the two tracts of land mentioned in a Deed which is hereto annexed and that she is willing the same shall be recorded... [Wit:] Jas Ball, James Gordon & Henry Towles. Recorded 16 Aug 1781 by Test Thads McCarty. [Page 266a]

4 Jun 1777. Bill of Sale with Receipt. Know all men by these presents that I John Wormeley of the county of Lancaster for and in consideration of the sum of one hundred and fifty five pounds lawfull money of Virginia to me in hand paid by William Brown of the said county at and before the sealing and delivery of these presents... for divers other good causes and considerations one thereunto moving have given... unto the said William Brown... the following negroe slaves with their future increase, to wit, Nanny and her two children Polly and Phill, Phillis and her three children Peggy Nelson and a young child a girl not yet christened all which negroe slaves I have delivered over to the said William Brown... [Wit:] Edwin Conway, Robert McCleay, & Jas W Ball. Received of the within named William Brown 4 Jun 1777 one hundred and fifty five pounds lawfull money of Virginia being the full consideration money within mentioned. Recorded 16 Aug 1781 by Test Thads McCarty CLC. [Pages 266a & 267]

18 Oct 1780. Deed of Trust. Between William Kent of the parish of Wiccomoco in the county of Lancaster of the one part and Edwin Conway of the parish of Christ Church in the said county of the other part... William Kent for and in consideration of the sum of five shillings current money to him in hand paid by the said Edwin Conway at and before the sealing and delivery of these presents and also for the performance of a contract or argument made by the said William Kent and his wife Ann at and before the Solemnization of their marriage as for divers other good causes and considerations him thereunto moving he the said William Kent hath given... unto the said Edwin Conway... one negroe girl slave

named Nanny and her increase, two feather beds and furniture or chest of
drawers, eight flag chairs, one walnut oval table, one large black leather trunk,
one small seal shim trunk, one square pine table, one tea table, seven silver tea
spoons, six pewter plates, two pewter dishes, one iron pot, one Dutch oven, eight
Queens china plates one small iron skillet, one tea kettle, five tea cups five
saucers one small china bowl... and the said Edwin Conway doth hereby signify
and declare that his name only is used in trust in this Indenture and to the intent
to permit and suffer the said Willm Kent and Ann his wife to hold and enjoy the
said negroe slave Nanny and her increase together with the above mentioned
articles for and during their natural lives and from and after their decease in
Trust to and for the only proper use and behalf of Ann Sarah and Isaac Taylor
Lucy Lee Legg and Mary Waddy children of the said Ann by her former
husband Isaac Taylor decd and also my daughter Charlotte to be equally divided
among them but at the death of the said Mary Waddy, her equal proportion of
the said negroe slave Nanny and her increase together with the above mentioned
articles to Clarissa Harlowe Taylor daughter of the said Mary Waddy... [Wit:]
John Heath Junr & Chas Lee. Recorded 18 Oct 1781 by Test Thads McCarty
CLC. [Pages 267 & 267a]

25 Sep 1781. Receipt. Then received on the within day and date of the within
Joseph Sampson the full sum of ninety pounds as written, it being the
consideration money for the within mentioned tract of land. Recd by me
Richard Payne. [Wit:] Peter Riveer, Richd Goodridge, Ailce Riveer, & Mary
ann Cundiff. This receipt from Richard Payne to Joseph Sampson was further
prov'd by Maryann Cundiff and ordered to be recorded previous to which at a
court held... 25 Sep 1781 was proved by Peter Riveer and Richd Goodridge and
ordered to lie for further proof [by] Test Thads McCarty CLC. [Pages 267a &
268]

9 Feb 1781. Bond. Know all men by these presents that we Bailie George and
Maurice Wheeler of the parish of Christ Church and the county of Lancaster are
held and firmly bound each to other in the just sum of ten thousand pounds of
crop tobacco for value received to which payment well and truly to be made...
The condition of this obligation is such that whereas there has been suits &
disputes between the above bound Bailie George and the above bound Maurice
Wheeler concerning the bounds and lines of their lands some were of opinion
that the lines run one course and some were of opinion that they run another way
and thereupon the processioning of the said lines were stop'd Now therefore to
establish the bounds and lines between the above parties we this day without any
regard to any former dispute or line We each of us agree... the line following to
be and continue between our land forever. The line begins at a locust (at the
upper end) a straight line between the said Bailie and Maurice and Mr Nathanl
Gordon and a corner between the said George and Wheeler thence runing a

straight line to a small spruce pine thence still in a straight line to the old chestnut stump mentioned in the deposition of Wm Scofield and others to a locust tree which is a straight line thence straight forward to a honey locust standing in an old brick kiln still forward straight to a chestnut sprout growing on an old stump, thence to a spruce pine a side line, thence to a dogwood tree, still straight to a locust fork thence straight to the creek side, the whole line being straight, 120W S....? it is that if the said Bailie George and Maurice Wheeler... shall at all times or forever be satisfied and contented with the abovesaid bounds and line without interrupting or molesting each other in peaceable possession of the land... [Wit:] Thos Hathaway, John Roberts, & James Kelly. At a court held for Lancaster County 17 May 1781... Bond... was proved by John Roberts and James Kelly and ordered to lie for further proof and at a court held for the said county 18ᵗʰ day October following was further proved by Thos Hathaway and ordered to be recorded Thads McCarty CLC. [Pages 268 & 268a]

17 Oct 1781. Deed of Bargain and Sale with Receipt. Between John Selden of the county of Lancaster Gent and Anne his wife of the one part and Richard Selden Gent of the same county of the other part... John Selden and Anne his wife for and in consideration of the sum of seventy thousand pounds of merchantable crop tobacco & casks in hand paid at or before the sealing and delivery of these presents... forever all that messuage tenement tract or parcel of land situate in the said county of Lancaster, formerly the property of Mr Thomas Lee decd who sold part thereof to William Griggs who sold the same to Col. Richard Selden from whom it descended to the said John Selden his Heir at Law, the remainder part thereof descended from the said Thomas Lee to his daughter Mary who with her husband Richard Hall conveyed the same to the said John Selden containing in the whole four hundred and twenty acres be it more or less and is bounded on the main branch of Mr Robert Clark Jacobs (formerly Col. Richard Seldens) Mill Pond & the lands of the Reverend Mr John Lelands, Capt William Montague and Mr William Warren... [also] part of the negroes, stocks, household furniture or other personal estate now in the possession of his mother Mary Selden, the use whereof devised unto her by her late husband Col. Richard Selden during her widowhood & at her death to be equally divided between his two sons the said John and Richard Selden parties to these presents...[Wit:] Jas W Ball, Elias Edmonds, & Jas Newby. Received the day of the date of the within Indenture of the within named Richard Selden the sum of seventy thousand pounds crop tobacco and cask in full consideration for the within granted parcel of land and premises negroes, stock, household furniture & other personal estate. [same witnesses as listed above]. Recorded 18 Oct 1781 by Thads McCarty CLC. [Pages 268a, 269, & 269a]

14 Nov 1781. Commission. The Commonwealth of Virginia To John Taylor, James W Ball & James Gordon Gent greetings Whereas Thomas Selden and Ann his wife by their certain Indenture of Bargain and Sale bearing date 17 Oct 1781 hath sold and conveyed unto Richard Selden an certain tract or parcel of land lying and being in the county of Lancaster containing 400 acres more or less, also negroes stocks & household furniture & C. and whereas Ann Selden the wife of the said John cannot conveniently travel to our said county court of Lancaster to make her acknowledgment of the same therefore we do give unto you or any two or more or you full power to receive the acknowledgment and relinquishment which the said Ann Selden shall be willing to make of her right aforesaid, and we do therefore command you that you personally go to the said Ann Selden and examine her privily and apart from her said husband whether she does the same freely and voluntarily without his persuasions or threats and whether she is willing the same shall be recorded... Thads McCarty. Recorded 18 Oct 1781 by Thads McCarty CLC. Recorded 18 Oct 1781 by Thads McCarty CLC. [Page 269a]

19 Dec 1781. Certificate. Agreeable to the within Commission to us directed we have examined Ann Selden relative to the annexed Indenture of Bargain and Sale privily and apart from her husband and she doth freely and voluntarily agree & acknowledge that she makes the conveyance without any persuasion or cumpulsion from her husband and also agrees the same shall be recorded... [Wit:] John Taylor & Jas W. Ball. Recorded 18 Oct 1781 by Thads McCarty CLC. [Page 269a]

16 Aug 1781. Deed of Bargain and Sale. ...and in the sixth year of the Commonwealth Between Rawleigh Hazard & Sarah his wife of the county of Lancaster and parish of Christ Church Silver Smith of the one part and Newton Brent of the same county and parish aforesaid of the other part... Rawleigh Hazard and Sarah his wife for and in consideration of the sum of fifteen thousand pounds current money of Virginia to him in hand paid... [for] a certain lott or parcell of land in the county and parish aforesaid known by the name of Kilmarnack containing by estimation five acres be the same more or less and is bounded as followeth, vizt Begining at the corner of the garden and runing as the ditch goes down the road that leads to the church to a corner at Mr Elmore Doggets line and from thence a cross the said Doggets old field as the ditch goes to the main road as leads down the county, and from thence up the said road as the ditch goes to the begining... [Wit:] John Parrott, William Yerby, & James Brent. August 16, 1781 received from Newton Brent the within mentioned sum of fifteen thousand pounds current money in full for the within mentioned premises. Recorded 20 Dec 1781 by Test Thads McCarty CLC. [Pages 270 & 270a]

4 Jun 1781. Deed of Bargain and Sale. Between Rawleigh Hazard of the parish of Christ Church and county of Lancaster and Sarah his wife of the one part and Alexander Hunton, William Haynie, Merideth Mahanes, Thomas Hammonds, William Norris and John Clayton Trustees of the Baptist Society and county of Lancaster & north of parish of Wiccomoco of the other part... Rawleigh Hazard and Sarah his wife for and in consideration of the sum of five hundred pounds current money to them in hand paid by the said Alexr Hunton, Wm Haynie, Merh Mahanes, Thos Hammonds, Wm Norris and John Clayton at or before the ensealing and delivery... for ever all that tract of land whereon stands the meeting house at Kilmarrock containing half an acre more or less and bounded as followeth Begining at a stake standing at the end of a ditch adjoining the Church Road north runing south fifty four yards from thence west runing east thirty yards along another ditch adjoining the Court Road from thence south along the said road north fifty four yards to a stake at the fork of the Church Road from thence east runing west thirty yards along the said Church Road to the begining... situate lying in the county of Lancaster and parish of Christ Church... [Wit:] Wm Hazard, James Hammonds, Maryann Coppedge, & Catherine Tapscott. Received the day of the date of the within Indenture of the within named Ten...? the sum of five hundred pounds currt money of Virginia being the consideration money within mentioned I say recd by me Rawh Hazard. Recorded 20 Dec 1781 by Thads McCarty CLC. [Pages 270a , 271 & 271a]

16 Dec 1781. Bill of Sale. Know all men by these presents that I Charles Rogers of Lancaster County for and in consideration of the sum of five shillings current money to me in hand paid have this day bargained and sold... to Joseph Sydnor of the county of Dinwiddie two negroes Judy and Gavin which said negroes... together with Judys increase... [Wit:] Henry Towles, Wm Chowning & Jno Chowning. Recorded 20 Dec 1781 by Thads McCarty CLC. [Page 272]

13 Aug 1781. Lease. Between John Moughon of the parish of Christ Church and county of Lancaster of the one part and George Brent of the said parish and county of the other part... for and in consideration of the sum of eighty pounds current money of Virginia to him the said John Moughon in hand paid by the said George Brent... [for] all that messuage or tenement plantation tract or parcel of land situate lying and being in the parish and county aforesaid and bounded by the lands of Nathaniel Gordon Jesse George and John Roberts containing by estimation fifty acres... from the first day of January next ensuing the date hereof for and during and unto the full end and term of ninety nine years from thence next ensuing and fully to be compleated and ended yielding and paying therefore yearly exclusive of the above consideration in hand paid and every year during the said term unto the said John Moughon... the yearly rent of one shilling current money of Virginia the first payment thereof to be made on the first day of January which shall happen and be in... 1783... [Wit:] John

Berryman, Robert Fergusson, Joseph Kem, John Parrott & William Merideth. Recorded 17 Jan 1782 by Test Thads McCarty CLC. [Pages 272, 272a & 273]

21 Dec 1781. Bond. Know all men by these presents that I John Moughon of the parish of Christ Church and county of Lancaster am holden and firmly bound unto George Brent of the said parish and county... in the just and full sum of one hundred and fifty pounds current money of Virginia... Whereas the said John Moughon hath leased to the said George Brent the tract of land lying and being in the county aforesaid whereon the said John Moughon lives containing by estimation fifty acres for the term of ninety nine years to commence from the first day of January next ensuing. Now the condition of the above obligation is such that if the said John Moughon will as soon as he has a good right and title in Fee Simple to the said land clear of all disputes... will whenever call'd upon by the said George Brent execute Deeds of Conveyance of the said lands to him the said George Brent... and in the mean time whenever calld upon by the said George Brent... will renew the said lease any time within the term of years mentioned in the lease for any other term of years or length of time the law will admit... [Wit:] John Berryman, Robert Fergusson, John Parrott, & William Merrideth. Recorded 17 Jan 1782 by Test Thads McCarty CLC. [Pages 273 & 273a]

5 Feb 1782. Deed of Trust. Between Corbin Griffin of the county of York Esquire and Mary his wife of the one part and the Honorable Ralph Wormeley of the other... for and in consideration of the sum of five thousand pounds... to him the said Corbin in hand paid by Nathaniel Burwill Esquire at and before the ensealing and delivery of these presents and also in the further consideration of the sum of five shillings... paid in like manner by the said Ralph to the said Corbin... unto the said Ralph all those tracts or parcels of land lying and being in the county of Lancaster being the lands which were devised to the said Corbin by his late brother Thomas Griffin and containing not only the old plantation but likewise those parcels of land adjoining which the said Thomas in his life time purchased of Newby and Oliver being partly bounded by the river Rappahannock Deep Creek and Mud Creek... the said Ralph... shall permit Nathaniell Burwell Esquire of the county of Lancaster to enter into said above conveyed lands and premises and to certain full seizen thereof and have hold and enjoy the same and take and receive the rents... during the continuence of the marriage of the said Nathaniel with his present wife Mary and if the said Nathaniel shall depart this life before his said wife then that the said Ralph shall permit the said Mary to enter into the premises and to retain certain full seizen thereof... after the decease of the said Mary he the said Ralph... shall reconvey the said premises to the said Nathaniel in fee if he shall then be alive, but if not, then to the Heir at Law of the said Nathaniel, if he shall have died intestate, and if not, then to such person to whom the said Nathaniel shall have devised the

same in his Will and Testament... [Wit:] William Ball, Eliza. Lee, & Martin Tapscott. Recorded 21 Feb 1782 by Test Thads McCarty CLC. [Pages 273, 273a & 274]

19 Jul 1781. Bill of Sale. Know all men by these presents that I William Kent of Lancaster County for and in consideration of the sum of ten thousand pounds current money in hand paid have this day bargained sold and delivered to George Brent youngr of the said county one negro girl calld Edy with her future increase... [Wit:] Henry Towles & Thads McCarty. Recorded 21 Feb 1782 by Test Thads McCarty CLC. [Page 274a]

13 Aug 1781. Bill of Sale. Know all men by these presents that I George Brent of the county of Lancaster for and in consideration of ten thousand pounds current money to me in hand paid by James Brent of the said county Planter have this day bargained sold and delivered unto the said Jas Brent one negro girl Edy with her future increase... [Wit:] Robert Fergusson & William Merrideth. Recorded 21 Feb 1782 by Test Thads McCarty CLC. [Page 274a]

21 Feb 1782. Certificates. I do certify that William Griggs the day before his decease that he devised me to take notice that the boat was Jesse Wilders. James Pollard. This is to certify that William Griggs told me that the boat his as long as he lived & at his death was for Jesse Wilders. Travers Lunceford. I do certify the Mr William Griggs told me that he had purchased Mr Isaac Currells schooner boat and that he had parted with her again to Jesse Wilder & had received full satisfaction of him for her, this happened some time in January last. Thos Pollard. James Pollard, Travers Lunceford and Thos Pollard severally made oath to the truth of each of the above writings to which their names are signed... before me Henry Lawson. Recorded 21 Feb 1782 by Test Thads McCarty CLC. [Page 275]

12 Nov 1781. Bill of Sale. Know all men by these presents that I William Griggs of the county of Lancaster for and in consideration of the sum of five shillings current money to me in hand paid by Jesse Wilder of the county aforesd as well as for divers other good causes and considerations one thereunto moving have given... nine hogsheads of tobacco now lying and being in my tobacco house and not yet inspected... [Wit:] Michael Wilder & Michael Wilder Junr. Recorded 21 Feb 1782 by Test Thads McCarty CLC. [Page 275a]

25 Mar 1782. Report. Pursuant to an order of Lancaster February court 1782. We the subscribers met and viewed the road Capt John Degge petitioned for and do report that the distance of the road to be about 120 steps further than the old road but equally as good and of little or no inconvenience to the publick...

[Wit:] William Schofield & John Cundiff. Recorded 21 Mar 1782 by Test Thads McCarty CLC. [Page 275a]

25 Mar 1779. Deed of Articles. Articles of Agreement Indented made concluded and agreed upon by and between Fortunatus Sydnor of the county of Northumberland and William Brown of the county of Lancaster... Whereas the said Forts Sydnor and William Brown agreed some time ago to build a water grist mill on a branch of the great Mil.... in Lancaster County and whereas the court of the said county have granted the sd Forts Sydnor leave to build the same... the said Fortunatus Sydnor hath granted unto the said William Brown... a joint interest... and agree to and with each other to build the said mill at their mutual cost and charge, and all costs... that have already accrued or shall hereafter acrue by means or on account... shall from time to time be mutually borne payed and defrayed by the said Fortunatus Sydnor and William Brown... share and share alike... and property of in and to the mill... shall from henceforth forever be vested and remain in the said Fortunatus Sydnor and William Brown jointly and severally... [Wit:] Bailie George, Benjamin George & Geo Phillips. At a court held 16 Aug 1781... proved by Bailie George & Geo Phillips and ordered to lye for further proof and in Mar 1782 was further proved by Benjamin George and recorded by Test Thads McCarty CLC. [Page 276]

INDEX

Elizabeth, 57; Ellen, 162; George, 2, 3, 34, 35, 38, 39, 41, 55, 56, 57, 109, 162, 163, 164, 168, 176, 177, 185, 197; John, 35, 57; Joseph, 16; Philip, 56; Sarah, 55, 56, 57, 162, 163, 164, 168, 197; William, 2, 56, 145

Heath, John, 1, 4, 12, 13, 17, 18, 19, 24, 25, 26, 27, 38, 39, 59, 60, 61, 73, 81, 82, 94, 95, 196, 197, 199; Judith, 94; Thomas, 12; William, 18, 60

Hendren, William, 139

Hening, Lewis, 23; Robert, 1, 23, 31, 32, 43

Henry, The, 4

Hewitt, Richard, 65

Heydon, John, 38, 39; Thomas, 38, 39

High Street, 93

Hill, Eliza, 97; George, 140; James, 20, 36, 38, 39, 97, 194; John, 6, 141; Sarah, 134

, Thomas, 141

Hills, The, 63

Hinton, Alexander, 196; Ann, 4; Fleet, 83; Henry, 4, 141; John, 112; Richard, 38, 39, 45, 46, 83, 84, 112, 140; Samuel, 15, 45, 46; Spencer, 66, 67, 164; Thomas, 46; William, 7, 140

Hoare, Roger, 23

Hoate, George, 9, 10; Sarah, 9, 10

Hollowing Point, 109

Holly Branch, 54

Horn, Henry M., 82, 83

Horne, Henry M., 140, 154

Horse Head Swamp, 107

Horton, George, 34, 55, 76

Hubbard, Joseph, 140; Joshua, 38, 39, 82, 83, 144, 154; Thomas, 72, 76, 144, 194; William, 38, 39, 83, 84,

155

Huckaby, Samuel, 26, 61

Hudson, Rodham, 178

Hull, Richard, 34

Hunt, Elizabeth, 104; George, 45, 46, 47, 111; John, 104; Samuel, 51, 140; William, 55, 122, 140, 193

Hunton, Alexander, 202; Charles, 92; Frances, 46, 53, 110, 111; John, 44, 45, 46, 47, 53, 83, 91, 92, 110, 111, 119; Thomas, 8, 45, 46, 66, 83, 92, 111, 140, 158, 164; William, 92

Hutcherson, John, 161

Hutchings, Joanna, 13; John, 178; Leanna, 113; Richard, 11, 13, 38, 39, 64, 82, 83, 113, 126, 130, 160

Hutching's Creek, 152

Hutchinson, John, 72, 171

Indian Creek, 20, 55, 76, 123, 126, 147, 195

Ingram, Thomas, 140

Isay, Mary, 94

Island Road, 109

Islington, 188

Ives Creek, 122

Jackson, Andrew, 20, 30

Jacob, Robert C., 188, 190; Robert Clark, 187, 188, 189, 190, 191

Jacobs, Robert Clark, 200

James, Bartlet, 82, 83; Bartley, 12, 38, 39, 62, 63; Isaac, 38, 39; John, 38, 39, 56, 72, 73, 78, 82, 83, 130, 141, 158, 178; Rawleigh, 141; Thomas, 33; Walter, 192; William, 192

Jones, Minitras, 141; Minitree, 141; Robert, 2, 22, 36, 140

Judith, The, 26

Keene, Newton, 115; William, 115, 116

Keets Bay, 147

221

Payne, Ailce, 187; Ailse, 187;
Captain, 13; Catharine, 15; Ellen,
158; George, 158, 188; Jane, 84,
85, 86, 87, 96, 98; Jean, 86, 87;
John, 15, 83, 84, 85, 86, 87, 114,
134, 158, 188; Judith, 63, 96;
Merryman, 2, 3, 15, 22, 32, 34,
35, 36, 63, 83, 84, 96, 132, 133,
140; Mrs., 3; Nicholas, 34; Philip,
182; Richard, 63, 82, 84, 187,
199; Richard Housing, 158; Sally,
98; William, 20, 63, 96, 188
Paynes Creek, 104
Pea Vine Neck, 36
Peach Orchard Cove, 92
Peachey, LeRoy, 88; Samuel, 82, 95
Pearcifull's Land, 197
Pearson, John, 140
Peed, Isaac, 197
Percifield, Eppeacus, 54; Mary, 54
Perciful, Elijah, 161, 171; William,
78
Percifull, Elijah, 14, 15, 82, 84, 170;
Thomas, 14, 15, 82, 84
Perkins, Thomas, 129, 140
Phillips, George, 16, 17, 174, 205
Pickett, William, 173, 174
Pierce, Joseph, 46
Pinchard, Robert, 13
Pinckard, Elizabeth, 120; James, 38,
39, 40, 73, 74, 82, 83, 120, 171,
182, 194; John, 120, 186; Mary,
74, 171, 194; Robert, 83, 100;
Thomas, 5, 38, 39, 40, 67, 74, 83,
120, 141, 180, 181, 186
Pinckards, Mr., 11
Pinckard's Line, 184
Pitman, Ambrose, 139; Thomas, 38,
40, 82, 84
Pollard, James, 53, 56, 77, 126, 140,
178, 183, 204; Mary, 53, 57, 118,
186; Thomas, 5, 6, 31, 33, 38, 39,

53, 56, 57, 72, 73, 77, 114, 118,
149, 186, 192, 204
Poorstock, 86
Pope, John, 38, 39, 45, 46, 47, 83;
Joseph, 95; LeRoy, 140
Poplar Neck, 8
Porringes Branch, 187
Porter, Ebbin, 33; Edward Sanders,
103; Peter, 103
Presbyterian Glebe, 114
Prices Creek, 132
Pricillas, 53
Prince William County, 181
Pritchards Swamp, 62, 64, 70, 131,
133
Pritchet, Rodham, 61
Pullen, Bettyanne, 30; Bryan, 30;
Elizabeth, 192, 193; Henry, 30;
James, 140; John, 9; Jonathan, 30,
36, 37, 83, 97, 144, 152, 153;
Mary, 30; Nathan, 192, 193
Purcel, Leanna, 36
Purcell, Charles, 109; Leanna, 97
Queens Town, 12
Quille, Sarah, 116
Rain, William, 65
Raines, William, 158
Randall, John, 6
Rappahannock, 5, 11
Rappahannock River, 22, 45, 46, 76,
98, 104, 126, 129, 131, 132, 133,
203
Reeves, John, 31, 140
Reid, James, 72; Thomas, 71
Rice, Augustin, 38, 40; Augustine,
83, 84
Rice's Creek, 133
Richmond, 14, 57
Richmond County, 5, 9, 16, 18, 22,
24, 25, 26, 35, 45, 57, 59, 60, 61,
80, 86, 94, 95, 133, 146, 178
Riley, William, 141

www.ingramcontent.com/pod-product-compliance
Lightning Source LLC
Chambersburg PA
CBHW070406270326

41926CB00014B/2727